Eldercare
FOR
DUMMIES®

Eldercare

FOR

DUMMIES®

by Rachelle Zukerman, PhD

Wiley Publishing, Inc.

Eldercare For Dummies®

Published by
Wiley Publishing, Inc.
111 River Street
Hoboken, NJ 07030
www.wiley.com

For general information on our other products and services or to obtain technical support, please contact our Customer Care Department within the U.S. at 800-762-2974, outside the U.S. at 317-572-3993, or fax 317-572-4002.

Wiley also publishes its books in a variety of electronic formats. Some content that appears in print may not be available in electronic books.

Library of Congress Cataloging-in-Publication Data:

Library of Congress Control Number: 2003101893

ISBN: 978-0-7645-2469-1

Manufactured in the United States of America

10 9 8

About the Author

Rachelle Zukerman, Ph.D. is Professor Emeritus of Social Welfare at UCLA, a gerontologist, and a clinical social worker. She is also a Visiting Professor at the University of Hong Kong and a Fulbright Scholar. For the past 20 years, her teaching, research, writing, and her heart have been fixed on the goal of helping to make the later years the best years.

She is the author of *Young at Heart: A Mature Woman's Guide to Finding and Keeping Romance* (Contemporary Books, division of McGraw-Hill) and *Aging Into the 21st Century* (Brunner/Mazel). She has also edited and authored four textbooks on counseling that are used in colleges and professional schools across the United States and have been translated into Japanese and Korean.

Dr. Zukerman is a sought-after lecturer and a speaker for seminars and workshops in the United States and abroad. Her audiences have included students on college campuses and in community education programs, cruise-ship passengers on all of the major cruise lines, and mature adults in senior centers and adult learning centers. She is a frequent and lively guest on television and radio talk shows.

Dedication

This book is dedicated to my brother, Harry Abramson, an extraordinary caregiver, who took care of our father and now looks after our mother with endless patience, utmost respect, and infinite love.

Author's Acknowledgments

I would like to thank Bubba Sally — the very first old person I ever knew. She has been gone from my life for over 40 years, but her wise and loving presence in my childhood shaped the very best parts of me, including my fascination, admiration, and compassion for our oldest citizens.

Elsa Efran has my deepest appreciation. She has edited nearly everything I have written in the last 15 years. I would be lost without her expertise and emotional support and, in this particular book, her willingness to share her personal experience in caregiving. Thanks also to Maria Carpiac, my very smart research assistant, who found answers for every "doozie" I sent her way.

Kelly Ewing, Project Editor, and I clicked immediately. This book is better for her guidance and editing. I was blessed to have a superb team at Wiley, including Kathy Cox, Acquisitions Editor, Kristie Rees, Project Coordinator, layout staff, proofreaders, and the indexer. Thanks also to my brilliant team of technical reviewers — Pat Lorne, Jim Davis, and Carol Akright. David Grady and Susan Payne also added their expertise to the reviewing process. Sheree Bykofsky, my agent, deserves a special thanks for bringing this project to me.

I am grateful to caregivers Herschel Rubin, Anna Maria Alverto, Tina Silver, Nancy Lippman, Leslie Ferebee, and Linda Newman who enlivened the text with their real-life stories. Bonnie Faherty, Karen Lee, and Renee Feiger (a nurse and two social workers) generously responded to my endless questions about their work with the elderly. Colleen Friend, who honors me with her unflinching support of my work, may not think she deserves mention. I assure you, she does.

I am especially grateful to the youngest in my family: Shawn (a talented writer), Brett (a gifted mathematician), and the baby girls, Lindsay, Skylar, and Tori (the smartest, most gorgeous toddlers in the whole world) — and I'm not prejudiced! These grandchildren, along with their great-grandmother, Frances Abramson, keep me in awe of the circle of life while they encircle me with their love.

But most of all, I thank my extraordinary husband, Jay Zukerman. Every day with Jay is a gift.

Publisher's Acknowledgments

We're proud of this book; please send us your comments through our Dummies online registration form located at www.dummies.com/register/.

Some of the people who helped bring this book to market include the following:

Acquisitions, Editorial, and Media Development

Project Editor: Kelly Ewing

Acquisitions Editor: Kathy Cox

General Reviewers: Patricia C. Lorne, RDH, MSG; James W. Davis, Jr., MD; and Carol Akright, CFP

Senior Permissions Editor: Carmen Krikorian

Editorial Manager: Michelle Hacker

Cover Photos: © Tom Stewart/CORBIS

Cartoons: Rich Tennant, www.the5thwave.com

Composition Services

Project Coordinator: Kristie Rees

Layout and Graphics: LeAndra Johnson, Kristin McMullan, Tiffany Muth, Jackie Nicholas, Jeremey Unger, Erin Zeltner

Proofreaders: John Tyler Connoley, Charles Spencer, TECHBOOKS Production Services

Indexer: Aptara

Publishing and Editorial for Consumer Dummies

Diane Graves Steele, Vice President and Publisher, Consumer Dummies

Joyce Pepple, Acquisitions Director, Consumer Dummies

Kristin A. Cocks, Product Development Director, Consumer Dummies

Michael Spring, Vice President and Publisher, Travel

Brice Gosnell, Publishing Director, Travel

Suzanne Jannetta, Editorial Director, Travel

Publishing for Technology Dummies

Andy Cummings, Vice President and Publisher, Dummies Technology/General User

Composition Services

Gerry Fahey, Vice President of Production Services

Debbie Stailey, Director of Composition Services

Contents at a Glance

Table of Contents

Introduction

My own baby daughter was the first person I ever took care of. I loved her immeasurably, but no amount of affection helped when she was colicky and irritable, or when she held her breath and turned blue. I had no clue about how to straighten her out when she got her days mixed up with her nights. Thank goodness, someone gave me a copy of *Dr. Spock's Baby and Child Care* (E.P. Dutton). The pages became dog-eared and the cover tattered before my children graduated from diapers. Dr. Spock's book lived on my nightstand for years — a good place for it, because most problems seemed to occur in the middle of the night.

Mind you, elders aren't babies, but I wrote *Eldercare For Dummies* with those long-ago memories still fresh in my mind, and I jam-packed it full of answers to eldercare questions, problems, and crises. Even if you've cared for an older person before, you always face new dilemmas. Think of *Eldercare For Dummies* as your new best friend, your partner in care, and your personal coach.

About This Book

This book covers a lot of ground. It covers eldercare in the home, in the community, and in an institution. It addresses chronic health problems and disability; financial and legal issues; and intricate family relationships. The tips, techniques, and strategies on these pages are for part-time caregivers, long-distance caregivers, and 24-hour-a-day caregivers.

Conventions Used in This Book

In this book, anyone who cares deeply for your elder is called *family*. The term *your elder* encompasses any older person (parent, spouse, relative, or friend) you care for. Many elders have illnesses that impair their memory and thinking. Wherever I can, I refer to such folks as simply *confused* rather than identifying them by the name of a specific dementing disease.

I also recommend a number of free pamphlets and guides throughout the book. In some instances, products do have costs. Keep in mind that the prices I quote are subject to change.

Lastly, the ☞ symbol within text tells you which links to click within a Web site to access critical information.

Foolish Assumptions

In one way or another, almost everyone is interested in eldercare. If you're not helping an elderly loved one now, you can probably look ahead to the day when you may.

How This Book Is Organized

Everybody's busy these days — especially if they're caregivers. I organized *Eldercare For Dummies* so that you can open it at practically any spot and get the information you need without having to read a whole chapter first. Here's an overview of what you can find in each of the six parts.

Part 1: Entering the World of Caregiving

"He's just not what he used to be," may describe your elder to a tee. In this part, I show you how to figure out what your older person needs to maintain or improve his or her functioning and stay independent for as long as possible. You discover ways to involve other family members in eldercare — without twisting their arms — and ways to cope with the painful realization that in-home care may no longer be doable.

Part 11: Mastering Everyday Challenges

Often, the best medicine is a good night's sleep, a hearty meal, a bit of activity for the body and brain, and a great big bear hug. This part shows you how to help your elder fully partake in these pleasures and how to get the eldercare assistance you need so that you, too, can eat, drink, and be merry.

Part 111: Keeping Elderly Folks Safe and Sound

A loose floor tile or dimly lit stairwell can change an older person's life. A misstep can lead to a broken hip, the loss of independence, and a decline in overall health. In another scenario, a neglected illness or mismanaged medication can land your loved one in a hospital bed. The chapters in this part present a potpourri of valuable tips for keeping the elder safe, healthy, and engaged in the world.

Part IV: The Blues, the "Good Old Days," and Other Senior Moments

The four chapters that comprise Part IV show what it's like to be sad, fearful, or bewildered in old age. In many ways, this part is a toolkit loaded with the tools to help your elder recover from overwhelming grief or anxiety and to assist you in understanding and managing the symptoms of Alzheimer's disease and other assaults on the brain.

Part V: Making the Final Years Golden

Most folks want to shape their own destiny — even when they depend on others for their care. I packed this part with information about how to fulfill last wishes and about applying for the health insurance and retirement income needed in the later years. Special attention is given to friendship, spirituality, and the final hours of life.

Part VI: The Part of Tens

Every *For Dummies* book has a part of tens — and this one is no exception! If you fancy yourself a bit of an undercover detective, you'll really like the chapters about the ten things elders do to hide their feelings and the ten ways to evaluate a nursing home.

Icons Used in This Book

I've sprinkled cute little icons throughout this book, but there's a method to my madness. The symbols in the margins help you weave your way through the book more efficiently. Here's an explanation of each icon.

This icon points out time-, energy-, and aggravation-savers that turn beginning caregivers into experts.

This icon is your guardian angel, helping you keep your elder out of harm's way.

 If you want to dazzle your friends and family with facts, figures, and scientific studies, read the technical information next to this icon. Otherwise, skip the information it highlights.

 This icon is your cybernetic pathway to more caregiving information, community resources, and a host of freebies.

 If you're caring for a confused elder, you need additional information and resources. This icon gives you just that, as well as a window into what it's like to suffer from memory loss and impaired thinking.

 This icon lets you know when it's time to consult a medical professional.

Where to Go from Here

You needn't read this book from cover to cover; feel free to skip around, letting your current caregiving needs and dilemmas direct you to relevant parts, chapters, and paragraphs. Although most of the content in *Eldercare For Dummies* focuses on taking care of your older adult, don't forget to take care of yourself! Chapter 8 tells you whether or not you're a victim of caregiver stress and, if so, what to do about it. Chapter 3 provides solutions for some of the emotional pitfalls of providing care (including guilt and despair), and Chapter 9 helps you achieve a sense of peace by showing you how to create a warmer, more intimate relationship with your older person.

Part I
Entering the World of Caregiving

The 5th Wave   By Rich Tennant

"It was one of the things they kept after selling the ski resort."

In this part . . .

If you feel bad because your elder is no longer as fit as a fiddle or raring to go, remember that it's no picnic for her either. In this part, you find out what your older person truly needs to remain independent and how to help in a way that preserves her dignity — and your sanity.

Chapter 1

Eldercare Basics

- -

In This Chapter

▶ Understanding the frailties of old age

▶ Uncovering your elder's needs

▶ Previewing housing options

▶ Making your elder's days safer and more meaningful

- -

Contrary to what many folks think, aging isn't a disease to overcome — it's simply a normal part of living. Declines in your long-living person's physical and mental functioning present new challenges. But chronic illnesses, family squabbles, and the sheer amount of work involved make caregiving one of the most difficult jobs anyone can have. It's important to know that you're not alone. The array of resources to help you cope is vast. In this book, I tell you everything I know to make your job easier.

Recognizing the Challenges of Aging

People over 65 are more diverse than people in any other age group. The varied life experiences of those who live a long time probably account for much of the individual uniqueness. People also age in different ways. Some folks remain healthy and active into their 80s, while others become frail early on. Even within an individual, organs age at different speeds. For example, Dad's ticker may be strong, but his digestive system seems to be falling apart.

A person who has smoked for decades, has rarely exercised, has eaten poorly, and has worked with hazardous materials as a young person probably will age differently than a person who has had another lifestyle.

How old is old?

If you feel old — you're old. If you feel young — you're young. Nothing is magical about the number 65. But that number has been the widely accepted jumping-off point for "old" since 1935, when President Franklin D. Roosevelt signed an act creating an insurance program that paid eligible retirees, *age 65* or older, a continuing income. You know it as Social Security.

Slowed reflexes, memory lapses, and "senior moments"

Even in the healthiest people, strength, flexibility, and reaction time diminish with age. The decline actually starts when you're a young adult but isn't noticeable until middle age, when knees aren't what they used to be and pesky memory lapses (senior moments) appear. (See Chapter 2 for help with understanding and coping with your elder's forgetfulness.)

Forgetfulness can signal a more serious illness, such as depression or Alzheimer's disease. (See Chapters 15, 17, and 18 to help you recognize, understand, and cope with Alzheimer's disease and depression in an elderly person.)

Dementiaphobia (an irrational fear of becoming a victim of Alzheimer's disease) can turn every missing pair of reading glasses or lost car keys into illogical "proof" that the Alzheimer's disease has taken hold. Reassure your elder that everybody loses things sometime and that senior moments are normal.

Diminished senses

In the normal healthy older adult, the five senses (vision, hearing, smell, taste, and touch) tend to decline somewhat with age. (See Chapter 2 for help with understanding and coping with your elder's vision and hearing problems.) A dulling in the perception of pain (the sense of touch) may cause an elderly person to ignore a bedsore, burn, or other injury increasing their risk of serious infection or disability. (See Chapter 10 for information on observing and detecting signs of illness in your older person.)

Age-related disease and disability

Lots of diseases strike older people more often than younger people. Interestingly, the same illnesses may produce different symptoms in older people than they produce in younger adults. For example, an underactive or overactive thyroid may cause confusion in an older patient but not in a younger one. When the confusion is mistaken as dementia, the elder may be unnecessarily institutionalized and the underlying illness left untreated.

Once upon a time, heart attacks, kidney problems, and diabetes were likely to cause an early death. Now they are simply considered "chronic" illnesses — controlled or treated, but not cured. Managing the medications, disabilities, and visits to medical specialists for multiple chronic illnesses can become a gargantuan caregiving task. (See Chapter 10 for help in understanding and managing various age-related chronic illnesses and the medications used to treat or control them.)

Changed family relationships

A parent who can't take care of himself or herself rattles the foundation of the family. Sometimes loved ones rise to the occasion with calmness and cooperation. More often, long-forgotten childhood rivalries and jealousies raise their ugly heads, creating chaos and strife. (See Chapter 3 for help in getting the caregiving best from family and friends.)

It's also common for spouses to deny that their husband or wife is in trouble — or that they're overwhelmed by caregiving responsibilities. Some spouses cover up or minimize their partner's problems, leaving treatable and potentially dangerous conditions unattended. It's sad to witness a loving marital relationship deteriorate because one spouse doesn't understand that the other spouse's "stubbornness" or "meanness" may be related to a medical condition — and not spite.

"Oh, Grandpa, what big ears you have."

The sense of hearing and sense of smell become less acute with the passing years — which makes one wonder if there's any connection between those losses and the fact that ears and noses continue to grow throughout life! I recently polled *orhinolaryngologists* (ear, nose, and throat doctors) in Los Angeles to make sure that this statement is true. Not only is it true, but one doctor offered an even more fascinating fact — hair continues to grow for a short time after death.

Avoid the mistaken belief that taking care of your frail parent is "parenting your parent." Even though many eldercare tasks are the same as child-care tasks (feeding, bathing, toileting), *emotionally* your elder is still your parent. Trying to parent a grown-up (for example, by speaking to him or her like a child) ends up with the parent feeling insulted and angry and the caregiver feeling frustrated and ineffectual. (See Chapters 2, 6, and 13 for ways of maintaining the dignity of the elder.)

Making Difficult End-of-Life Decisions

Helping frail elderly people retain a say about what happens to them in the last months of life or to their bodies after death is noble. I have helped dozens of older people legally document what actions they want or don't want taken to keep them alive. I have also helped them appoint the person they would like to make their medical decisions when they no longer can do it themselves. Most elderly are grateful for the opportunity. A few wanted no part of such talk — but that's a decision, too!

I recall one sweet nursing home resident who said she wanted to be cremated and have her ashes scattered on the ocean. "But," she said, "I want to be double-fired. That way there'll be no big pieces of my bones to wash ashore and scare the little children playing on the beach." And so it was written. Most older adults are far more at ease discussing end-of-life decisions than are their younger family members. (See Chapter 20 for information on estate planning, wills, advance directives, and funeral preplanning.)

Acknowledging That Help Is Needed

It's sometimes hard to admit — even to yourself — that your older person is failing, especially when that person assures you that everything is fine and dandy. It's heartbreaking to see a father who could fix any broken appliance be reduced to a trembling man who can't fix his own breakfast. Figuring out what's needed and then offering help may prolong your elderly person's independence and avoid a later crisis.

Recognizing the telltale signs

Taking early action prevents more serious problems. If you observe the following warning signs, a thorough assessment of your older person's situation is in order:

Who are the caregivers?

It's estimated that over ten million older people require some sort of assistance to carry out their everyday activities. Family members provide 80 to 90 percent of that help. Three-quarters of these family members are women (mostly daughters). Sons (and daughters-in-law) who provide care are often *only children* or the ones who live closest to the aged person.

In many cases, spouses are the first primary caregivers. Many eventually relinquish that role to their adult daughters and sons when increasing demands overwhelm their capacities or affect their own health.

- Extreme clutter, especially in a former neatnik's home
- Clothes strewn about
- Items that used to be in drawers and cupboards now crowding countertops and other surfaces
- Medication bottles left open
- Uncertainty about what medications he or she is taking, and when and why medications are supposed to be taken
- Unfilled prescriptions
- Unpaid bills
- Penalties for overdue bills
- Bill-collection dunning notices
- Disheveled and dirty clothes
- The same outfit worn over and over again
- Dangerous driving (see "Chapter 2)
- Unkempt hair
- Body odor (indications of loss of bowel and bladder control or difficulty bathing)
- Bad breath (inability to brush or floss, gum disease, or infection in nose, throat, windpipe, or lungs)
- Not much food in the house
- No nutritious or fresh food in the house
- Decayed food in the refrigerator
- Burnt pots and pans

> ✔ Confusion, sadness, anxiety, no interest in friends and former pastimes (see Chapters 15 and 16 to sort out what these symptoms may mean)
>
> ✔ Evidence of falling prey to a telephone scam or door-to-door fraud
>
> ✔ Compensation for losses in sometimes clever but dangerous ways
>
> ✔ Bruises on body (could be a sign of falls)

It's always best to double-check. Ask neighbors and friends if they've observed similar problems or have concerns.

Making an assessment

When your elder appears to be struggling with some tasks but you're not sure if you have the full picture, the time is ripe for an organized assessment of his or her capabilities. The key to locating trouble spots is to list all the basic activities that people need to do to keep themselves healthy, safe, happy, and financially solvent. Then go down the list, one item at a time, determining whether your elderly person can manage each item without help. (See Chapter 2 for more information on assessment.)

Preventing caregiver stress

A doctor, nurse, or social worker who treats an elderly person actually has two patients — the older person and his or her caregiver. The demands of eldercare place caregivers at risk for all sorts of health and family problems. (Refer to Chapter 8 for ways to protect yourself from caregiver stress and stress-related illness.)

A study reported in *The Lancet* (an international medical journal) showed that 61 percent of caregivers who provided at least 21 hours of care per week suffer from depression. Other studies have shown that caregiver stress inhibits healing. It's also been shown that half of the caregivers looking after people with Alzheimer's disease develop signs of psychological distress.

Understanding Your Options

Eldercare involves an ever-changing set of chores. Needs almost always grow. As frailty increases, more decisions about care need to be made.

Why provide eldercare?

A man took early retirement from a hard-sought prestigious position to take care of his wife (an Alzheimer's victim). When his wife required total care and no longer recognized him, his friends and colleagues said, "Why do you do it? She doesn't even know who you are." The man replied, "But *I* know who *she* is. She is my wife and the mother of my children — that's why I do it."

Remaining in his or her own home

Most American want to "age in place," but doing so may take creative thinking. Like all adults, elders want to be surrounded by their own things and enjoy the freedom and privacy to do as exactly as they please. (See Chapter 3 for ideas about obtaining income from the elder's home and exploring other options. Chapter 8 outlines the ins and outs of bringing care into the elder's home.)

Living with you

When worrying about your Mom affects your work and a phone ringing late at night gives you the shudders, entertaining thoughts of moving your elderly parent into your own household is only natural. The arrangement has its benefits, to be sure. It's less expensive to provide care yourself than to hire others to come. Having Mom close by can alleviate your fears that she will burn her house down, not eat properly, or forget to take her medication. Such a move may seem especially right when a parent loses his or her spouse and is depressed and lonely.

A multigenerational household may work for you. Mom may be able to help with the housework or contribute financially to the family's coffers. Then again, it may be a disaster. (Read Chapter 3 to help you separate the fantasy from the reality so that you and your older person make the right decision.)

Assisted living

Approximately one million elderly reside in assisted-living facilities. The premise behind this option is that living in a homelike group setting (with a menu of services available) enhances and extends an older adult's ability to live with dignity. Residents have private or shared rooms and receive only the services that they need or want. Services (some requiring an extra charge) include meals, housekeeping, laundry, transportation, recreational activities, shopping assistance, and reminders to take medications. Assisted-living facilities do not provide medical care.

These homes vary tremendously in what they offer, and the smart shopper has to know what to look for to weed out the ones that put up a good front but don't deliver. (See Chapter 4 for the nitty-gritty on assisted living and other housing alternatives.)

Nursing homes

Some people go to nursing homes for a short while to recuperate after a hospitalization. For the elderly who become residents, the nursing home will be the last place they will live in. I know no nursing home residents who live in nursing homes because they simply like the lifestyle. They live there because their medical conditions are such that they need to have skilled nursing care and supervision within reach 24 hours a day. In the face of all the problems facing the nursing home industry (including finding and retaining good staff, cuts in federal reimbursement funding, and frequent changes in ownership), many nursing homes are undesirable. But good ones exist among the 17,000 nursing homes in the United States. (See Chapter 4 for help in locating a good one and making sure that the care *stays* good.)

A rose by any other name

Some find the term "old" insulting, while others wear it proudly. Ask your elderly person how he or she likes to be thought of. Consider the following:

- ✔ Senior
- ✔ Senior citizen
- ✔ Older person
- ✔ Older adult
- ✔ Oldster
- ✔ Elder
- ✔ Old-timer
- ✔ Golden-ager
- ✔ Grandpa
- ✔ Grandfather
- ✔ Pop
- ✔ Grandma
- ✔ Granny
- ✔ Auntie
- ✔ Patriarch
- ✔ Matriarch
- ✔ Age-advantaged person
- ✔ Long-living person (not to be confused with a "long liver," short kidney, or any other misshapen organ)

Enhancing the Quality of Life

The average life expectancy in the United States today is 72.5 for men and 79.3 for women, which averages out to 76 years. It's expected that by 2050, the average life expectancy will be 80 years. You may have to take an array of pills to control a collection of chronic illnesses — but life will be long.

The next important area for research is not keeping people living longer (that's pretty near been accomplished!), it's helping them to make those extra years as good as they can be.

Retaining health

Getting sufficient sleep, exercising regularly, eating a well-balanced diet (including breakfast), and not smoking helps ward off disease — important advice at any age. Having a satisfying relationship with those closest to you has been shown to also be a factor in health promotion and disease prevention for the age-advantaged person and his or her caregiver. (See Chapter 9 for ways to improve your relationship with your elder.)

Understanding emotions

Sometimes it's clear why Grandpa is depressed or worried — he has lost his spouse, his health, or his confidence. On the other hand, it's sometimes a mystery. Sadness and apprehension can come without warning, seemingly unrelated to anything in daily life. It takes some investigation, perhaps medical intervention, and a whole lot of love and patience to identify and treat emotional upsets. (See Chapters 15 and 16 for ways to help your elder overcome his or her grief, depression, and anxiety.)

Keeping your loved one out of harm's way

A kitten underfoot, throw rugs, appliance cords tangled like spaghetti, and shag rugs on stairs are accidents waiting to happen. A kitchen fire or a broken hip can signal the premature end of independent living. Elder-proofing Mom's home can add months and years to her autonomy — and who knows how many fewer gray hairs you will have saved! (See Chapter 12 for ways to make elders safe in their own homes.)

Taking advantage of assistive devices

My father's workshop was something to behold. I recall that he was particularly pleased with his collection of bits — whatever they are. Dad had plastic boxes with slide-out drawers filled with nails, screws, and bolts sorted by size. He told me once that the secret to being able to fix anything was having the proper tools. Perhaps that's why Dad so easily accepted first a cane, then a walker, and eventually a wheelchair. Maybe that's why he never balked when we bought him a magnifying glass to help him read and a device to help him pull up his socks. He even grew to love the electrically powered armchair that raised him from a seating to a standing position. To Dad, these devices were not reminders of his growing frailness; they were simply the proper tools. (See Chapter 12 for finding the right assistive devices for your loved one.)

Preparing for a meaningful goodbye

Helping a dying person remain lucid and painfree in his last months, weeks, or hours of life opens the way for a dignified death. With pain management and comfort as priorities, the stage is set for richly meaningful discussions between the dying person and his loved ones. Elders and the family share past hurts, regrets, and unexpressed love and ask for and return forgiveness. (See Chapter 23 to find out how you can make your elder's final hours full of grace.)

Chapter 2

The Elderly Are Like Vintage Computers

At 90, Daniel's mind is razor sharp, but his body is falling apart. Esther is strikingly healthy and vital at 87, but she can't keep up with the house-cleaning or shopping. Wheelchair-bound 70-year-old Ted whips around the neighborhood in his motorized "buggy" but can't read the little numbers on a syringe well enough to manage his daily insulin injections. And Tillie, age 75, can't remember where she lives, but the doctor says she has the heart and lungs of a 50-year-old.

Generally speaking, older adults suffer from far more chronic illnesses, disabilities, and difficulties with everyday tasks than younger people. But no two elders are alike. Some folks need a helping hand only now and then, while many depend on others to bathe, feed, and dress them.

In this chapter, I help you figure out what your particular older person's needs are. You also discover how to overcome the communication problems that accompany forgetfulness, low vision, and hearing loss.

Understanding Slower, Older Models

When I think of my elderly mother, I visualize an older computer. But don't get the wrong idea — I don't really think elderly people are like computers or vacuum cleaners or any household appliance. That would be sheer nonsense — and disrespectful, to boot. But I'm sure you'll agree that aging human "machines" function less efficiently than the slicker, slimmer, shinier, newer versions.

Minds and bodies work a little more slowly. Elders tend to "poop out" fast, in part because their hearts simply pump significantly less blood (when pushed to the max) than younger tickers. Keep in mind, though, that this generalization isn't true for all older people. Some people in their 70s and 80s can complete marathons. To accommodate for weariness, pace activities and allow for frequent short rests. But avoid lengthy snoozes. (See Chapter 5 for the low-down on naps.)

Old dogs *can* learn new tricks. Healthy age-advantaged minds continue learning if given extra time to master new information. Thinking ability doesn't change drastically in healthy older people. It simply slows down. This delay means that you have to allow 15 percent longer for elders to respond to a question.

My mom, impatient with my father's long pauses, used to shout, "Think, Frank, think!" which flustered Pop even more.

Internal organs and most senses reach peak performance at about age 30 and then begin to decline. People hardly perceive the cumulative changes until their later years. The main reason people don't notice the change is because they have more organ capacity than they need. Half a liver gets you by just fine. One kidney can do a splendid job. And you have one lung plus a spare. Should illness or trauma strike, extra capacity gets you over the hump. Unfortunately, age and lifestyle choices like drug and alcohol abuse, a sedentary existence, and smoking diminish these reserves. When reserves are low and serious illness strikes, a person has very little to fall back on.

Identifying needs

Mom falls and breaks a hip. Grandpa has a stroke. Aunt Hortense passes on, leaving Uncle Jack a domestically challenged widower. It's crises like these that set off alarms, even though assistance may have been needed for some time.

Signs of trouble often go unheeded because no one realizes that these signs may indicate serious problems. For example, stained or smelly clothing is a warning sign for worsening vision or other sensory loss, disease, depression, and a host of other possibilities, including poor lighting. Another example is weight loss. Although not unusual in advanced age, it may be a tip-off for emotional distress, poorly fitting dentures, gum disease, inability to shop or prepare meals, an underlying illness, or medication side effects.

Behavior and personality changes, weight loss, weight gains, or sudden changes in appetite are not part of normal aging and should be reported to the doctor.

Follow your gut. If something doesn't seem quite right, it probably isn't. Losses may be so gradual that the older adult is unaware that a problem exists. Pride, cultural traditions, shame, or fears of being "put away" or losing privacy and independence may keep elders from asking for help or even admitting to themselves that they need it.

To complicate matters, loved ones are often so busy that they fail to notice deterioration — or wrongly attribute the changes to "old age." Confusion, for example, is not part of normal aging. It is a symptom of a disease process or other often-treatable condition. Left unattended, things can spiral downward.

Observe, ask questions, and diplomatically poke your nose into things around the home, looking for risky situations. First, make a list of things that can be improved with a simple intervention, such as installing ramps and railings. Then, make a list of areas where ongoing help is needed, such as giving daily eye drops. Finally (after reading Chapters 3 and 8), organize a plan to accomplish these tasks, enlisting family, friends, and neighbors and drawing on professional caregivers and services. Include your long-living person in the decision-making. Expect some resistance. Some elders refuse assistance at first and have to be coached to accept help.

Cover all the bases by finding out whether your older person can manage the aspects of his or her life listed in Table 2-1.

Table 2-1	What Can My Elder Do? A Geriatric Assessment
Health	
Recognize symptoms of physical illness and emotional problems	
Arrange and get to regular physical and dental appointments	
Take medications properly	
Obtain and prepare nourishing food and follow special diets	

(continued)

Table 2-1 *(continued)*

Daily activities

Get up and down safely from a chair, bed, or toilet

Bathe

Dress

Safely navigate stairs

Use the telephone

Shop

Prepare meals

Do housework

Drive safely

Safety

Obtain and use assistive devices (walkers, reaching gadgets, grab bars, hearing aids)

Avoid con artists who prey on the elderly

Summon emergency help

Appearance

Wear appropriate clothing and footwear

Wash their hair

Shave

Trim their nails

Social life

Visit with friends and neighbors

Attend community events (movies, senior center, religious services, and clubs)

Mental health

Cope with everyday stress

Discuss fears and worries

Continue with their hobbies and interests

Finances
Pay bills on time
Make financial decisions
Locate legal documents and assets
Take advantage of outside financial assistance and benefits

You can do an assessment yourself, or you can hire a professional. *Geriatric care managers* conduct assessments, offer recommendations, and create plans for short-term and long-term goals. They can also coordinate, implement, and monitor the services if you want. Professionals are especially helpful if you're a long-distance caregiver and can't personally monitor the situation frequently. (Be sure to read Chapter 8 before employing anyone.)

For a listing of geriatric care managers in your area, contact National Association of Professional Geriatric Care Managers, 1604 N. Country Club Road, Tucson, AZ 85716-3102; phone: 520-881-8008; fax: 520-325-7925. Or visit the Web site at www.caremanager.org and click Find A Care Manager.

Another resource is The American Board of Examiners in Clinical Social Work. The Web site is www.abecsw.org. Click Directory Of BCD Clinicians ☞ I Accept The Rules And Would Like To Begin My Search at the bottom of the screen. On the next screen, enter your city (or zip code). Check off Family, Case Management, and Aging. Click search, and you're provided with a list of highly qualified social workers.

Helping when help is refused

Seniors refuse help for the same reasons that they deny they need it — pride, shame, and fears of being "put away," parting with their home, or losing privacy and self-esteem. Approach them gently but frankly. They may be offended. Then again, they may be relieved. Express your concerns firmly but compassionately. The following suggestions can increase the likelihood that your offers of help will be well-received. (See Chapter 3 for more suggestions about offering help.)

  ✔ **Take advantage of a casual complaint about not seeing or hearing as well as they used to by asking questions.** Ask "How does that affect your reading [driving, taking medication]?" Don't tell them you suspect a problem; ask them whether they think *may* be a problem.

✔ **Before suggesting outside help, do your homework.** Gather resources, Web sites, and phone numbers of community services so that you can suggest practical options.

✔ **Offer help, but beware of fostering the perception that you are "taking over."** Then *don't take over.* See the sidebar "Signs that you may be trying to take over," later in this chapter.

✔ **When they make it clear they don't want to discuss it, wait and then bring up the subject again on another day.** Press the issue only when health or safety is at risk.

✔ **Help them to accept help by having someone they respect be the one to suggest it.** Options include a doctor, clergy, trusted friend, or relative.

✔ **Explain how assistance will keep them more independent.** For example, assisting an elder who has low vision by organizing a week's worth of his medications in a pill dispenser may cut the risk of illness (and even falls) caused by overdoses, missed doses, or wrong drugs.

✔ **Introduce any person who comes in to help as someone hired to help you with your work.** Don't say, "They will help me take care of you," which tends to make the oldster feel like a burden.

✔ **Make the most of their need to help *you*.** For example, you can say, "I found a bargain on light bulbs and bought too many. Will you do me a favor by taking some off my hands and letting me replace some of your lower wattage ones for these new brighter ones?"

✔ **Elicit their wisdom.** For example, mention a neighbor whose sight or hearing has made it dangerous for her to keep driving. Ask your older person what she thinks would be the best way to handle the situation.

Signs that you may be trying to take over

There's a thin line between providing help and trying to take over. If you answer yes to any of the following questions, it may be time to step back:

✔ Do you sometimes sound like a parent talking to a child rather than an adult talking to another adult?

✔ Do you make assumptions about your elder's needs and wants without consulting him?

✔ Do you make appointments and other arrangements for your elder without asking for his preferences first?

✔ Are you quick to offer suggestions before gathering your elder's views on whether he even thinks a problem exists and, if so, his ideas for solutions?

✔ Does your elder accuse you of trying to run his life?

✔ Do you do things for him that he could do for himself given a little more time, a helping hand or assistive devices (see Chapter 12 about assistive devices)?

Encourage seniors to make their own decisions unless they suffer from dementia, or they insist on driving when it's clear that it's no longer safe for them to get behind the wheel.

Determining when it's time to turn in the car keys

Deciding when to send the Chevy out to pasture, turn in the driver's license, and melt down the car keys is never easy. Certainly, many people in their 70s, 80s, and 90s are still safe drivers. But for a good many others, failing vision, slower reflexes, and other physical problems (including dementia) mean it's time to call it quits.

People older than 70 are more likely to be involved in a crash while driving and are more likely to die in a crash than young and middle-aged adults.

Recognizing when its time to evaluate your elder's driving skills

You need to make a serious appraisal of driving ability if your elderly person:

- Is involved in frequent fender-benders
- Receives multiple tickets
- Becomes lost in familiar places
- Loses the car in parking lots
- Gets locked out of the car with the keys in it (maybe with the motor running)
- Experiences episodes of lightheadedness, fainting, or drowsiness
- Comes home with scrapes on the family car and is unaware of how they got there

Asking your older adult to take you for a ride

If any of these warning signs have occurred, make sure that your life insurance is paid up, take a really deep breath, and invite your elderly person to chauffeur you somewhere (in their car). During the ride, watch for these danger signs:

- Straying into other lanes
- Stopping at a green light
- Signaling incorrectly or not at all
- Driving so slowly that it's dangerous

- Reacting slowly to the sirens and flashing lights of emergency vehicles
- Showing confusion about traffic signs and signals
- Making wide turns
- Stopping in the middle of intersections
- Mistaking the gas pedal for the brake pedal
- Complaining about night blindness (sensitivity to glare, trouble seeing white lines)
- Slamming brakes without warning for no apparent reason
- Having near misses (almost hitting people, other cars, and objects without realizing it)
- Backing into and over curbs
- Parking inappropriately
- Having difficulty turning his or her head to look back (due to stiffness)
- Being frightened by the noise or speed of passing cars
- Finding that other drivers are honking and giving them "the finger"

After the ride is over, tune in to your feelings. Is your heart in your mouth, are your knuckles white, is sweat pouring down your face, and are you thanking higher powers for sparing your life? Go for another drive on another day just to make sure that your elder's driving is as bad as you think — or ask someone else to do it.

You should also ask your older person how he feels about his driving. First, express your concerns and ask him what he thinks would help. Also talk with the doctor about your concerns and schedule an eye exam.

If the situation is not as bad as you thought but still clear that your elder's skills and reflexes are slipping, urge him to limit *himself* — for example, by driving only during the day for short distances to familiar places and avoiding traffic, heavily traveled roads, and bad weather. Frequent stops and regular meals make longer trips more manageable. Couch these suggestions as "ideas to keep you on the road" rather than as condescending admonitions.

The AAA Foundation for Traffic Safety publishes two outstanding free publications, *A Flexibility Training Package For Improving Older Driver Performance* and *How to Help an Older Driver*. You can order directly from AAA Foundation for Traffic Safety, 1440 New York Avenue, NW, Suite 201, Washington, DC 20005; phone: 202-638-5944). You can also go online to www.aaafts.org and click Products ☞ Free Materials. AARP sponsors a Web site that offers dozens of tips and video demonstrations of flexibility exercises. Visit www.seniordrivers.org.

AARP sponsors 55 ALIVE, a low-cost driving-refresher course. To find a class in your area, call 888-227-7669 or go online to www.aarp.org/55alive/class.html.

When driving is no longer a safe option for your elder, gently and with great empathy, urge her to give up her "wheels." You can also appeal to her conscience by showing her articles in the newspaper about older drivers injuring or killing themselves and others. Tell her that you don't want to see her name in such an article.

If your elder still won't agree to give up driving, next ask the doctor to order "no more driving" for health reasons (to save face). As a last resort, you may have to disable the car or put a "club" on the steering wheel.

In most states, physicians are required to report a driver who has dementia to the health department, which then notifies the department of motor vehicles. A detailed medical report, and in some cases a driving exam, is required to maintain the license.

Finding other ways to get out and about

Giving up his or her wheels doesn't mean that your elder has to be stuck in the house. With a little planning, the following strategies can keep your long-living person from being a homebody.

- ✔ Offer rides.
- ✔ Arrange for Paratransit. See Chapter 8 for information about transportation services and Chapter 14 for ideas about traveling by train, bus, and Paratransit.
- ✔ Recruit volunteer chauffeurs.

If your elder injured or killed herself or someone else, and you had the power to stop her from driving, you will be haunted forever. Regrettably, you may have to forcibly take keys away from unsafe or confused drivers who refuse to quit.

Partners in crime

Wives often cover up for their husbands' poor vision or spatial judgment by being front-seat drivers. I suppose this compensation is better than nothing, but in my mind, using someone else's eyes and judgment when your own is faulty is an accident waiting to happen.

Who are you?

An overlooked consequence of giving up driving is that without a current driver's license, an elder has no handy identification. Mom's credit card may not be accepted without a current driver's license or I.D card. She can't have her signature notarized or put her adult child's name on her checking account if she wants.

The answer may be a senior citizen I.D. card. Each state has a different policy regarding these cards. For example, in California, for a small fee, an adult with a birth certificate or Social Security card can qualify for a senior I.D. at age 62. A senior who is turning in his license can get a free I.D. Idaho will also provide a free I.D. in exchange for a valid driver's license. In Florida, an I.D. costs $3, and in Nebraska, it costs $18.75. Check with your local Department of Motor Vehicles to see what its policies are.

After my dad stopped driving, I often invited him to shop with me at the supermarket just for the pleasure of seeing him enjoy cruising the grocery aisles in one of those motorized carts for disabled shoppers. Many elders who can no longer drive a car can still manage these carts. Find out which stores in your area have them.

Managing with Less Memory

The incredible human brain consists of a hundred billion nerve cells inter-connected in a fabulous weblike communication system. After adolescence, cells begin to die off, and links sever. By the time you're 70 or 80 years old, 10 percent of your brain cells may be gone. Math, verbal, and spatial skills decline, and vocabularies shrink. Thinking and remembering take more time.

Not to worry — these normal losses are harmless. So much so, in fact, that old and young alike have adopted the expression, "I'm having a 'senior moment'" to excuse a minor bout of forgetfulness.

Physical and neurological testing can determine whether forgetfulness is a result of normal aging or is caused by Alzheimer's disease, hypertension, diabetes, insomnia, stress, or medication side effects.

Mild Cognitive Impairment (MCI) is a medical condition often thought of as a "transitional state" because 12 to 15 percent of people over 65 who are diag-nosed with MCI go on to develop Alzheimer's disease each year. On the other hand, only 1 to 2 percent of people over 65 who *don't* have MCI go on to develop Alzheimer's disease each year.

Only a doctor can make a diagnosis, but some people with Mild Cognitive Impairment report

- ✔ Problems with recent memory (learning new information or recalling previously learned material)
- ✔ Bouts of forgetfulness
- ✔ Retaining little information after reading a book or article
- ✔ Trouble understanding plots of movies
- ✔ Difficulty playing familiar games or managing hobbies
- ✔ More than the usual difficulty recalling names, finding the right word, or completing sentences

If memory losses are worrisome to you or to your older adult, get him or her to the doctor, pronto! There's no cure yet, but drugs can delay decline, especially if they're started early. (See Chapter 17 for information about Alzheimer's disease treatment.)

Communicating with the memory-impaired

How you act toward the elder with memory loss can affect his or her performance. It's best to follow these guidelines:

- ✔ Steer clear of arguments about forgotten details. Don't say things like "Don't you remember?" or "How could you forget?"
- ✔ Avoid quizzing or testing memory.
- ✔ Talk about only one idea at a time.

The most loving tactic is to come up with strategies to jog your elder's memory.

Creating reminders and prompts

Searching frantically for items, looking in the same places hundreds of times to no avail, can make anybody doubt his or her sanity. Employing the follow strategies may make a difference:

- ✔ **Set aside a "memory place" for your age-advantaged person.** This place can be a permanent spot (box, shelf, or drawer) to put things that always get misplaced (keys, glasses, purse, reminder notes, shopping lists).

✔ **Post helpful notes in obvious places.** An Alzheimer's disease sufferer (the mother of a dear friend) asked to be taken to church every day until her clever grandson began writing a daily note on her mirror that reads "Today is Monday, no church," or the more welcome one, "Today is Sunday. Church today."

✔ **Think about what you'll need when the two of you go out and then place the item where it can't be missed.** (You can hang an umbrella on a door knob or place outgoing mail or dry cleaning in the car.) The secret is to do the task when you think about it.

✔ **Create "a place for everything and everything in its place."** This age-old adage still works.

✔ **Set timers whenever you can.** Use travel alarms, pill-dispenser timers, or kitchen timers and put them in pockets to announce that it's time for medication or time to pop the meatloaf in the oven.

✔ **Make lists.** Then stick your to-do list, to-remember list, or appointment list on the refrigerator or a bulletin board.

✔ **Put all important and emergency information in one place.** You'll want to include important names, phone numbers, and medications.

✔ **Encourage your elder to remember what he went into a room for by retracing his steps.** When retracing steps doesn't work, refresh his memory by asking him what he was doing just before he left the room.

Older people with serious memory impairments often ask repeatedly for a meal (even though they just ate) or for some other pleasure like a back rub or a walk. Help them wait by hanging two clocks on the wall. Set one at the accurate time and the other (unplugged or with batteries removed) with the hands positioned at the time when lunch will be served or when it's a convenient time for a back rub or walk. Tell them that when the hands of the first clock are at the same position as the hands of the second clock, it's time to do what they like.

Never underestimate an older person

Grandpa's memory was not what it used to be. When his newest great-grandchild, Carly, was born, Grandpa traveled a hundred miles with his daughter Grace to meet the newborn. Grace, fearing that Grandpa wouldn't remember the baby's name, prompted him on the journey.

"Just remember," she said. "Her name is Carly. Car like an automobile." Grandpa nodded. When the little baby girl was presented to him, Grandpa said, "Hi, Automobile" and then looked up with a twinkle in his eye to see what kind of a reaction he provoked.

Making the Most Out of What You've Got!

Some years ago, while studying aging, I lived for a few months among older adults in a residential facility for the elderly. I was most impressed by the long-living people who were able to adapt to their losses and challenges by replacing old pastimes and pleasures with less demanding ones. One lady, no longer able to play Chopin waltzes on the piano, switched to simple folk songs. When that was no longer possible, she regularly attended concerts and listened to other people's music-making.

Finding new pleasures to replace familiar ones is not an easy task, but once accomplished, the results can be life-enhancing.

Shedding light on common vision problems

According to the American Foundation for the Blind, 5.5 million Americans age 65 and older are blind or visually impaired. Annual ophthalmologist visits are crucial for early detection and treatment of eye diseases. Neglect can result in permanent vision loss.

Presbyopia (difficulty focusing on close objects and reading materials) takes hold at about age 40. Eyeglasses with bifocal lens can take care of this problem, but other vision problems are more serious.

Blurred vision or dry eyes may be caused by medication side effects.

Cataracts

The transparent lens of the eye becomes cloudy, impairing vision. About 95 percent of people over 65 have cataracts. Most cases are mild and don't need treatment until they "ripen." The cause of cataracts is usually unknown, although they sometimes result from exposure to x-rays or sunlight.

Don't wait for your age-advantaged person to complain of cloudiness before going to the doctor. The change is so slow that most don't even realize that it's a vision change behind their inability to do the things they used to do. Outpatient surgery is painless and has a success rate of about 95 percent.

Glaucoma

Fluid inside the eyeball fails to drain sufficiently. Pressure in the eyeball builds up, ultimately damaging the optic nerve and causing vision loss.

Because no warning symptoms occur, people don't realize they have this condition until the damage is irreversible. Early detection and medication can stop the damage or slow it down.

Macular degeneration

The macula is the part of the eye responsible for seeing fine details in the center of your vision as opposed to the details on the periphery. In this condition, the macula breaks down, creating a blind or fuzzy spot smack in the middle of the field of vision. It usually affects both eyes. Little treatment is available. If the macular degeneration is the type that's associated with leaking blood vessels in the center of the macula, and vision is worse than 20/70, laser surgery can often reduce further vision loss. Unfortunately, the surgery won't bring back the vision that's already lost.

Diabetic retinopathy

In one form of this condition, capillaries in the retina break and leak, causing blurry vision. In the second form, damage to the retina stimulates new capillaries to emerge. The latter sounds good, but isn't — the new capillaries grow abnormally and can result in total or near total blindness. The best management for both forms is keeping diabetes under control to prevent further damage. Laser treatments can seal off leaky capillaries and destroy the new abnormal ones.

Combating failing vision

Tweaking the environment makes a difference for folks with low or failing vision. Try the following:

- **Paint woodwork around doorways with bright colors.** Because bright colors are easier to see than pale ones, you may want to paint steps, too, or apply colorful tape on their edges.

- **Place extra light on stairs and in reading areas.** (Oldsters need three times more light to see as clearly as younger people.) More lamps help. You may also want to try increasing the wattage in the lamps you have, but stay within the manufacturer's recommendations for each fixture.

- **Evenly distribute light throughout the home.** (Old eyes lose some capacity to refocus when they shift from light areas to darker ones.)

- **Check to be sure that every room has at least one light that can be turned on by a switch that is within easy reach of the doorway.** You don't want your elder fumbling around in a dark room looking for a lamp to turn on.

- **Use night lights generously.** Night lights that go on automatically at nightfall provide extra safety.

✔ **Pop a tiny flashlight into your pocket or purse to help make menus in dim restaurants and programs in dark theaters readable.** Come to think of it, this strategy is one anybody can appreciate.

✔ **Light a table with a portable lamp when your older person has trouble seeing his plate.** A small, portable, battery-operated camp lantern works well. I used to hang one on a banana stand (a curved holder with a hook) near Dad's place setting, and no restaurateur ever objected.

✔ **Call ahead to reserve a well-lit table.** If you explain the reason for your request, you'll ensure an honest answer — which in some cases may be "There aren't any well-lit tables."

✔ **When the old TV is on the fritz, buy a new large-screen set.** Some folks with low vision also report that a black-and-white TV is easier to see than a color TV.

✔ **Investigate magnifying devices for reading.** You can find hand-held magnifiers (some have built-in lights) or ones on swinging stands. Look in craft or medical-supply stores.

✔ **Borrow large-print books from the library.** While you're at the library, ask whether it rents or loans books on tape, too.

✔ **Look for raised lettering when buying new kitchen utensils, such as measuring cups and spoons.** Buy items that have distinctive and easy-to-remember shapes. For example, a pepper shaker shaped like a pear is easy to distinguish from a salt shaker shaped like an apple. P is for pear and pepper!

The National Library Service for the Blind and Physically Handicapped lends Braille books and books on tape. These items and specially designed phonographs and cassette players are also loaned for free. They're delivered and returned by postage-free mail. Call 800-424-8567 (TDD 202-707-0744) or go online (www.loc.gov/nls).

You can join The National Association for the Visually Handicapped for an annual membership of $50. Benefits include discounts on low-vision products, access to a lending library of 6,500 large-print books, and a newsletter. Call 212-889-3141 for the New York office and 415-221-3201 for the San Francisco office or go online (www.navh.org).

State commissions for people with disabilities provide many free services for people who are blind or have low vision, including home assessments, mobility training (how to use a cane and how to use transportation services), and home safety (including placing labels with raised letters and numbers on the oven, microwave, and washing machine dials and buttons, which make it possible to select on and off switches, temperatures and other features. Some commissions will set up your elder's home (for example, putting dry goods on left and canned vegetables on right in cupboards, or tagging clothing to make coordinating outfits easier). To find your state's organization, look under "Disabilities, commission on" in the County Government pages (usually blue) in your local white pages telephone directory or, using the search function on the Internet, type the name of your state and the words "state services for the blind."

Suffering from vision problems is compounded by confusion. These folks can't see well, and they have trouble making sense of what they *do* see. Because anything black can seem like a hole, a checkered linoleum floor can seem like a floor made of Swiss cheese. Stepping onto a very dark floor may seem like stepping into an abyss.

Patterns and prints are bewildering. If all you have is busy furniture, drape solid-color throws on them.

For extra insurance, make sure that others can also see your elder. For example, a colorful flag atop a pole attached to a wheelchair makes crossing the street safer for the person in the wheelchair. For those on foot, a "white" cane announces to others that this person has impaired vision. You must have a doctor's note verifying that you are legally blind to obtain a "white cane."

Communicating with the vision-impaired

Elders with low vision sometimes have trouble following normal conversation despite the fact that their hearing is perfectly fine. Adopting the following practices can make communication flow.

- ✔ Avoid nonverbal responses, such as nods and head shakes.
- ✔ Don't depend on facial gestures for emphasis or nuance.
- ✔ Smile. Even though the gesture may not be seen, the feeling comes through.

Communicating with the hearing-impaired

Conservative estimates say that 23 percent of people between ages 65 and 74 experience hearing loss. That percentage increases to 33 percent for people between ages 74 and 84, and 48 percent for those 85 and older. Most hearing loss is so gradual that people are unaware of it. They just turn up the television or say "What?" a lot. Sudden loss of hearing may indicate an infection, an accumulation of earwax, or even a buildup of hairspray. (The latter happened to my mom.)

Presbycusis (nerve damage associated with aging) makes it tough to hear high-pitched voices and tones. Violin music, for example, becomes less stirring, and women and children's voices sound murky.

You should suspect that your elder's hearing is waning if she behaves in one or more of these ways:

- ✔ Complains that people don't speak up on the phone.

- ✔ Claims the phone is not working right.

- ✔ Becomes suspicious, thinking people are talking about her (misunderstood or unheard conversation causes the brain to fill in the blanks with negative assumptions).

- ✔ Withdraws from social interaction.

- ✔ Hears you but doesn't understand you.

- ✔ Plays the TV or radio too loudly.

- ✔ Strains to hear (squints her eyes, juts her chin forward, cups her ear).

- ✔ Becomes unable to hear conversation when noise is in the background.

- ✔ Accuses people of mumbling or whispering.

Once you suspect hearing loss, get your older person to the doctor. After ruling out such things as obstructions and infections, the doctor will refer him or her to an *otolaryngologist* (doctor who specializes in disorders of the ear) or an *audiologist* (a health-care professional who identifies, evaluates, and manages hearing problems, often by dispensing the proper hearing aid or listening devices).

Communicating with hearing-impaired people often goes better if you follow these guidelines:

- ✔ **Sit or stand within three feet and face the person.** Never yell from another room.

- ✔ **Make sure that your face is in the light.** By doing so, you'll facilitate lip reading.

- ✔ **Understand that some words are more difficult to hear than other words.** For example, it's hard to distinguish between *c*, *d*, *e*, *t*, and *v*.

- ✔ **Enunciate as clearly as possible.** Expressions like "didjaeat" or "halzit-goin'" are difficult to understand.

- ✔ **Appreciate that some letters and numbers are more problematic than others.** For example, if letters and numbers seem to cause a problem in situations like taking down phone numbers, say "M as in Mary, B as in boy." Say each number separately. Instead of "56," say "five six."

- ✔ **Don't eat, chew, or smoke while talking.** These activities may muffle your words.

- ✔ **Keep your hands away from your face.** For example, leaning your chin on your hand may distort your words.

- ✔ **Point and touch.** Use facial expressions and gestures to provide clues.

- ✔ **Paraphrase.** If your elderly person doesn't hear a phrase, do not repeat it over and over again. Just say it another way. I repeat: Don't just repeat!

- ✔ **Understand that a high pitch is harder to hear than a lower one.** If you're a woman, try lowering the pitch of your voice.

- ✔ **Eliminate TV noises and nearby conversations.** (This guideline is especially important for hearing-aid wearers because hearing aids magnify extraneous sounds.)

- ✔ **Check hearing aids frequently.** Are the batteries installed? Is the hearing aid switched on? Is it clean and free of earwax?

- ✔ **Try to talk to "the good side."** Sometimes it's obvious that one ear works better than the other. If the person is not overly sensitive about his or her loss, you might ask which is the "best" side. Never ask which is the "good" or "wrong" side.

- ✔ **Seat the person where he or she can see everyone.** For example, you may want to seat him at the head of a rectangular table at family dinners.

- ✔ **Make sure that the person is wearing glasses if she needs them.** It's easier to hear with your glasses on because unconscious lip reading fills in the missing blanks.

- ✔ **Always announce that you're going to talk about a particular subject, such as tomorrow's trip to the doctor.** Also announce when you're switching subjects — for example, "I want to talk about the garden now."

Guess who wears two hearing aids?

Fewer than 25 percent of the people who need hearing aids actually wear them. This low number may be because of vanity or because it takes considerable perseverance to adapt to one. Another reason is dissatisfaction with the performance of the hearing aid because of unscrupulous, untrained hearing aid salespeople who promise much and deliver little. Finally, if your older person refuses to talk about being assessed for a hearing aid, he or she may be envisioning the clunky models of yesteryear, not the tinier and more powerful ones of today. Some of these high-tech numbers are partially or entirely implanted in the ear.

Try pointing out that former President Clinton has worn two hearing aids since 1997 — the kind that fit well inside the ear. His hearing loss is due from nerve damage partly attributed to age and also to too much saxophone playing!

Consider installing a TTD/TTY system for an elder who has difficulty using the telephone. TTY stands for teletype writer and is a "telecommunications device with a keyboard and visual display for people who are deaf, hard of hearing, or speech disabled." TDD stands for "telecommunications device for the deaf." It is exactly the same thing as the TTY. Call your local telephone company or Public Utilities Commission to inquire about a state program for free TTY/TDD equipment. Medicare does not cover TTY/TDD equipment, but some state programs provide free equipment.

AARP will send you a free *Consumer Guide to Hearing Aids* (Stock #D17177). Write to AARP Fulfillment EEO1531, 601 E. St., NW, Washington, DC 20049. Or send an e-mail to `member@aarp.org` with your name, mailing address, the title, and the stock number, or call 202-434-2277.

Urge your elder not to buy a hearing aid unless the hearing aid dispenser is willing to give her a refund if she's not satisfied after a month of use. A nonrefundable fee for the ear mold is reasonable.

Preserving Dignity

Many elders have a sense of worthlessness and low self-esteem — lost dignity — when they can't function as well as before and must depend on caregivers. Every bit of advice in this book is written with your long-living person's dignity in mind. (See Chapters 6, 13, and 23 for information on how to maintain dignity in the face of particular situations, such as being spoon-fed, being incontinent, or dying.)

You can help maintain your elder's dignity with the following strategies:

- Squat down or pull up a chair so that you're on the same eye level, especially if he's in a wheelchair (to avoid being in a "one-up" position).
- Always try to sit at a good conversational distance.
- Invite your elder to help with chores (for example, folding laundry, watering plants, bringing in the mail).
- Show appreciation for her possessions, opinions, and preferences.
- Encourage him to make choices and offer input into his own care.
- Never insist on helping, only offer to help.

- Make sure that your confused elder has money in her purse or his wallet. Ten one-dollar bills make quite a wad and help your oldster retain adult status.

Chapter 3

Old Age Is a Family Affair: Deciding Who, What, Where, and When

. . . .

In This Chapter

▶ Bringing out the caregiving best in family and friends

▶ Taking on long-distance caregiving

▶ Using an elder's home to finance care

▶ Moving the elder in with adult children

. . . .

Few older people aspire to be "taken in." Most want to live out their days in their *own* home — often past the time when it's safe or economically sound to do so.

What's a family to do? You don't want your older person living in a potentially risky situation. On the other hand, most elders find it demoralizing, demeaning, and downright infuriating to have to put up with family members who are hell-bent on moving them from the comfort and privacy of their own home into the "safekeeping" of an adult child's home.

In this chapter, I discuss how you and your family can help an older person support and maintain independence *in his or her own home.* I also demonstrate the usefulness of "the family conference" for motivating each family member's caregiving efforts. Finally, I explore the cons of adult children living with their parents.

Surviving Caregiving

Understanding the dollar value of what you're providing — for free — is important to your sense of accomplishment. For example, care provided to

Alzheimer disease sufferers by their family members would cost about $31,000 to $35,000 a year if that care was purchased from professional service providers.

Eldercare is difficult. Shouldering the work by yourself is like being "it" in the game of tag. If you're lucky or swift, someone else will take his or her turn. Lots of caregivers remain "it" simply because no one else is within tagging distance or because they don't know how to get anyone else involved in the game. As your elderly person grows ever more frail, the health, sanity, and well-being of you and your immediate family depends on getting others to pitch in. Anticipating the situations you're likely to encounter can help a lot, too!

Recognizing the Pitfalls of Providing Care

Unlike professional caregivers who go home after their shift, you're always "on call," facing some of the following situations:

Handling a resentful spouse and angry children

Every hour spent on caregiving represents an hour you don't have available for family and friends (for example, less time to attend hockey games, less time to help with homework, and perhaps less time to share a hobby or interest with your partner). It's natural for your family members to start to feel cheated, even if they don't admit it.

One solution is to include a spouse and kids in eldercare to enhance their understanding of the demands you face every day. Make it fun. For example, grandchildren love assisting with exercise. They count the repetitions and cheer Grandpa on. Young teenage girls may get a kick out of doing their grandma's nails. Not only does it lighten your load a bit, it helps young people become more compassionate human beings.

Feeling unappreciated by the rest of the family

If you're the one who takes care of most of your elder's needs, others may eventually take your hard work for granted — especially when you do the job so well. Over time, you may begin to feel unappreciated and believe that sacrificing your life is your only option. You may find yourself dwelling on all the things that you're missing because eldercare dominants your days.

Consider joining a support group. Your despair will be met with emotional support and helpful resources and ideas. (See more about caregiver support groups in Chapter 8.)

Feeling unappreciated by your elder

Family members' lack of appreciation stings, but criticism, complaints, and the lack of gratitude from your elder cuts even deeper! If you're in this situation, you may find yourself visiting less and offering less care, even though the age-advantaged person needs it as much as ever.

Share your pain with someone close and take an objective look at the situation. If the older person has always been ungrateful, it's unrealistic to expect anything different now. If the oldster is newly unappreciative, cruelly critical, or apathetic, it's her *illness* making her so.

Confused elderly may be unaware of what you do for them or may misunderstand it. For example, a gentle man endured his mother calling him "monster" every time he tenderly cleaned her and changed her diaper.

Making do with lower future earnings

Eldercare responsibilities lead to stress-related illness, lost time from work, lost career opportunities, and poor productivity on the job — all bound to affect earnings. Approximately one-third to one-half of all caregivers are employed.

Under the 1993 Family and Medical Leave Act, companies with 50 or more employees must allow up to 12 weeks of leave for employees to care for a seriously ill parent or spouse. The leave is unpaid, but your job is secured. If your elder's problem is a time-limited acute illness (heart attack) or condition (broken hip), and you can manage 12 weeks without pay, take advantage of family leave. Ask your boss whether you can take your 12 weeks in small chunks. Ask the Human Resources Department at work for information about family leave, flexible work hours, or job sharing.

Suffering from unemployment

Approximately 12 percent of working caregivers eventually find they have to quit their jobs to provide full-time care. Sometimes the people receiving the care want to make up the lost wages but they don't have the money. Even if they do have the money, an unwritten code says that accepting pay for family care is wrong. A study actually attempted to tally up how much all this free care (to impaired relatives of all ages) would cost if families had to pay for it. They estimated that the services provided each year are worth a whooping $196 billion.

A full accounting of your lost income as well as the cost of care (food, medication, transportation, and formal services) should be on the family conference agenda. (See the upcoming section in this chapter titled "Asking Family Members to 'Chip In.'")

Dealing with feelings of guilt

The bane of eldercare is that no matter how much you do, you always feel that you could have done more. Even worse is the guilt felt when angry words toward the elder occasionally leap from your lips in the frustration and fatigue of the moment.

Be realistic — you can't change your feelings. Nasty feelings are occupational hazards. All caregivers have them! Realize that you're doing the best you can with what's available. Think of unpleasant emotions as clouds that float in and float out. One goes away only to be replaced by another. Your guilt will flow in and out along with other negative and positive feelings.

If you find that sadness and guilt persist, see your doctor. (You may have a treatable depression.)

If you earn your livelihood by caring for confused elders, you can get a free booklet, *Nurturing a Family Partnership: Alzheimer's Home Health Care Aides Guide.* It's chock full of advice on how to develop a great relationship with a confused elder and his or her family. Call 800-424-3410 and ask for publication number D17624. Or write to AARP Fulfillment EEO1531, 601 E. St., NW, Washington, DC 20049.

Ensuring Care When the Caregiver Lives in Another City or State

Far-away caregivers come in different flavors — ones who *do it all* from a distance and ones who, while not in the driver's seat, are eager to lend a hand. (Read the section "Conducting a family meeting" in this chapter for ways to inspire another group to cooperate — the uninvolved and unwilling relatives.)

The following suggestions are for the far-away caregivers who are trying to do it all:

- Resist the "relocation reaction." Before moving your elder to your home, allow lots of time to consider other options.

- Do an on-site comprehensive assessment of your elder's situation (see Chapter 2).

- Arrange for home health-care providers and special programs like Meals on Wheels and transportation services for the frail elderly. (See Chapter 8 for assistance.)

- Enlist family members and friends to fill in the gaps.

- Ask neighbors, friends, or relatives to visit your elder regularly to spot problems impossible for you to detect by phone, such as mail or newspapers piling up outside the home.

- Contact the local postmaster. Informing the local letter-carrier that a frail elder is on her route may encourage her to report worrisome signs on the property.

- Tell the local police department that an elder lives alone in the community. This knowledge may encourage officers (especially in small towns) to give the oldster a little extra attention, like checking up on him during heat waves, cold spells, earthquakes, hurricanes, and tsunamis.

- Check with local utility companies, which may have "elder-watch" programs designed to be sensitive to signs that something may be amiss with an elderly person or couple.

The following suggestions are for far-away caregivers who play second fiddle to the primary caregiver but nevertheless want to help:

- Save vacation days and personal holidays for emergency visits.

- Squirrel away funds for crisis air travel (or save frequent-flier miles).

  Check your airline to find out how to get a ticket on short notice. Frequent-flier programs vary, and airlines policies change frequently, but I have found that agents try to help you plan for emergency travel — before the emergency!

- Don't wait for eleventh-hour predicaments. Visit as much as possible.

- Call often.

- Give the primary caregiver a welcome break by bringing the elder to your home or staying with her in her home.

- Avoid stepping on the primary caregiver's toes. She is closest to the situation and knows things you don't. Be diplomatic. Tread lightly when disagreeing or intervening.

✔ Offer to research these areas:

- Medical conditions (a task made in heaven for Internet surfers!)

- Assistive devices (a task made in heaven for technology freaks!)

- Benefits and entitlement programs (a task made in heaven for number crunchers!)

- Health and social services providers (a task made in heaven for born organizers!)

The Eldercare Locator is a free national directory-assistance public service that can help you locate aging services in every community throughout the United States, including Alzheimer's hotlines, transportation, housing options, home health services, home delivered meals, legal assistance, adult day care, respite services, and long-term-care ombudsmen. Call 800-677-1116. The hours are Monday through Friday 9 a.m. to 8 p.m. (Eastern time). After hours, callers may leave a message, and calls are returned the next business day. Or go online (www.eldercare.gov).

Rotating Care When Necessary

Handing off caregiving chores to others can help you survive. One method of rotating care reminds me of the arrangements that divorced parents have. For example, little Suzie has Christmas with Mom and Thanksgiving with Dad. Bobby spends weekends with Dad and weekdays with Mom, or the first four weeks of summer with one parent and the second four weeks with the other parent. Glitches always occur, but if familiar things are in both homes, and the routines in both places are similar, it generally works out — at least for a while.

As long as Mom agrees and doesn't get stressed out by travel or adjusting to different settings, six months at her daughter's home and then six months at her son's place can be fun for her and doable for both families. Family members can also take turns helping Mom in her own home.

Don't rotate personal care (bathing, feeding, dressing) unless absolutely necessary. Otherwise, you may find that your older person's symptoms worsen, and his or her emotional upsets become more frequent. Instead, focus on rotating behind-the-scenes activities (making doctor's appointments, keeping financial records, hiring help, shopping, and emotionally supporting the primary caregiver).

In the early stages of caregiving, others usually say, "Let me know whether I can do anything to help." When they're not called on, they stop offering — probably because they assume that you're managing just fine. If nothing else, ask them to stop by for short social visits, which can boost an elder's ego and ease loneliness. Encourage visitors to note changes or potential problems. For example, a nephew makes a daily 15-minute evening stop to visit his aunt, a long-time MS sufferer. Before he bids her goodnight, he helps her transfer from her wheelchair to her bed. This close physical contact makes him acutely aware of changes in her strength, her personal hygiene, and her weight (losses or gains). Once he spotted a skin rash that his aunt ignored but that needed medical attention.

Don't allow offers of help to dry up. Every time someone offers, respond graciously with a specific task. Keep a list in your pocket or purse for just these occasions and add to your "chore list" whenever you think of something that needs doing.

Keeping uninvolved relatives in the loop about medical conditions, treatments, and finances increases the likelihood of their involvement. At the very least, it prevents later complaints that "nobody told me" or "I'd have never agreed to that had I'd known."

If it was good enough for Blondie and Dagwood, it's good enough for you

Create a job jar for people who ask to help. The jar can be filled with little slips of paper (each one with a particular chore written on it) like the one Blondie kept for Dagwood in the famous comic strip. I love the image of someone sticking his or her arm up to the elbow in a deep jar and pulling out an assignment.

The best tasks are the ones you would get to if you had the time (not the ones that border on emergencies). For example:

- Fix the screen door.
- Pick up cans of food supplement at the discount store.
- Rake the leaves.
- Press Mom's blouses.
- Shop for a bathtub bench.
- Play gin rummy with Dad.
- Visit for two hours so that you can get a haircut or go to lunch with friends.
- Organize the medical bills.
- Organize the medicine cabinet.
- Reconcile the checkbook.

Determining When You Need a Family Conference

A family conference is the best way to let everyone put his or her two cents in and get an opportunity to contribute to the elder's care.

Perfect reasons to have a family conference include the following:

✔ The care-receiver looks healthier than the caregiver.

✔ A progressive disease or terminal illness has been diagnosed.

✔ Rehabilitation from a broken hip or other trauma renders the elder dependent.

✔ Elder abuse is suspected. (See the section "Watching Out for Abuse and Neglect" in Chapter 4.)

✔ Grandma's activities seem to have been elevated to the stuff of urban legends. Is she really giving away huge amounts of money to the good-looking young man next door, or is Cousin Henry's concern unfounded and none of his business anyway?

✔ Childhood rivalries, jealousies, and personality conflicts have raised their ugly heads after decades of "relative" peace. For example, your brother's tone makes you feel like a dunce or a black sheep, and you would like nothing better to smack him "upside the head."

✔ You believe that eldercare is your sole responsibility because you're the spouse or the only child or "the only one who can do it right."

✔ Your sister thinks Mom needs a full-time nurse, and you think a weekly ride to the beauty shop would do the trick.

You can pick a date and invite the others to a gathering, but people generally hate being told what to do. Planting seeds about a get-together is usually a better first step. Causally mention a few of your observations. Pondering aloud about the usefulness of getting together is much more likely to rally enthusiasm and cooperation. For example, "Dad seems to be having trouble taking care of himself and the house since Mom passed. I wonder if you've noticed that, too?" or "Aunt Dottie complains of pain, but she refuses to see the doctor. I'm at a loss for what to do" or "I wonder if we should all put our heads together on this one?"

Holidays or celebrations when everyone's in town are ideal times for a gathering. Conference calls are okay, but nothing beats the effectiveness of face-to-face encounters.

It may be a good idea to include your older person in the conference, but that really depends on the situation. Inviting older people to a family meeting in which their problems and care needs are the only agenda is risky business — especially if they've refused help in the past or deny they need it. On the other hand, making plans for people of any age without their involvement invites anger. You know your own elder. If such a meeting would be upsetting for her to attend, brainstorm without her first so that you can encourage everyone to voice their concerns freely. Once some options are agreed on, get together with Mom for her input.

Studies show that an elder is more satisfied with care when he has had an opportunity to express his values and standards and is convinced that the care he's getting matches those preferences.

When the decision is *not* to invite your older person to the family conference, don't even think about swearing people to secrecy. There's no such thing as a family secret!

Conducting a family meeting

A few agreed-upon guidelines set up at the beginning of the first meeting can make the difference between running a productive family conference and trying to referee a chaotic, useless meeting.

Ground rules:

- Everyone speaks for himself or herself. Don't preface your point of view with "we think" or "my family thinks."

- Interruptions aren't permitted. Stop interrupters cold with a "Please let Uncle Joe speak. We'll all have a chance to talk."

- Everyone's opinions count (from the youngest to the oldest, from the shyest to the boldest). Words like "Joan, we haven't heard from you yet" or "If anyone has anything to add, please do so" encourage participation.

- Pick a facilitator. He or she can be the oldest, bravest, most respected person or the one with the loudest voice or the owner of the *For Dummies* book — as long as he or she is willing.

- Talk about feelings. When family members open up in this way, they often discover that others share their feelings, which helps the family draw closer emotionally.

- Blaming and criticizing aren't allowed. Family members stop listening, get defensive, or withdraw from the task at hand when they've been insulted or verbally attacked.

When the family is too emotional or too distraught to manage a conference on its own, a geriatric care manager or clinical social worker can help. (See Chapter 2 for information on finding a geriatric care manager and a social worker.)

Once the ground rules are agreed to, the facilitator can

1. **State the reason for the powwow.**

   For example, the facilitator may describe the meeting's purpose as "Getting the loved one the help he or she needs to enjoy life and stay as independent as possible."

2. **Ask someone to take notes.**

3. **Invite each person to identify what he or she understands to be the elder's pressing needs, niceties, and wishes.**

   • Pressing needs (essentials). For example, meal preparation.

   • Niceties (things to make life more comfortable and fun). For example, weekly visits to the hairdresser.

   • Wish list (sort of the cherry on the top). For example, reconnecting Mom with her long-lost brother.

4. **Write the pressing needs, niceties, and wishes on a blackboard or a large pad of paper.**

   Read Chapter 2 to make sure that you've covered all the bases.

5. **Invite each member to voice his or her opinions about remedies for each pressing need, nicety, and wish and write down possible remedies next to each one.**

6. **Ask for volunteers to help satisfy each need.**

   Niceties and wishes are optional.

7. **Invite everyone to volunteer according to his or her strengths, abilities, skills, and other responsibilities.**

It's infuriating when others don't do their share, but ultimately you must accept that even though it makes sense to request their help, you can't force people to do anything they don't want to do. In the long run, you're better off not spending time stewing which only results in more anger, bitterness, and family feuds.

8. **Decide what pressing needs, niceties, and wishes may be accomplished by outside sources like social service agencies, church, volunteer groups, or entitlement or assistance programs.**

   One person may be able to coordinate services.

9. **Close with a summary of the meeting, thanking every person for his or her contribution.**

10. **Revisit the situation again later, when circumstances change for better or worse for all involved.**

Understand that guidelines are just that — guidelines. Your family may come up with creative ways of organizing assistance that work just as well or better.

Offering the elder family assistance

Designing a fabulous program for caregiving doesn't guarantee that your older person will greet the plan with enthusiasm. Take the following advice from a long-time social worker — me — and you'll have a better chance of getting a positive response to the family's plan:

- Make sure that your elderly person is well-rested and well-fed before presenting the plans.

- Voice your concerns carefully and gradually. (It's demoralizing to be confronted with a multitude of things that you can't do or have trouble with.)

- When your elder's perceptions of his or her abilities don't match your observations and understanding, resist the urge to contradict.

- Offer assistance in an off-handed or humorous manner. For example, ask her whether she has difficulty managing medications, adding, "It would take a rocket scientist to keep it all straight — I know I could never do it."

- Step aside. Invite someone else to try. The elder may be more willing to talk to someone older than you or of a different sex or someone who has a history of being more influential with the elder. (See Chapter 2 for additional ways to ways to help when help is refused.)

Underestimating an older person's abilities has grave consequences. For example, buttering Dad's toast is quicker, neater, and more efficient, but it reduces him to child status.

No one should take control of a mentally competent adult, no matter how frail. Think of the offers of family help to the older person as merely selections on a smorgasbord. Adults have the right to pick and choose what they want and pass over what they don't want.

Asking Family Members to "Chip In"

Care costs money. Most families fall into one of the following categories.

The elder has

- ✔ Sufficient financial resources to cover his or her needs. (See Chapter 21 for advice on how to help the older person disclose and organize personal finances.)

- ✔ No financial resources. The cost of care is beyond the family's ability or willingness to pay for it. (See Chapter 21 for information on qualifying for Medicaid, SSI, and other means of keeping the wolf from the door.)

- ✔ Some financial resources. The family may or may not be equipped make up the monthly difference.

Talking about money is taboo in many families. The average Joe would rather talk about his sex life than his financial statement. The older generation is reluctant to let the young 'uns know their "business." And the young 'uns loathe disclosing their financial situation to their siblings. If the money question is not handled with kid gloves, all sorts of ugliness can erupt.

The best approach is to take a businesslike unemotional stance, using the following steps:

1. **Determine the total cost of home care or care delivered in a facility.**

2. **Establish whether your older person has sufficient resources to pay for care.**

3. **Discuss the costs with him or her, being sensitive to how difficult it is for some older folks to discuss their finances and care needs.**

4. **Explore the "chipping in" option at a family conference.**

   Include the older person if possible. Be tender. It's extremely difficult for parents to accept financial help from their children.

5. **Before pledging a monthly amount, each person should ask himself or herself the following questions:**

   - Do I really understand the elder's financial situation?

   - Will "chipping in" jeopardize my children's education, my own financial stability, or my retirement nest egg?

   - Am I willing to make those sacrifices?

   - Am I clear about my own financial situation?

   - Can I spare money for the short term?

   - Can I spare money for the long term?

   - Is my immediate family willing to make the lifestyle changes "chipping in" may require?

Put a cap on how much you can contribute. Tell the family what the cap is so that they know the limit you can give.

Don't keep contributions secret from siblings. Family secrets (even benevolent ones) tend to boomerang.

Keeping the Elderly Person in His or Her Own Home

Eighty-year-old Adie lives in the house she's occupied for 52 years. She's not about to move now. The house overflows with memories, and it's near shopping, church, and friends. She needs increasingly more help with the basic tasks of living, but she has little room in her paltry income to pay for it. Before throwing the towel in, Adie needs to explore the options. The home itself may produce income.

Getting income from the home

Thousands of elderly people like Adie have only one asset — their house. The mortgage may have been paid off decades earlier, and the value of the house may have climbed over the years. Such homeowners are often short on cash, a little lonely, and struggling to keep up the property and manage the basic activities of daily living. They could sell their homes, but many elders want to stay put. Adie puts it this way, "I want to stay here until they carry me out."

Reverse mortgage

A federally insured *reverse mortgage* feels like the opposite of a mortgage. Instead of making a payment to the mortgage company every month, a qualified mortgage lender makes monthly cash payments to *your elder!* Of course, the monthly sum comes out of the equity of his home. How much that amount is depends on the value of the house (the mortgage must be paid off or nearly paid off to qualify), the location of the house, the current interest rate assumptions, and the age of the homeowner (at least 62). The beauty of this arrangement is that the long-living person continues to occupy the house and receive monthly payments even after the equity in the house gets used up.

A meeting with an independent accredited counselor is required for anyone applying for a federally insured reverse mortgage. The counseling session takes about an hour and may require a second session.

Before making an appointment with a counselor, read AARP's booklet, *Home Made Money: A Consumer's Guide to Reverse Mortgages*, which explains the pros and cons of different types of reverse mortgages. Call 800-424-3410 and ask for publication D15601or order from the Web site (www.aarp.org/revmort).

To request reverse mortgage counseling from AARP Reverse Counseling Referral Request Line, call 202-434-6082 from 10 a.m. to 3 p.m. EST Monday through Friday.

Calls made during off hours will be returned within 24 to 48 hours. A telephone counselor may determine your eligibility for a reverse mortgage, and you may receive a quick quote. A counselor from a nonprofit agency may be assigned for more in-depth assistance.

Federally insured reverse mortgages are also called *Home Equity Conversion Mortgages*.

Counseling is highly recommended for a reverse mortgage product owned by a private company as well. Different features and complexities must be mulled over. For example, some options advance a large lump sum at the outset plus a monthly payment.

A down side to reverse mortgages is that, because mortgage borrowers continue to own their own homes, they remain responsible for property taxes, insurance, and repairs. Failing to carry out those responsibilities can result in big trouble — the loan can become due and payable in full.

Sales-leaseback

A *sales-leaseback agreement* may be just the ticket for a house-rich, cash-poor senior citizen. It goes something like this scenario: The home is sold to a buyer (often someone in the family who thinks it's a good investment and wants to help out his relative). The buyer leases it back to the elder, who now becomes a tenant with a guarantee (in writing, of course!) that he may remain in the house for as long as he lives.

The good news is that Pop gets to stay in the house he is attached to, has the cash he desperately needs, and is no longer responsible for the expenses, aggravation, and responsibility that come with home ownership. The bad news is that he loses control of his home.

These arrangements (also referred to as *lifetime tenancies*) are often made with charitable organizations (also referred to as *life estates*). Is it advisable? It depends. There are all sorts of legal and tax ramifications. A consultation with an estate-planning attorney is the first step to seeing whether this option makes sense for your older person and his family.

House-sharing

Deborah, a social work student from a small town in South Dakota, house-shares with Emmy, an elderly family friend living in Los Angeles. For the price of a modest monthly rent, a share of the household expenses, a little house-work, and a few errands, Deborah gets her own room and bath and the use of the kitchen and living room — within walking distance to campus. The extra income allows Emmy to remain in her beloved home. She considers Deborah's companionship a bonus, not to mention the greater feeling of security from having a young person in the house.

House-sharing between two or more unrelated people is growing by leaps and bounds. You may be able to find a suitable housemate for your older person by checking with friends and family members for leads.

Lots of communities have services to match up people who would like to share an apartment or house and pool their resources. For help, contact the National Shared Housing Resource Center in Maryland online at www.nationalsharedhousing.org.

Before jumping into a shared housing situation, verify the zoning restrictions in your community. More than two unrelated people living together may violate zoning regulations in particular neighborhoods.

Check with your local Department of Social Services to make sure that house-sharing doesn't jeopardize any public welfare benefits, such as SSI or food stamps, received by the elder.

Letting others do the watching

Dad doesn't answer the telephone; you're worried sick because he never goes out after dark. With rush-hour traffic it will be over an hour before you can get to his house. To avoid going nuts during times like these (with Dad's permission), seek out a kind-hearted, trustworthy neighbor who is willing to stop by now and then to check on him or let herself into Dad's house in an emergency. Then, if you can't reach your elder by telephone (and have reason to worry), you can call the neighbor and ask her to make sure that Dad's okay. Be sure you remind her to knock first.

A *telephone reassurance program* is a service in which someone calls your elder daily to check up on him and have a warm howdy-do. The same program often has a "friendly visitor" component (a volunteer drops by for an occasional brief visit). Places to check for this service include senior centers, churches, synagogues, and religious organizations.

Call the national Eldercare Locator at 800-677-1116 for the number of the local Area Agency on Aging or your state's Department of Aging, which in turn should be able to tell you about nearby telephone reassurance and friendly visitor programs.

Moving Your Elder in with Adult Children

Mini-crises and medical emergencies deprive your immediate family of your presence and leave you washed out at the end of the day. Perhaps it breaks your heart to see Mom struggling to manage her life by herself. You *know* that moving Dad into the warmth of your home and the loving arms of your family would end his depression. These are just a few of the thoughts that motivate caring people to invite their elders to live with them.

Among the benefits are

- Saving money. Caring for someone in your home is less expensive than having care delivered by care workers in the elder's home. It's also usually less costly than institutional care — unless, of course, you're quitting your job to care for your elder!

- Gaining peace of mind, knowing that he or she is getting high-quality care.

- Spending more time with the long-living person.

- Receiving help from your healthier oldster (such as light housework, childcare, or assistance with household expenses).

- Modeling responsibility and respect toward the older generation for the younger generation.

Opening your home to your elder is a noble and loving thing to do — but unfortunately it's often done impulsively, without anticipating the negatives. All sorts of unintended consequences are bound to occur — for example, anger and resentment from a child who may have to give up his room, or the husband or wife who "didn't bargain for this."

Differences in personal habits and family practices cause friction. For example, Grandpa's smelly cigars and his habit of saving newspapers are intolerable to your wife, and your teenager's pierced nose and habit of sleeping until noon on Sunday are revolting to Grandpa. And everyone knows about the potential for fireworks when two adult women try to use the same kitchen!

Unless you really have no other choice or you've worked out all the kinks well in advance, support your elder's autonomy *in his or her own home.* This book is packed with resources to keep your age-advantaged person independent as long as possible and lighten your burden at the same time

The Family Caregiver Alliance provides free information about family caregiving. The main office is 690 Market St., Suite 600, San Francisco, CA 94104. Call 800-445-8106 to be referred to one of its local branches or visit online (www. caregiver.org).

Questions to ponder before making a move

The last thing you want is to move your elder into your home and have the new arrangement fail miserably. To prevent such heartbreak, ask yourself the following questions before you invite your elder to live with you:

✔ Is your place big enough to accommodate another person's belongings and treasures?

✔ What construction changes (to ensure safety, mobility, and privacy) are possible and affordable? Consult with a carpenter or handyman to discuss present or future alterations. You may just need to make simple changes, such as widening doorways and installing ramps for a wheelchair, or complex and costly changes, such as converting a garage into a small apartment.

✔ Do you know all you can about your older adult's medical conditions and what changes to expect over time? (See Chapters 10 and 17.)

✔ Have all family members voiced their feelings about the move? Unconditional acceptance of *all* feelings is crucial for a successful adjustment.

✔ Have you given the family members a "heads up" about potential problems? Some people say giving advance warning is borrowing trouble. I say it's being smart.

✔ Is a plan in place to resolve problems? A regular family conference can't be beat. (See the section earlier in this chapter titled "Conducting a family meeting.")

✔ Does everyone understand and accept the personal sacrifices that will have to be made, including additional chores, less personal space and privacy, and disrupted routines?

✔ Will anyone's habits, preferences, or pets disturb anyone else? You're better off mediating those problems before the move rather than after.

✔ How will the move affect your employment? Investigate a part-time option, job sharing, flextime, and family leave.

Chapter 4

Where to Turn When Your Elder Needs a New Home

In This Chapter

▶ Finding the right place to live when home is no longer possible

▶ Considering nursing home placement

▶ Ensuring quality nursing home care

▶ Protecting your elder from abuse and neglect

*W*hen I was a child, Grandma Sally came to live with us. Despite a disabling heart condition, she managed her basic needs. On her good days, she also tidied up after my brother and me. Grandma Bess, my other grandmother, suffered from dementia (we called it senility) and lived in a nursing home where people knew how to care for her and keep her safe. In those days, families had few options — when you couldn't take care of yourself anymore, you moved in with family or went to a home.

Today, all kinds of alternatives exist — from homelike independent settings with a host of services to choose from, to specialized institutional settings with around-the-clock medical care and special units to keep confused elderly and Alzheimer's disease victims like my grandma secure and involved in stimulating activities.

In this chapter, I explain the various kinds of long-term care settings and explain what's good and what's not so good about each of them.

Understanding the Differences Between Housing Options for Seniors

The day may come when your elder needs a different living arrangement than the one she has now — ideally a home that provides just the right amount of care (not too much and not too little!). In this section, I familiarize you with popular options, including senior housing, assisted living, board and care, and continuing-care retirement communities. And in the section "Being in the Know about Nursing Home Care," later in this chapter, I guide you through the entire nursing home care process, including decision-making, finding a place, financing care, and managing the moving day.

Government-subsidized senior housing

Government-subsidized *senior housing* (Section 202 housing), also called the Supportive Housing for the Elderly program, is administered by the U.S. Department of Housing and Urban Development, better known as HUD. Section 202 housing is a good deal for eligible older people lucky enough to get it. Most units are studio or one-bedroom apartments with small kitchens and bathrooms. Most buildings have elder-friendly features, such as nonskid flooring, elevators, ramps, railings, wide doorways for wheelchairs, emergency buttons in the bathrooms and bedrooms, and grab bars. Transportation, shopping, and laundry services are usually available (for additional fees). Whether your elder chooses any of the limited services available is entirely up to him. Some, but not all, of these settings provide meals.

Buildings range from small one-floor structures to large high-rise complexes usually located near shopping and public transportation.

Who is a candidate?

The low-income older person who can get out of bed, dress, bathe, and generally take care of himself (perhaps even prepare a light breakfast or snack) is a perfect candidate as long as he meets eligibility requirements. Applicant must at least 62 years old and have an income of less than 50 percent of the median income in their area. The typical resident is a single woman in her mid-70s with an annual income of less than $10,000.

What are the pros and cons?

Extremely low rent is the major benefit, and you can have plenty of privacy when it's wanted.

Unfortunately, this setting is not equipped to support a frail elder who can't manage the basic tasks of everyday living. When the elderly person reaches that point, he must relocate to a place that offers more care, leaving familiar surroundings and friends behind. Waiting lists for government-subsidized senior housing tend to be years long. (On average, nine applicants are waiting for each vacancy that occurs in any given year.) Sometimes, the buildings aren't well maintained.

Assisted living

Assisted-living facilities — sometimes called "nursing homes light" — are popping up all over the country. There's no common definition for assisted living. The term covers a wide range of facilities, but most states require a license. Living spaces can be as modest as a shared bedroom in a small group-housing arrangement or as great as a small apartment with a tiny kitchen in a large complex. For additional fees, residents can choose from a range of possible services, including meals, laundry, cleaning, bathing, dressing, toileting, and other personal care. Although assisted-living facilities don't provide medical care, sometimes a staff member provides a medication reminder.

Assisted living is a marketing term that means different things in different states. Ask whether the facility is licensed and what kind of care and level of supervision is provided. Specific questions, such as how many staff members are on duty at night, whether there's assistance with medication, and whether the residents are regularly checked on, help you determine whether your loved one will get what she needs to live as independently as possible. It's best for your older person to live in a place that has additional services and supervision available as her needs grows.

Who is a candidate?

Elders who require help and support in managing their daily activities but who don't need medical oversight (for catheters) or intense supervision for incontinence or dementia are the best candidates for assisted living.

What are the pros and cons?

Assisted-living arrangements can potentially extend an elder's capacity to live independently. Social butterflies seem to especially enjoy the opportunity to mix with others. Because the staff tends to be small, supervision and oversight may be insufficient. For example, I got a call once from a heartbroken daughter whose father, an assisted-living resident, fell in his bathroom. He lay on the cold tile floor for three days before anyone realized that he wasn't showing up for meals in the dining room. Fortunately, he recovered from his injuries, and everyone agreed, including the father, that it was time to move in with his daughter's family.

Medicare doesn't pay for assisted-living arrangements. Most tenants — about 90 percent — pay with their money or out of their family's pockets. Even when long-term care insurance policies pay, they may allow only a specified amount of money to cover assisted living, after which no insurance funds are left for nursing home care — the next move for 40 percent of assisted-living residents.

Some states provide limited Medicaid coverage for assisted-living residents. Unfortunately, those states limit the number of people who can get this kind of assistance through Medicaid. So, although your elderly person may be eligible for assisted-living benefits (called *waivers*) in your state, he may find himself on a very long waiting list.

Family members sometimes supplement inadequate services with home health-care workers and hired companions, only to eventually abandon that remedy because the cost becomes prohibitive. (See Chapter 8 for more information about hiring caregiving help.)

The people who market assisted living can be quite aggressive and a little lax about presenting the details. Check the cost for each and every service. What exactly is included? How many meals? How often is the room or apartment cleaned? Are the bedrooms and bathrooms cleaned, or just the community areas?

Board and care

Board-and-care homes are group living arrangements for people who can't survive independently. Often, the setting is a house with four to six residents and a few staff members. Help with walking, bathing, and toileting may be available. Then again, it may not. This option is hard to describe because board-and-care settings are so diverse. The range of services varies widely and wildly — and so does the quality!

Who is a candidate?

The key motivator for moving into a board-and-care home is cost. These settings are often, but not always, less expensive than assisted living.

What are the pros and cons?

Low-cost board-and-care homes in which a handful of adults (often confused elderly) receive good care from kindly proprietors or employees do exist. When you find one, it's a blessing. The poorly run ones are short on privacy, space, activities, and well-trained staff. Licensing varies from state to state. Be sure to check your state's licensing requirements. Medicaid may pay.

Continuing-care retirement communities

In many ways, continuing-care retirement communities (sometimes called life-care or multilevel-care facilities) are the Cadillacs of long-term care. Independent seniors pay an admission fee (hefty by most standards) and then a monthly charge. Housing, meals, activities, housekeeping services, and medical care are provided on site. People must plan well ahead for this option because they must be fully independent to qualify for admission. Once a person has been admitted, care continues for the rest of his or her life at whatever level of care is needed. Some facilities charge less up front but then charge additional fees as more care is needed.

Who is a candidate?

Candidates are fully independent and tend to be well-heeled, although I have known several residents who were teachers, nurses, and accountants and were by no means rich. But because they knew early on what they wanted, they saved and invested wisely in order to have the funds to pay for this option when they reached retirement age. The most common reason given for living in a continuing-care retirement community is that "this arrangement assures that I will never be a burden to my children."

What are the pros and cons?

These self-contained senior communities are unique in that residents are able to receive more intensive levels of care as they grow frailer without ever having to relocate. For example, a person may move from an independent house or apartment to an assisted-living setting and then to a skilled-nursing unit (keeping some of their furniture along the way) within the same campus. Couples can remain in close proximity even if one is healthy and the other needs intensive medical care. Some residents feel optimistic and cheered by the mix of elders at all levels of functioning, while others become depressed seeing impaired elders who are painful reminders of their own futures.

The significant investment in a multilevel facility must be made cautiously. An attorney should review the contract before any money is plunked down. Ask questions about increases in monthly fees and the financial stability of the community. Regulations vary from state to state.

The American Association of Homes and Services for the Aging provides information and referrals to over 5,500 not-for-profit member nursing homes, continuing-care retirement communities, assisted-living arrangements, and senior-housing facilities. Call 202-783-2242 to get the phone number for your state office, write to the American Association of Homes and Services for the Aging, 2519 Connecticut Ave. NW, Washington, DC 20008, or visit online (www. aahsa.org).

Being in the Know about Nursing Home Care

Nursing homes are facilities that provide residents with a bed, meals, rehabilitation services, medical care, and protective supervision. The distinguishing characteristic is the availability of around-the-clock, seven-days-a-week skilled nursing care. Because 22 percent of Americans over 85 years old live in nursing homes, it makes sense to familiarize yourself with the ins and outs of nursing home care *before* one is needed. Imagine facing any of the following scenarios without preparation:

- A formerly active grandfather suffers a massive stroke. After the hospital stay, he requires around-the-clock skilled nursing care.

- An older man undergoes heart bypass surgery. For an unknown reason, he never regains functioning. He needs total care.

- A near tragedy occurs before it's determined that an 80-year-old woman with advanced Alzheimer's requires 24-hour supervision in a secure environment to keep her safe.

The emotionally distraught families of these loved ones have to find nursing homes for their elders — and fast. They don't know the best way to locate them or how to distinguish good ones from bad ones. Worse yet, family members are under pressure because the hospital wants the patient discharged pronto. Under these circumstances, family members often surrender their responsibility to the hospital discharge worker and accept the first available bed that he or she comes up with. No discredit to the discharge worker, but it's far better if caregivers gain knowledge about local nursing homes in advance of a crisis so that their choices are well-informed and are not made under pressure, by default, at the 11th hour.

Making the decision

Caregivers are forced to confront the dreaded nursing-home placement decision when their loved ones become extremely frail, lose mobility, become incontinent, or exhibit dangerous behavior such as wandering away or striking out in violent outbursts. Regret, uncertainty, and guilt tend to shadow the decision. The nursing home decision is less gut-wrenching (but no less heartbreaking) when a sudden trauma lands an elder in the hospital and a return to home care becomes out of the question.

Once the nursing home placement decision has been made, you're likely to be plagued with some unpleasant thoughts and feelings. Every caregiver has them! You're absolutely normal if you feel any or all of these emotions:

- Relief that you no longer have the responsibility of eldercare

- Guilt because you feel relief

- Selfish because you look forward to reclaiming your life

- Self-reproach for failing to keep the promise "You will never have to live in a 'home.'"

✔ Remorse for "abandoning" your elder

✔ Embarrassment because you can't afford a better nursing home

✔ Anger because the costs of care are a financial drain

✔ Fear that the nursing home administrator will tell you to take Mom home

✔ Guilt because you don't want to take Mom home

Finding a place

It's hard to believe that 17,000 nursing homes are in the United States. Luckily, you have to check out only the ones that are located in a convenient area. Location is one of the most important deciding factors to consider. Despite the quality of care they receive, elders who aren't visited by their loved ones grow ever more despondent and feel abandoned and hopeless.

Quality nursing homes and caring staff exist, but it takes a little research to find them. Gather recommendations from any or all of these sources:

✔ Friends, coworkers, and acquaintances

✔ Doctors or other health-care providers

✔ Clergy (they and their colleagues may visit or hold services at local facilities)

✔ Geriatric care managers

✔ Hospital discharge planners

✔ The World Wide Web

Special-care wings in nursing homes and assisted-living facilities or freestanding facilities for Alzheimer's disease suffers (and elders with other dementing illnesses) are becoming more available. When evaluating these settings, look for a high staff-to-resident ratio (one staff member to every four to five residents), a calm, secure atmosphere, and a building design with user-friendly features — for example, protected walkways that lead back to the building and visual cues to help residents find their rooms.

Check your elder's affiliations (past and present). Religious, ethnic, fraternal, or professional organizations often operate nursing homes. Acceptance is likely to be easier, and your older person may enjoy living with people who share common experiences or values.

Call the Veterans' Administration at 800-827-1000 and ask to speak to the Enrollment Coordinator to find out whether your veteran is eligible for free or low-cost nursing home care or go online (www.va.gov). Click Frequently Asked Questions and then click Eligibility.

A nursing home is a nursing home is a nursing home

I recently had a "to-do" with an acquaintance who insisted that her relative was *not* in a nursing home but was in a "health center." Believe me, all of the following are euphemisms for nursing homes:

✔ Old folks home

✔ Rest home

✔ Convalescent home

✔ Health center

✔ Rehabilitation center

✔ Home for the aged

✔ Living center

✔ Nursing center

✔ Care center

Nursing homes offer similar services, although some may have hospice services (see Chapter 23) or other special accommodations, including wings for residents with dementia. In most cases, the nursing facility becomes home — but not always. Many elders receive rehabilitation at the nursing home after surgery or stroke during a brief stay and then return home.

You can get information about every Medicare and Medicaid-certified nursing home in the country, including inspection results, staff size, and number of beds by calling 800-Medicare (800-633-4227). A brand new feature on the Medicare Web site allows you to compare the quality of care in each nursing home in your area (called *quality measures*). Ten quality measures include the percentages of residents in each facility experiencing pressure sores, pain, infection, and daily physical restraints. Go online to www.medicare.gov/NHCompare/home.asp. Click Nursing Home Compare. Select your state from the drop-down menu and then click Next Step. Refine your search by selecting your specific county, city, or zip code and then click the Search button. A list of your local nursing homes appears. Click the check box next to each facility's name that interests you and then click Next Step. A side by side summary for each facility appears. To get additional details for any one facility, click View All Information.

Once you have chosen a few homes in your area, call and ask the following questions:

✔ Do they have Medicaid-certified beds? How many? (See the next section, "Costs of Care," to understand why this number is important.)

✔ Does the home meet your elder's needs?

✔ What is the base cost? What services are included in the base cost?

✔ What extra services (such as hairstyling, cable TV, private telephone, or personal laundry) are available? How much do they cost?

Visit the top three or four contenders on your list and do the following at each place:

1. **Take the formal tour.**

   Trust your senses and intuition. Does the nursing home *feel* good, smell good, and appear clean and bright? Does the noise level make it feel too institutional?

2. **Ask to see the facility's most recent survey report.**

   Every Medicare and Medicaid-certified nursing home submits to yearly inspections. The investigating team arrives unannounced once a year and for three to five days (on average) leaves no stone unturned looking for violations. Team members interview residents and observe how care is delivered. They poke into the kitchen and bathrooms, test the food temperature, and look for problems and signs of abuse or neglect. The report contains a statement of deficiencies, plus the plan for corrective action that the facility has agreed to.

   The detailed inspection report found at each nursing home is the most useful. But it's also a good idea to take a look at the shorter versions online (www.medicare.gov/NHCompare/home.asp).

   Don't expect to find a home without any violations. The average is eight violations found during an inspection. Violations that are intolerable are the ones that put the well-being or the very lives of residents in danger. Ask the administrator about anything in the report that troubles you. Note his or her reaction. If the administrator balks at showing you the report, cross the home off your list! The law requires this report to be made public. Any administrator who tries to tell you that the report is unfair or unimportant is simple to deal with — just run for the nearest exit.

3. **Ask for permission to attend a monthly residents' council meeting or monthly family meeting at any home remaining on the list.**

   These meetings are wonderful opportunities to uncover what the care is *really* like.

4. **Drop in unannounced at different times — for example, during mealtime to see how the food looks and if residents are getting help eating.**

   Is the staff cheerful and warm? Drop in on a weekend, evening, or morning. Chat with lucid residents in the public rooms as well as family members and staff. (See Chapter 24 for more ways to assess a nursing home.)

5. **Revisit the nursing homes you like — with your elder, if possible.**

You can obtain a handy free booklet, *Your Guide to Choosing a Nursing Home*, published by The Centers for Medicare and Medicaid Services. Call 800-633-4227 and ask for publication #02174. You can also download this booklet or order it online at www.medicare.gov — click Publications.

Paying for care

The *average* cost of nursing home care will knock your socks off — $50,000 per year. Despite what many people think, Medicare does *not* "take care of it." Medicare pays only for a brief period of nursing home care under certain conditions. The following sections explore the methods many families use to pay for the care.

Personal resources

When people are admitted to a nursing home, the initial monthly fees commonly come out of their own pockets. Within six months or so, most pockets are darn near threadbare. Money squirreled away for decades to fund a carefree retirement or to leave behind for children and grandkids goes like a flash! Approximately 75 percent of those who receive nursing home care become impoverished after one year. At that point, they can apply for Medicaid. (This process is referred to as "spending down.") (See Chapter 21 to find out more about Medicaid eligibility and how to apply.)

Medicaid

Medicaid is a joint federal and state program that pays for health and long-term custodial care for people with low incomes and limited resources. Elderly Medicaid recipients are required to pay a "share of cost" (from their fixed incomes) toward their nursing home cost. For example, Pop receives a monthly Social Security check of $600. He also receives a monthly pension check of $400, for a total income of $1,000. Medicaid makes up the difference between Pop's $1,000 and the cost of the nursing home (at the Medicaid rate). Medicaid allows Pop to keep a very small amount each month for his personal use. Last time I looked, it was $35 in California. Medicaid programs vary from state to state. (See Chapter 21 for more information on Medicaid.)

Make sure that the nursing home you choose is certified to accept Medicaid patients. A scenario you want to avoid is to have your elder "spend down" to get on Medicaid only to hear, "Sorry, you'll have to find another place to live because we don't have Medicaid beds here."

Medicare

Medicare federal health insurance program for people over 65 (and others with certain disabilities). It's not limited to low- or limited-income elderly. The program has two parts. Part A (hospital insurance) covers most hospital bills, but covers very limited nursing home care. The patient is responsible for some deductibles and copayments. Part B (medical insurance) covers medical bills, most doctor's fees, some medical equipment, diagnostic tests, and outpatient care. Part A has no charge, but Part B requires a monthly premium. (See Chapter 21 for more information on Medicare.)

House of horrors

When your elder moves into a nursing home, you may find yourself blessed with yet one more task — disposing of her house and its contents. The following tips can keep your loved one's house from turning into a "house of horrors."

✔ **Urge your elder to finalize her will as soon as possible.** That way, items designated in the will can be given to the heirs right away, saving on storage costs.

✔ **Line up the professionals.** You need a lawyer (to protect your elder and you), a Realtor (preferably in the same city as the house), a termite exterminator, and a home inspector (to identify and help remedy "deal breakers").

✔ **Maintain the property.** Clear out the squirrels in the garage and cart away dead tree limbs and the trash that gathers in an unoccupied property.

✔ **Contact the county, city, or township sanitation department.** You need to find out its pick-up dates and rules (and the fines if you don't comply).

✔ **Call a dumpster company for the big cleanout.** Do not cart trash around to local gas station dumpsters at night. Dumpsters don't cost as much as you'd think (especially relative to a fine for illegal dumping).

✔ **Keep the power on.** That way, you don't freeze to death in winter and cook in the summer while you're clearing the house, and you can see what you're doing.

✔ **Collect boxes, tape, heavy-duty leaf and garbage bags, and newspapers.** You'll need them to clear out the house.

✔ **Empty the fridge.** Don't take the mayonnaise 300 miles back home — you already have two jars in your pantry! Donate unopened food to shelters. The police or fire station may accept it for the next food drive.

✔ **Prepare for relatives to come out of the woodwork!** Videotape every inch of every room, including knickknacks, chairs, mirrors, the piano, the TVs, and fur coat and then date the tapes. Certain relatives who have come to help have greasy fingers. Don't let them come to town with an empty car!

✔ **Look for lockboxes full of cash and who knows what, stashed who knows where, such as in the basement under the floorboards.** Go through pockets and drawers and look behind drawers, in old cans of nails, and between the pages of books, checking for money, receipts, insurance papers, prescriptions, and jewelry.

✔ **Gather old family mementos and photos in one place and invite family members to review them later.** (Look for photos behind photos.) You can also put the photos on a Web site for all to see and download.

✔ **Throw a *house cooling*.** Give friends and neighbors the chance to bid on items like furniture. Resist dwelling on whether or not to hold on to the junk your elder doesn't want. Put a box of junk on the lawn and mark it "free."

The excellent booklet *Medicare Coverage of Skilled Nursing Facility Care*, published by The Centers for Medicare and Medicaid Services, explains exactly what's covered and where to get help with your specific questions. Call 800-633-4227 and ask for publication #10153. You can also order this booklet online or download it from the Web site www.medicare.gov — click Publications.

Long-term care insurance

There's currently an explosion of private *long-term care insurance* policies on the market. If you purchase a policy when you're fairly young and in good health, the premiums are piddling. When you're no longer a spring chicken and have certain medical conditions, premiums will be very large — that is, if you can get the insurance at all. For example, a 64-year-old whose diabetes is not well controlled probably will be turned down, even if he is an otherwise healthy nonsmoker.

The most difficult problem is figuring out what kind of coverage you need. A crystal ball would help. For example, you may only need an aide who comes in daily to help with dressing, eating, and bathing. On the other hand, you may need 24-hour skilled care in a nursing home facility. Or you may need something in between.

How do you pick options when you have no idea what the future holds? Some folks say, "I'm never going to an institution, so I just need a policy that will pay for someone to come in now and then to help me out." Others say, "Nursing home care will wipe me out fast. I don't want to become impoverished. I'll pay the high premiums now to protect me and my family later." Even with that last option, you'll have to decide how long the custodial coverage should last. Some policies have caps. For example, they'll pay only for three years of coverage, a certain lifetime dollar amount, or whichever comes first. Although the average nursing home stay is two years, no one knows how long he or she will last. Many policies also have deductibles. For example, the first 100 days may have to be paid out of pocket before the policy kicks in. (See Chapter 21 for more information on long-term care insurance.)

Medigap

Medigap, a private insurance, pays for the gaps in Medicare coverage (such as deductibles and co-payments). However, Medigap policies pay only when nursing home care is covered by Medicare (usually a brief period under certain conditions). (See Chapter 21 for more information on Medigap coverage.)

Managed-care plans

Managed-care plans (also called HMOs) provide comprehensive health coverage at low rates to its members. The downside for some folks is that their medical care is limited to the physicians and other health-care professionals who have contracts with the managed-care organization. In addition, the member must use only the hospitals and nursing homes that have contracts with the managed-care company. (See Chapter 21 for information on the Medicare managed care option.)

Each state has its own free State Health Insurance Counseling and Assistance Program (SHIP). Counselors can answer your questions about choosing a managed-care plan and deciding between original (fee-for-service) Medicare and the newer managed-care plan. A counselor can help you understand the new health plan choices, Medicare bills, the appeal process for payment denials, and Medicare rights and protections. To find your state's SHIP go online to www.medicare.gov and click Nursing Homes ↱ Nursing Home Related Sites.

Making moving day okay

Leaving home isn't ever easy. For the young, it's filled with great expectations, hopes, and plans. For the old, leaving home to live in a nursing facility represents loss. Don't *try* to make it cheerful. Make it warm and dignified. The following strategies diminish feelings of helplessness, confusion, and anxiety for your elder (and you):

- ✓ **Plan to spend the day together.** Stay for a meal or two and participate in or observe an activity.

- ✓ **Introduce your elder to her roommate.** Then back off. They'll get to know each other at their own speed.

- ✓ **Personalize her area with things from home (photos, a piece of furniture, a quilt).** Encourage your elder to decide where she wants her things.

- ✓ **Make sure that the call light or bed buzzer works and is within reach — and that your elder knows how to use it.**

  If your elder doesn't understand when or how to use a call light or buzzer, ask the head nurse how the staff intends to deal with this problem. In one facility, for example, confused residents wear electronic devices pinned on their bed clothing. The devices alert the nurses if they get up from bed.

- ✓ **Introduce the new resident to her nurse or nurse assistant.** Try to stay until the next shift so that you can introduce the night people as well. Unfortunately, some homes rotate nursing staff regularly so your elder will have lots of staff members to get to know.

- ✓ **Tell your older person when the next meal will be served.** Make sure that the dietary department is aware of any special diets and food preferences.

- ✓ **Tell your elder when you or someone else will visit — and stick to it!** A calendar with big squares allows you to write the names of who will be coming and when.

- ✓ **Watch for nonverbal signs of fatigue or upset.** Respond to your elder's tears, sighs, and second thoughts about the wisdom of the move with understanding (for example, "Anyone would be unnerved by a big move.")

- ✓ **Tell no lies.** (For example, "It's only for a little while.") Keep in mind that the initial period is but a trial. If things don't go well at this place, you can find other places whose policies, residents, environment, or staff may fit better.

A few things to do before moving day

Try to ease the transition from the old home into the new home with as much advance work as possible. A little preparation can avert problems later:

✔ Ask for a conference with the administrator to discuss matching your elder with a roommate who has a compatible personality and similar level of mental alertness.

✔ Find out what personal items are allowed so that you don't have to take home things that your elder had planned on having with her.

✔ Sew name labels on clothing and mark all belongings.

Moving to a nursing home is particularly difficult for the confused person who is leaving behind the comfort of familiar cues and surroundings that help him function. The following ideas may help with the transition:

✔ Allow him to pick a few things to take with him.

✔ Be matter-of-fact about the move.

✔ Leave information for the staff (in writing), such as his usual evening rituals, the people he might ask for, and the customary ways you comfort him when he's upset.

✔ Should he get upset, don't argue or try to convince him that he'll like it.

✔ Don't take angry accusations personally. His illness may have robbed him of the capacity to express his loss and anxiety in any other way.

✔ Above all, tell no lies such as, "We are just going to stay a little while" or "I'll take you home tomorrow."

Be patient. The period of adjustment can be six months or longer. An illness, a fall, a new roommate, or clashes with a staff member or other resident are only a few of the situations that can trigger setbacks.

Monitoring and evaluating care

When your elder becomes a nursing home resident, you exchange your familiar caregiver role for a guardian angel role. The features of a good nursing home that are presented in Chapter 24 provide a starting place to measure how things *should* be against what you actually observe. The following guidelines can help:

✔ **Visit frequently.** There's absolutely no better way of ensuring good care than becoming a fixture at the facility! Your presence virtually says, "I care deeply about my loved one, and I won't be shy about advocating for him or her." When you can't visit, call the nursing station to see how your elder is doing. Call in between your visits when your long-living person has a cold, has had a bad day, or has had any change in condition.

✔ **Nurture relations with staff members.** Thank them for their work — as you know so well, it's not easy. Get to know them. Remember them at Christmas and Valentine's Day. A small gift, such as a plant or a box of candy, is appreciated, but check with the administration before giving tips.

✔ **Develop friendly relations with family members of other residents.** Family members can be extra eyes and ears, informing one another if something seems amiss.

✔ **Take your elder's complaints seriously, but validate them wherever possible.** For example, when Mother complains that it takes too long for someone to respond to her call light, time how long it takes yourself. Better yet, when you see a call light on for another room (where no visitors present), time that response, too. Ask Mother whether this problem is a continuing one or whether it happens only on certain shifts or with certain nursing assistants. If she complains about the quality of the food, randomly check the appearance, taste, and temperature of several meals at different times over a couple of weeks.

✔ **Understand that unfounded complaints may be indicative of your elder's efforts to get attention or regain power and control in the face of his or her losses.** Look for ways to restore control. Some facilities allow their residents to do volunteer work (delivering mail to other residents, visiting more impaired residents, or distributing materials during craft activities). One wheelchair-bound lady crochets booties for other residents. Having a plant to care for and being able to make choices about her own activities may help as well.

✔ **Discuss any concerns with the appropriate staff members (nursing aide, director of nursing, physical therapist) and with the administrator.** A calm, collaborative "we're all in this together" approach gets much more action than a condescending or angry approach. Mama was right about catching more flies with honey than vinegar!

✔ **Make sure that a Comprehensive Assessment is done.** The law is very clear about this assessment. Two weeks after being admitted, each resident must receive a *Comprehensive Assessment,* including an evaluation of skin condition, mobility, nutritional and medical status, and daily habits. The assessment is revised after significant changes in the elder's condition or at least every three months.

Next, a team of health-care professionals puts together the *Care Plan* (sometimes called a Plan of Care), which states the senior's current medical, nursing, mental, psychological, and social needs and how the facility will meet those needs. The resident (if he is willing and able), his representative, and family members are invited to the Care Plan Meetings to share their perspectives. Your attendance ensures that your elder's wishes will be observed.

Obtain a copy of the Plan of Care and make sure that it's being followed! The nursing home is legally accountable for providing the treatment and services listed in the Plan of Care.

✔ **Be familiar with Nursing Home Resident's Rights.** You should be given a copy when your elder is admitted. If you don't get one, ask for it.

✔ **Document your concerns.** Keep notes of conversations you have with the administrator and other staff members. Record your efforts to get the problem fixed and your contacts with other agencies. Take photos if necessary to document injuries or signs of neglect.

✔ **Contact your ombudsman.** Long-term-care ombudsmen are advocates for the elderly. While they have no power of enforcement, they're experienced and are trained to investigate and resolve a wide range of problems in nursing homes and other adult-care facilities.

To get the telephone number for your local ombudsman, call the Eldercare Locator (800-677-1116) and ask for the local ombudsman program nearest the nursing home or facility where your elder lives or visit online (www.ltcombudsman.org).

✔ **Raise community problems at the family council meeting.** If the facility doesn't have a monthly meeting for interested family members, talk to the social worker, social service designee, or administrator about starting one.

Watching Out for Abuse and Neglect

Most abuse and neglect takes place in private homes, *not* in institutions. The victims are typically women over age 74 who are living with their abuser. Wherever abuse and neglect occur, victims tend to suffer silently, believing that if they tell anyone, unpleasant consequences will occur, such as:

✔ They'll lose the care they depend on.

✔ The abuse will get worse.

✔ No one will believe them.

✔ "Nothing will be done anyway."

✔ They'll feel ashamed and embarrassed.

Bruises (from hitting and pinching) and injuries (from rough handling) are more obvious than the mental suffering caused by emotional abuse and neglect. But even bruises aren't completely reliable. (Old skin is thin and fragile, and it bruises and splits easily.) Ask about any unusual or new marks you notice. If you're told that your elder fell, ask why you weren't notified immediately, as required.

Neglect (intentional or unintentional) is the most common form of abuse in nursing facilities. Examples include

- ✔ Allowing the elder to have soiled or inappropriate clothing, an unshaven appearance, dirty or broken fingernails, and greasy hair. Lack of attention to personal appearance can lead to social isolation, loss of dignity, and despair.

- ✔ Not assisting with eating and drinking (which leads to malnutrition and dehydration)

- ✔ Not assisting with personal hygiene (which leads to offensive odor and social isolation, oral infections, skin breakdown, infection, and loss of dignity)

- ✔ Positioning or turning the elder's body incorrectly (which leads to limb contractures and bedsores)

- ✔ Ignoring call lights, buzzers, and cries for help

- ✔ Not assisting with walking and range of motion exercises (which leads to loss of mobility)

Also be on the lookout for financial exploitation:

- ✔ Misusing the elder's money by taking it with promises to do something that isn't done

- ✔ Not providing the personal allowance allowed to Medicaid recipients

- ✔ Forging checks

- ✔ Not allowing the older person to have access to his or her money

 Valuables, sums of cash, ATM cards, and blank checks should not be kept in the resident's room. (Unfortunately, even other residents have been known to exploit confused or vulnerable elderly.) If your older person wants access to these items, the administrator can keep them in the facility's safe. Some nursing homes even allow a small safe to be installed in an alert resident's room.

Although not usually life-threatening, "mental suffering" (caused by emotional and psychological abuse) can be the most damaging to elders. This form of abuse includes

- ✔ Name-calling

- ✔ Giving the "silent treatment" as punishment

✔ Insults

✔ Threats

✔ Teasing

When you suspect abuse or neglect or your elder tells you about it, report it immediately to prevent continued suffering. States vary on abuse reporting requirements and procedures. Put every detail and all dates down in writing as soon as possible. Keep a copy and give the report to the following authorities:

✔ The nursing home administrator

✔ The state or local ombudsman

✔ The local police department

✔ The appropriate agency in your area. The Eldercare Locator (800-677-1116) can refer you to the right agency.

What is abuse?

How many of the following examples are abusive?

✔ A nursing assistant brings a resident a black banana for her snack. When the old woman won't eat it, the nursing assistant laughs at her and says that the banana is good, and the old lady's eyes must be bad.

✔ A confused man, mistaking a chair for a toilet, urinates on the chair. The aide yells at him and calls him stupid.

✔ A difficult resident makes frequent demands and never says "Thank you." Lately she has been calling her nurse insulting names. The overworked nurse is tired of it, so the next time she dresses the resident, she is a little rough, to "teach her a lesson."

✔ A resident reports his nursing assistant to the administrator because she took an hour to respond to his buzzer. When the nursing assistant goes into the resident's room later that day, she says to the resident, "I'm mad at you. You better not do that again, or you'll be sorry."

✔ An old lady complains that her leg hurts. Her aide responds, "Well, we'll just have to cut if off, then."

All these situations are examples of abuse. Better training may have prevented some of them.

Part II
Mastering Everyday Challenges

The 5th Wave   By Rich Tennant

"I tried stimulating Mom's appetite by reading her a long article about the food of Italy. I then ate two frozen pizzas and a jar of olives while preparing her lunch."

In this part . . .

Helping a frail elder bathe, dress, and eat while you're keeping a lid on the muss and fuss requires an extraordinary amount of skill. Just when you figure out the best way of satisfying your elder's needs, those needs change. Not to worry! This part helps you accomplish the most basic caregiving tasks while drawing closer and dearer to your elder in the process.

Chapter 5

Sleeping Well Means Doing Well

. . . .

In This Chapter

▶ Making the connection between sleep and mood

▶ Dealing with insomnia

▶ Becoming aware of common sleeping disorders in the elderly

. . . .

Most adults need six to eight hours of sleep. Elders who don't get suffi-cient sleep are more likely to get sick, be exhausted and cantankerous, and have memory and judgment lapses. When they already have chronic health problems — as many elderly people do — their conditions may flare up. This chapter shows you how to help your elderly person overcome the obstacles that keep him and you from getting a good night's sleep.

Setting the Stage for the Sandman

People normally cycle through different stages of sleep throughout the night. Sometimes they drift in and out of light slumber, while at other times they're in such a deep sleep that nothing short of a volcanic explosion wakes them. As people age, they spend less time in deep sleep and more time in light sleep. So when the elderly person you care for wakes up when you hiccup two rooms away, consider it normal.

Block out sleep-disrupting noises with good old-fashioned earplugs or "white noise" from a fan or window-unit air conditioner, a radio, or a special device that plays continuous soothing sounds.

Few things are worse than getting into your pajamas, sliding under the covers, plumping up the pillow, flicking off the lamp, and then staring into the dark-ness for hours like a deer caught in the headlights. *Insomnia* (difficulty falling asleep or staying asleep) is the most common sleep complaint among elderly people.

When life events (such as the death of a loved one) interfere with sleep, many doctors prescribe sleeping tablets to get over the hump. Unfortunately, these "magic" pills tend to stop working after several weeks and often have unpleasant or dangerous side effects, so most doctors suggest only intermit-tent use, even for insomnia that isn't related to stress. (For more about drug side effects, see Chapter 11.)

Most sleeping medications cause grogginess, which puts older people at risk for falling (and breaking a hip) when they get up to use the bathroom in the middle of the night. For more safety, have the older person call you for help (with a bell, buzzer, or intercom). When the elderly person lives alone, a bedside commode helps. Check with your doctor before allowing your elder to try herbal sleep remedies and other alternatives to sleeping pills.

Tossing, turning, and cussing because sleep is elusive only serves to associate bedtime with frustration. If your older person can get out of bed safely, encourage him to read, watch TV, listen to music, or whatever else pleases him (except running the vacuum) — and then return to bed a little later.

Fortunately, lots of sleep-promoting strategies don't involve sleeping pills. Some will work for the person you care for; some won't. But every one of the following suggestions has helped someone sometime, so they're worth a shot:

- **Make sure that the older person feels safe.** Reassuring devices include call bells, bedside lamps, smoke alarms, locks on doors, and telephones (especially ones with big numbers) by the bed.

- **Set a comfortable room temperature.** You may need to experiment with different settings. Generally cool is best, but some folks feel better sleeping "hot" (socks, undershirt, extra covers).

- **Darken the room.** Most people find that a dark or semidark room is more sleep enhancing than a room that has light flowing into it. Use an eyeshade to block out unwanted light.

- **Keep the house as quiet as possible.** Older people are generally light sleepers.

- **Give them a hot water bottle.** Warmth soothes. Hot water bottles are safer than a heating pad. Many elders can't tell when a heating pad becomes dangerously hot. If the pad stays in one place, they can be burned fairly quickly.

- **Plan regular bedtime routines (a favorite poem, a nostalgic mini-review of the day, a warm bath).** Rituals signal the body that it's time to wind down.

- **Stroke your elderly person's head and hands, but only if he or she likes it.** Some people are oversensitive to touch. Done nightly, the elder associates this relaxing routine with sleep, which makes it easier to drift off.

- **Play tape-recorded soft music or tune the radio to easy-listening music or call-in shows.** Music and the hum-drum of radio voices calm jangles nerves.

- **Allow a pet to sleep nearby or tuck in a snuggly stuffed animal.** Cuddling makes everyone feel safer and more relaxed.

✔ **Keep bedtime snacks light — perhaps a little warm milk and a cracker.** Milk and other dairy products contain *tryptophan,* an amino acid, which has been shown to help induce sleep. A cracker, a piece of toast, or other carbohydrate enhances the effect.

✔ **Encourage exercise during the day (with the doctor's approval).** Exercise relieves tension, eases stress, and keeps body parts "well-oiled." But avoid exercise close to bedtime unless you enjoy staying up with your elderly person into the wee hours.

Napping or Not, That Is the Question

Faced with a zillion chores, most caregivers are thrilled to see their older person grabbing 40 winks a couple of times a day, but be careful what you wish for. A brief "power nap" — 20 minutes or less — does no harm now and then, but lengthy midday napping comes with heavy consequences. A nap that's more than an hour long is sure to cause sleeping troubles and, in fact, indicates that your elderly person is already having sleeping problems at night.

Here's the vicious cycle you want to steer clear of: Dad takes frequent or lengthy snoozes during the day. Because of all his napping, at bedtime he is wide awake — tossing, turning, and punching the pillow. The next day, he is sleep-deprived and compelled to take frequent or lengthy naps. Getting Dad back on track may call for rousing him after a short doze or coming up with interesting activities (including some exercise) to encourage daytime wakefulness.

Your goal should be the 20-minute nap — long enough to refresh, but short enough not to interfere with nighttime sleep. If your elderly person is used to lengthy naps, slowly ease him into shorter snoozes over several days (or risk getting your head bitten off).

Awakening at the crack of dawn and then not being able to fall asleep again can be a consequence of the dreaded frequent nap — or it can be a sign of depression. (See Chapter 15 for help in determining which it is.)

Make sure that your older person gets some natural light every day. Open the drapes or lift the window shades in the morning so he or she can wake up to a bright, sunny room. Sunlight helps to reset your biological clock; this is crucial when sleep routines are upset because of illness, family visits, or (once again) the dreaded nap.

If you've tried everything and your elderly person is still nodding off, drug side effects may be the culprit. When medication can't be changed, ask whether it can be given at bedtime instead of during the day. Excessive sleepiness during the day or persistent sleeping difficulty begs for a doctor's attention. (See Chapter 11 for more information on medication side effects.)

When Staying Asleep Is Easier Said Than Done

The frequent urge to urinate wakes elders up and is often accompanied by difficulty falling asleep again. After being up and down several times a night, the older person is likely to fall victim to fatigue, grouchiness, and — here you go again — the troublesome long nap.

Frequent urination during the night could be a result of diabetes, bladder infection, prostate trouble, or other medical problems. Remedies are available.

You can buy plastic urinals (they look like curved beakers with a large handle) in most medical supply stores. Both male and female versions are available. These urinals are lifesavers for folks with frequent bladder calls. They can use them throughout the night and empty them in the morning. (See Chapter 13 for more information on dealing with plumbing problems.)

In addition, changes in the room temperature may also wake someone up. During certain stages of sleep, people lose some of their ability to regulate body temperature. Older people naturally lose some temperature regulatory ability even when they're awake. Have you noticed that elderly people don't sweat (a natural cooling-off mechanism) or shiver (a natural heating-up mechanism)? This inability to regulate body temperature efficiently explains why Grandma clings to her cardigan even on warm days and why age-advantaged folks are more vulnerable to hypothermia in cold weather.

Remaining Wide-Eyed and Miserable All Night

When you want your elder to sleep through the night (and who wouldn't), urge him to stick to the following guidelines:

- **Don't drink caffeinated beverages (coffee, chocolate, soft drinks, and nonherbal teas) late in the day.** Experiment to discover how many hours before bedtime your elder has to refrain from caffeine (which is a stimulant) to get a good night's sleep. Decrease fluid intake in the evening to reduce the need to wake up at night to urinate. Encourage him to drink more fluids early in the day.

- **Don't keep an irregular schedule (for example, going to sleep at different times every night).** Doing the same things (like having a bedtime snack and brushing teeth) at the same time every evening signals your elder's body that it's time to go to sleep.

- **Don't enjoy a late supper of fried chicken and dumplings with gravy or other heavy or spicy foods before bedtime.** Eating rich or spicy foods late in the day can trigger *heartburn* (a burning or searing pain in the chest caused by acid flowing upward from the stomach). This condition is especially common when lying down. (See Chapter 10 for more information.)

> ✔ **Don't drink alcohol before bedtime.** Although a nightcap may cause drowsiness, it interrupts sleep as the effects of the alcohol wear off.
>
> ✔ **Don't keep on smoking.** Cravings for a dose of nicotine (even while asleep) will disturb your elder throughout the night and have him up with the roosters, the hens, and the guy who makes the donuts. The nicotine in cigarettes is also a stimulant.

Bona Fide Sleeping Disorders

At last count, at least 70 different kinds of sleeping disorders exist — but fortunately, most of them are rare. The creepy ones like sleepwalking and nightmares mostly terrorize children and teens. Sleep apnea and restless leg syndrome are conditions that are more common in older people (especially in those who suffer from heart disease, obesity, heart failure, and cerebrovascular disease). Sleep apnea and restless leg syndrome tend to be underdiagnosed.

Sleep apnea

Repeated snorting or gasping and then a return to snoring (or normal breathing) as well as excessive sleepiness during the day may indicate a condition called *sleep apnea*. This condition, in which the person stops and starts breathing during sleep, can be life-threatening. It can also lead to hypertension and daytime confusion. The most common form of sleep apnea occurs when the airways collapse. It happens more in men than women and more in heavy people than thin ones.

Sleep medications, sedatives, and alcohol (even in modest quantities) can make sleep apnea worse. Driving can be dangerous.

Losing weight, exercising, and changing sleeping positions are lifestyle changes that often help. Dental appliances that hold the tongue or jaw forward during sleep (so that the airway stays open) may be effective. Some folks get relief from a breathing machine (dubbed CPAP for Continuous Positive Airway Pressure) that pumps air through the nasal passages. In rare, extreme cases, surgeons operate to widen the airways.

Diagnosis of sleep apnea requires a polysomnograph. As long as the sleep specialist you see is from a sleep center accredited by the American Academy of Sleep Medicine, Medicare should cover the initial consultation, tests, follow-up visits, and CPAP equipment.

Check out the Web site `www.assmnet.org/listing.htm` to find your nearest accredited sleep center.

Sleeping pills can prevent sleep apnea sufferers from awakening enough to restart their breathing. Avoid them!

Restless leg syndrome

This condition, which runs in some families and is more commonly found in the old than the young, compels the person to keep legs and feet moving to relieve unpleasant crawling or tingling sensations. Sufferers don't get much sleep — nor do their caregivers.

No known cure exists, but some people get a measure of relief with medication. Ask the doctor whether benzodiazepine drugs would help.

Chapter 6

Helping Finicky Eaters

. . . .

In This Chapter

▶ Understanding why older adults refuse food

▶ Overcoming appetite and swallowing problems

▶ Maintaining the dignity of elders who must be fed

▶ Preventing dehydration

. . . .

My mother, Frances, has always been a robust eater. She can out-eat anyone — and is proud of it! At 84, she is an odd bird — a widow who lives alone and cooks big meals for herself. When I telephone her, she is often stuffing a chicken or making a pot of vegetable soup (from scratch, no less). Mom's not thin — she never was — but she's not fat, either. Age has not quelled her appetite, her cooking ability, or her pleasure in cleaning her plate and taking seconds. Unfortunately, not all elderly people are like Frances.

Many elders find it difficult to eat and drink even when they know they must. This chapter gives you strategies for getting nourishment into your loved one and making meal time more enjoyable for everyone.

Metabolism slows down with age. Older people need fewer calories but require the same vitamins as always.

The majority of older people (especially those who require help to eat or who have disabling illnesses) show diminishing interest in food and eating, many times refusing food altogether or eating too little for optimum health.

Refusing Food

When you understand the reasons behind this disinterest in food, you can take steps to make food interesting again. Elderly people can't, won't, and don't eat because:

✔ **Mouth sores, poorly fitting dentures, gum disease, or dry mouth makes the act of eating difficult.** Older mouths produce less saliva than younger mouths, which makes chewing difficult and swallowing a chore. Sipping fluid between each and every bite makes a big difference. Gravies, broths, sauces, and syrups — over, under, and mixed into foods — help enormously. See the section "Swallowing Difficulties," later in this chapter, for more ways to ease swallowing.

✔ **Cardboard would taste better.** The senses of taste and smell diminish with age. More salt and seasonings — and sometimes a little bit of sweetening (as long as the doctor approves) — can wake up worn-out taste buds. Now you know why Grandma's special stews and soups sometimes taste too salty.

✔ **The food lacks eye appeal.** Set the table with a flourish. Flowers (real or fake) work, as long as they're colorful. Bright napkins, patterned table coverings, and seasonal decorations are inviting — that is, if the older adult isn't confused or demented. In that case, it's best to go for simplicity — avoid patterned plates and tablecloths. Solid-colored bowls are less distracting.

Add some natural food coloring to drab-looking food and try to serve foods with contrasting textures.

✔ **They have trouble using silverware.** If your elderly person has trouble using a knife because of muscle weakness or neurological disease such as stroke, Parkinson's disease, or essential tremor (or in the case of dementia, has forgotten how), cutting the food before you serve it and setting the table with only a fork or a spoon avoids frustration. Plates with raised sides (called *scoop plates*) can be purchased in most medical supply stores. (See Chapter 12 for assistive devices.)

✔ **They're depressed or mourning a loss.** Appetite loss and a drop in weight may signify a serious depression that needs treatment (see Chapter 15).

✔ **They can't poop.** Constipation in older folks can be serious. Severe cases can cause mental confusion and temporary memory loss — or worse (see Chapter 13).

✔ **They are worried or distracted.** Jangled nerves cause some people to overeat and others to disdain food. (See Chapter 16 to help you decide what to do when you suspect anxiety is causing the elder to refuse food.)

✔ **Medication side effects and illnesses (such as infection and heart attack) interfere with appetites.** Are they taking a new medicine? Is a chronic illness flaring up? Alert doctors about weight loss (or gain) and any appetite changes.

✔ **Somebody's rushing them.** Caregivers are an overworked bunch. A relaxed meal with your older person is worth more than tidiness, efficiency, and the prized "beds made before noon" award.

✔ **The amount of food on the plate is intimidating.** It could feed half the population of a third-world country — or so it seems to the person with a pea-sized tiny appetite.

✔ **They live alone.** When you don't have anyone to break bread with, appetites tend to wane, along with the motivation to prepare nutritious meals.

Stimulating the Appetite When All Else Fails

If you still can't get your elder to eat, try these appetite-stimulating ideas:

✔ **Invite your older person to participate in meal preparation.** Let them stir the soup, beat the eggs, and wash the veggies.

✔ **Allow a short "guilt-free" break from the meal.** Return to try again in a few minutes.

✔ **Take a walk or do light exercise before the meal.** Exercise can often stimulate appetite.

✔ **Serve several small meals throughout the day rather than three large ones.** Large portions of food can seem insurmountable and ruin an already small appetite.

✔ **Serve comfort food, such as mashed potatoes, meat loaf, and chicken soup.** Comfort foods are usually familiar dishes that Mother used to make herself. They are associated with family, love, and fond memories — all appetite enhancers.

✔ **Cook favorite foods or ethnic dishes.** This one may take some investigation, because not everyone knows how to prepare collard greens, gefilte fish, or tabbouleh. Better yet, if your elderly person likes to cook, invite her to teach you how to fix her favorite dishes or at least oversee part of the preparation process.

✔ **Try "finger foods" or elegant but nutritious tea-size sandwiches.** Difficulty manipulating eating utensils causes some elders to dread meals. Finger foods eliminate any anxiety about wayward forks and preserve dignity at the same time.

✔ **Offer a glass of juice or a nip of wine, if it's not too close to bedtime.** A nip of wine may be just enough to create a little appetite-enhancing relaxation, but get the green light from the doctor first. As little as one drink may pose a problem to an elder taking certain medications or already at risk of falling. (A drink is 1½ ounces of spirits, 4 to 6 ounces of wine, or 12 ounces of beer.) Depending on size and other factors, an older person should have no more than one drink per day.

> ✒ **Fill the house with wonderful smells.** Successful real estate agents advise sellers to bake cookies or bread before an open house. The same principle works here. The aromas are mood enhancing and help people to be more agreeable to buying a house — or eating their dinner.

Left to their own devices, many elderly people will try to survive on tea and toast or cereal. It's easy to prepare, and they're not hungry anyway. One man I know survived for months on Twinkies. Although Twinkies are tasty, they hardly cover all the food groups. Stock the cupboards and the refrigerator with healthy accessible snacks that an older person can help himself or herself to.

Thick milkshake-like food supplements, such as Ensure and Boost, go down easily. The sweetness pleases the taste buds, and they're ready to use right out of the can. Experiment with different brands and flavors. One woman I know rejected Ensure unless it was chocolate and "on the rocks."

You can give food supplements between or after meals, as long as weight control is not an issue. They provide calories and nutrients, especially for finicky eaters and elderly people who have swallowing difficulties.

Swallowing Difficulties

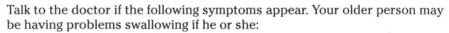

Talk to the doctor if the following symptoms appear. Your older person may be having problems swallowing if he or she:

- ✒ Seems to have difficulty moving food to the back of the mouth
- ✒ Holds food in the mouth
- ✒ Refuses food or drink
- ✒ Coughs or chokes on food or drink
- ✒ Complains that food is stuck in the throat
- ✒ Has a "wet" sounding voice after swallowing
- ✒ Has great difficulty getting pills down
- ✒ Drools

Solutions do exist, however. Although dunking has always been considered poor manners, it isn't anymore. Steeping, sloshing, or submerging finger-food in tea or milk is a great idea for old folks — or anyone who is having trouble swallowing. Mashing food with a fork or pureeing it in a blender helps a lot, too.

A choke is no joke

When tiny particles of food "go down the wrong way" (we've all experienced this problem), you merely cough it up. You may be embarrassed, but no true harm is done. However, such occurrences can be dangerous for elderly people. I know of a number of cases in which a frail older person could not cough up the tiny pieces of food they inhaled (or their own vomit); as a result, they developed aspiration pneumonia.

Inhaled stomach acid and vomit create a breeding ground for lung infection. Running a fever, coughing up blood-tinged sputum, choking while swallowing, difficult breathing, or chest pain signals that a case of life-threatening aspiration pneumonia may have taken hold. Antibiotics and oxygen therapy are the standard treatment.

Sometimes the pieces of food are not so minuscule — like a hunk of bread or a piece of meat. These bigger obstacles block the airway and deprive the brain of oxygen. Brain damage or death can occur if the food is not dislodged and expelled. Choking is most likely to occur when someone is eating too fast, talking while chewing, or consuming alcohol. Here's where the Heimlich maneuver can save the day.

Contrary to what you may think, thin liquids are difficult to get down and are more likely than thicker liquids to cause choking or to be aspirated into the lungs. Products like Thick-It or Thick & Easy Instant Food Thickener add a thicker consistency to hot or cold, thin or thick liquids and purees. Generally, the thicker the fluid, the easier it is to swallow, but go lightly on the amount of thickener used at first because you don't want to thicken more than you have to. Fruit juices, carbonated beverages, tea, coffee, lemonade, broth, and pureed vegetables can all be thickened to the consistency of nectar, honey, or pudding, depending on the amounts of thickener used. You can even thicken drinking water. Drinking thick water seems weird (I've tried it), but it's such a relief to elderly people with swallowing difficulties. You can buy Thick-It, Thick & Easy Instant Food Thickener, and similar products in medical supply stores and some pharmacies.

If you notice signs of swallowing problems, avoid anything that can get stuck in the airways, especially raw carrots, corn, raisins, nuts, peas, and popcorn. If the person is really choking, use the Heimlich maneuver. However, make sure that the person is really choking, because although the maneuver can save a life, the abdominal thrusts can also damage the liver or other internal organs. People who are truly choking cannot talk, cough, or breathe.

Here's the basic Heimlich maneuver, shown in Figure 6-1:

1. **Stand behind the choking person and wrap your arms around his or her waist.**

   If the victim is sitting, bend your knees and waist behind the chair to circle both the victim and the chair.

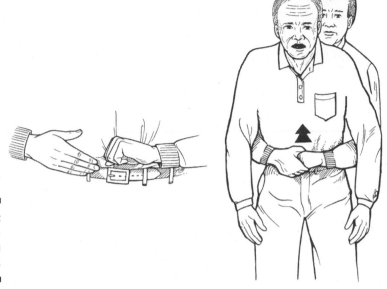

Figure 6-1:
The basic
Heimlich
maneuver.

2. **Make a fist and place the thumb side of your fist against the victim's upper abdomen, below the ribcage and above the navel (about an inch above the belly button).**

3. **Grasp your fist with your other hand and press into the victim's upper abdomen with a quick upward thrust. Repeat until the object is expelled.**

After it's all over and they are breathing again, get a medical evaluation to check on those internal organs.

The Heimlich maneuver is taught in every CPR course. This rescue training can save your elderly person's life.

Heimlich's marvelous maneuver

Dr. Heimlich is one of the cleverest guys around, the kind of person who comes up with brilliant but simple solutions to serious problems. Thirty years ago, the Red Cross taught people to whack a choking person on the back. The problem was that the whack forced the offending object to drop further down into the airway, which then grew even tighter around it. So in 1974, Henry Heimlich invented his now-famous maneuver. The Red Cross retracted its "back whack" recommendation in 1984, and the Heimlich maneuver went on to save an estimated 50,000 lives in the United States and to make the good doctor's name a household word.

You can locate a Red Cross Adult CPR course in your community by going to the Web site `www.redcross.org`.

Spoon-Feeding with Dignity

Eating is far more than just putting substances in the mouth to stay alive. Tasting food is one of life's great pleasures — or should be. The act of eating is steeped with meaning and memories. Food is associated with love, Mother, family life, and grace.

Self-feeding is often one of the last activities that an ailing person can perform. Being fed (like a baby) can result in low self-esteem, poor self-image, and increasing despair. That's why feeding your aged person has to be done with the utmost care, respect, skill, and dignity.

When an older person is unable to feed himself or herself, it's helpful to:

- **Announce what the meal will be and when it will be ready.** Always use positive comments to describe the meal. For example, "This is meatloaf — and boy, does it smell yummy!" Small courtesies promote self-esteem and dignity.

- **Develop a routine before the meal, including hand-washing and toileting.** If they're used to it, saying grace is comforting.

- **Make sure that his glasses are on and his dentures are in.** It's also a good idea to make sure that hearing aids are turned on so that your elder can hear your warm words, which helps eating become associated with pleasant socialization.

- **Prop up her head, neck, back, and sides with foam supports if necessary.** Position her as close to a 90-degree angle as possible, even in bed.

- **Use a table that allows wheelchair arms to slide underneath easily.** Clear bedside tables of all the odds and ends, such as tissue boxes, mail, and the television remote control.

- **Test the food temperature by placing a drop on the inside of your wrist.** Warn that the food may be hot, icy cold, or spicy. Always ask your elder how he or she likes the temperature of his or her food. For example, some folks like soup piping hot, while others prefer it lukewarm.

- **Stir food to cool it or wait for it to cool, but do not blow on it.** (Who knows what microorganisms lurk in your mouth? You can fight them off — but perhaps your fragile elder can't.)

- **Keep foods separate unless your elder asks for them to be mixed together.** Moistening the chicken breast with pudding may get the food down but doing so without asking permission ignores the elder's preference.

- Unless you're absolutely certain, don't assume that the entire meal has to be spoon-fed; ask whether help is needed. Hand him the fork or spoon and request that he try to feed himself.

- Vary the spoonfuls — a bite of meat, a bite of vegetable. Spoonfuls of dessert in the middle of the meal may break up the monotony of the main courses. Then again, it may disturb the elder's sense of order. Ask first.

- Offer liquids between bites to wash down the food. When the meal is over, check your elder's mouth to be sure it's empty. Have the older person spit out the remaining particles if necessary. Food remaining in the mouth may be aspirated later with grave results.

- Don't threaten, beg, plead, or force your elderly person to eat. That coerced extra mouthful may come with serious psychological cost. Spouses, in particular, can often be heard to say, "You'll have to go to the hospital if you don't eat your lamb chop" or "Eat to make me happy" or "I'm begging you — just a little more" — all no-no's.

Keep your elder upright for 30 minutes after the meal to prevent aspiration pneumonia.

Creating a "no-shoveling" zone

Feeding a frail elder demands finesse:

- Fill the spoon halfway, with the food mostly toward the tip of the bowl.

- Touch the person's lower lip to stimulate opening if his mouth is clenched.

- Position the spoon on the middle of your elder's tongue.

- Place an empty spoon in his mouth to trigger the swallowing mechanism if the food from the last spoonful hasn't gone down yet.

- Encourage him to finish, but don't force the issue.

Because there's always so much to do and so little time to do it, you may develop a tendency to rush through meals. You and your elder will enjoy this time much more if you:

- Keep a relaxed pace.

- Be vigilant for your own unconscious nonverbal clues that reveal your impatience (tongue clucking, sighs, checking the clock).

- Allow time to chew, swallow, and take a few breaths in between mouthfuls.

Clearing the table of extra dishes and utensils and turning off a noisy television or radio makes for a more soothing meal experience for an easily distracted and excitable confused elder.

Caring for the Never-Thirsty Elderly

Older folks tend to be a dry bunch. They store less water (but more fat) in their bodies than when they were younger, and their ability to detect thirst (that is, feel thirsty) diminishes with every passing year. Taking in too little fluid, medication side-effects, and illness increase their risk for dehydration.

Ask the doctor about the appropriate fluid intake for your elder. Some medical conditions require restricted fluid.

Water is essential for moving food through the digestive tract and preventing constipation (the scourge of old age). Water regulates body temperature and sodium levels and other elements in the bloodstream. Organs function better. Bad stuff (toxins and impurities) is flushed from cells.

Tea and coffee are fluids, but they are also *diuretics* (substances that increase urination).

Elders taking in less than the recommended 6 to 8 cups of noncaffeinated liquid a day risk dehydration. Warning signs may not be heeded because it's assumed that they're merely part of the normal aging process or chronic illness. Warning signs of dehydration include the following:

- ✔ Headache
- ✔ Dry mouth
- ✔ Cracked lips
- ✔ Dry skin
- ✔ Sunken eyes
- ✔ Nausea
- ✔ Vomiting
- ✔ Diarrhea
- ✔ Weight loss
- ✔ Fast heartbeat
- ✔ Low blood pressure
- ✔ Confusion

✔ Dizziness

✔ Dark urine

✔ Strong-smelling urine

✔ Constipation

✔ Confusion

✔ Lethargy

Waiting for your long-living person to ask for a drink doesn't cut it. Many voluntarily restrict their fluids because of incontinence or fear that they will wet themselves or the bed, which only makes matters worse.

Appealing fluids have to be within in reach at all times — cold if they like cold, hot if they like hot. Don't ask, just offer. For example, "Here's some nice old-fashioned pink lemonade for you" is far better than "Do you want a drink?" Straws that bend are a necessity for bed-bound elders unless they have swallowing problems and are at risk for aspiration pneumonia. You can purchase extra-long straws in medical-supply stores.

Offer a range of fluids, such as water, ice chips, sugar-free popsicles, juice bars, gelatin, ice cream, sherbet, soup, broth, juices, and lemonade.

Chapter 7

Helping Elderly People Be All That They Can Be

*N*ot counting wrinkles, gray hair, and tired bones, America's elderly people are in pretty good shape. Most live well into their 70s, 80s, and beyond. This longevity was not the case 100 years ago, when the average life expectancy was only 47 years — hardly old enough to be called "old as the hills." But living a long time doesn't guarantee that the aged can take care of themselves. No one knows this better than you — the caregiver. You have signed on to be another pair of hands and to lend your heart and mind to caring for an elderly person who needs you.

Seeing that doctors' appointments are kept, meals are cooked, and bills are paid is only part of your job description. Your main job — and most important work — is helping your older person be all he or she can be for as long as possible.

Although I can't promise that your Mom will live to be 102, I can assure you that if you incorporate the recommendations in this book into your daily eldercare routines, she will get the best out of her remaining years, and your job will be considerably easier than you ever imagined.

For most elders, depending on others to help them clean and groom their bodies is painful and embarrassing at best — especially when the person performing the service is a son or daughter.

Bathing Made Easy

Preparing the bath and standing nearby for emergencies may be all that's required to help with personal care. On the other hand, you may have to do *everything,* including toweling dry an embarrassed elderly parent or cajoling a confused spouse into the shower.

First and foremost, act casual — even if you don't feel it. A laid-back attitude helps relax your elder in what may be a disconcerting situation for both of you. Calmness is infectious. Remain unruffled if they say they don't need a bath (despite the fact that potatoes are growing out of their ears).

Resistant bathers will frequently submit to the "power of the prescription pad." When all else fails, work with the doctor to get him or her to write a prescription to take a shower.

Have a frank discussion about bathing. Does your older person prefer a family member to assist, or would she like it better if a stranger did it? How about someone of the same sex, or opposite sex? (Many choose to hire a trained person to come in regularly to do personal hygiene like bathing and shaving.)

It's good practice to:

- ✔ **Ask about usual bathing routines (morning or night, shower or bath, washcloth versus sponge).** Incorporate as many preferences as possible. (See Chapter 12 for ideas to make bathing safe.)

- ✔ **Suggest a tub bath.** Tubs are less dangerous than showers (unless it's a stall shower) and are easier on the caregiver. But don't insist on the tub if she's a shower person.

- ✔ **Get everything — towels, sponges, soap, and shampoo — for a smoother process.** Liquid soaps are more convenient than slippery bars of soap.

- ✔ **Clean under every skin fold and wrinkle — including breasts, neck, and genitalia.** Dry these hard to reach places well to avoid fungal infections. (See Chapter 12 for information on skin care.)

- ✔ **Allow modest elders to hold a towel around their bodies while they're being showered.** Admittedly, this practice seems awkward to me. Nevertheless, I feel compelled to pay attention to what experienced caregivers have told me. They say it works. But what about cleaning those private parts? You decide.

- ✔ **Use a hand-held shower attachment for rinsing.** (See Chapter 12 for other assistive devices.) Protect your clothing with a plastic apron unless you want a shower, too.

✔ **Install nonslip adhesives or the floor and grab bars in the bathtub.** Most medical-supply stores stock a variety of shower stools and bathtub benches for safer bathing.

✔ **Pat dry sensitive, fragile skin.** Applying a moisturizer (one without drying alcohol) after a shower or bath helps to prevent furthering drying.

✔ **Sponge-bathe your elder on some days.** Daily baths aren't usually necessary, and they tend to draw moisture from the skin, especially if the water is hot and the bath or shower is long.

Dressing Challenges

Leroy was a dashing figure in 1938 with his three-piece pin-stripe suit, wing-tipped shoes, and felt hat. He still likes to dress up. His sister Marge is the same way. She accessorizes with colored beads and silk scarves. While other older folks may be quite content with easy-care casual clothes, sweat suits and such hold no appeal for Leroy and Marge.

Determine whether your elder is a "dresser," a "sweat-suiter," or something in between and help him maintain his style as long as possible by:

✔ Encouraging self-dressing and assisting only when needed

✔ Laying out all clothing in the order it should be put on

✔ Buying duplicates if they insist on wearing the same thing every day

✔ Replacing tricky buttons, snaps, and zippers with Velcro

✔ Maintaining dignity by providing a couple of clothing choices

✔ Complimenting his or her appearance, but only when the flattering remark is genuine

For disabled elderly, put the painful or weak arm or leg into the clothing first, minimizing stress on the weaker side. When removing clothes, take the stronger arm or leg out first.

 As women age, their tummies protrude, and their behinds flatten. Finding pants to fit becomes a chore. An easy solution, especially with elastic-waist pull-up pants, is to wear them backwards so that the extra seat room now covers the tummy.

In addition, if your elder's underwear is uncomfortable, substitute a camisole or undershirt for a bra, or boxers for briefs. Swap pantyhose for knee-highs or socks, but only if your elder lady agrees.

When they become angry or confused . . .

Bathing a confused older adult may become more difficult because the person may have forgotten what bathing is for and perceives the whole experience as distressing. She may feel threatened, get angry, and react with resistance, screaming or even hitting.

For confused elders:

✔ **Increase the room temperature.** Being cold sometimes ignites a strong emotional reaction.

✔ **Test the water temperature.** The elder may be unable to tell you that it's too hot or too cold.

✔ **Don't get bent out of shape if personal care provokes an inappropriate sexual behavior.** Try distraction or counter with a firm but gentle "no." (See more about inappropriate sexual behavior in Chapter18.)

Look out for tight clothes. Advanced age affects the ability to detect the discomfort associated with tight belts and binding sleeves that can interfere with circulation.

Keeping Smiles Bright and Mouths Healthy

Old age, illness, and dentures don't diminish the need for oral hygiene and regular dental checkups. The amount of saliva (which cleans teeth) decreases with age, leaving the mouth more vulnerable to tooth decay and infection. Pair that with the inability to brush and floss, and the risk soars.

Dentures should be checked regularly for proper fit. Long-living people are also at high risk for oral cancer — another reason for regular dental visits.

When your elder's loss of dexterity or lack of a firm grip make holding a toothbrush akin to holding a greased pig, try to:

✔ Attach the brush to the elder's hand with a wide elastic band.

✔ Enlarge the brush handle with a sponge, rubber ball, or bicycle handle grip.

✔ Wind adhesive tape around the handle.

✔ Lengthen the handle with a piece of wood, such as a ruler or tongue depressor.

✔ Introduce an electric toothbrush.

✔ Brush his or her teeth with a wet toothbrush or an electric toothbrush.

✔ Clean her mouth with swabs designed for this purpose; oral swabs can be found in most medical supply stores.

✔ Clean his mouth with a damp cloth.

For confused elderly, you can stand by the person and give several short simple instructions: "Hold your brush," "Now put toothpaste on the brush," "Now raise the brush to your teeth," "Now brush your top teeth," or "Now brush your bottom teeth." You can even brush along with him, mirroring what to do.

Skip the toothpaste if the elder is at risk for aspiration pneumonia.

Keeping an Old Brain "Young at Heart"

Contrary to what researchers always thought, evidence shows mental stimulation can cause new cell growth in some areas of the brain.

Day after day of lying about with nothing new or exciting happening decreases the likelihood of hanging on to one's mental abilities. On the other hand, physical activity (which increases blood flow to the brain) increases the ability to think and solve problems. Chalk up yet another benefit for exercise. Above all, exercise the brain!

To help your older person hang on to his mental abilities (and maybe improve them):

✔ Stimulate his senses with new sights, sounds, and feelings. (How about a weekly massage?)

✔ Reduce stress with meditation, prayer, music, and a good night's sleep.

✔ Seek immediate help for depression. (See Chapter 15 for more information.)

✔ Obtain treatment for blood pressure, high cholesterol, and other cardiovascular conditions.

✔ Get diabetes, heart disease, and other medical conditions under control.

✔ Plan a day trip to a local event and then discuss it.

✔ Take a trip to visit a relative or see a new or familiar location. (See Chapter 14 for travel tips.)

✔ Encourage him to learn something new.

✔ Create opportunities to socialize with family and friends.

Remembering and reflecting on the past is associated with advancing years. Some regard it as the play or work of old age. (You can find out more about the healing aspects of reminiscence in Chapter 15.) Not only that, it's educational. (See the section in Chapter 20 about creating family histories.) Your elder can exercise his or her brain by attacking crossword puzzles, identifying old photos, recalling song lyrics, and playing board games and card games.

Exercising

Don't give in to the temptation to skip this section because your elder person is disabled, suffers from a chronic medical condition, or is a lifelong couch potato. Those are exactly the reasons why your age-advantaged person *should* exercise.

Physical activity (with few exceptions) carries enormous benefits for older people in all sorts of shape. For example, walking strengthens the heart and cardiovascular system, reducing the risk of heart disease. Twenty minutes of exercise three times a week may be all that's necessary for health benefits.

When older adults combine endurance activities (walking or other activities that increase heart rate and breathing), strength-building exercises (for example hoisting a weight as light as a soup can), and flexibility exercises (stretching) on a regular basis, they can

- Reverse bone loss (even if bones have already become brittle)
- Improve chronic diseases
- Positively affect disabilities
- Relieve depression
- Enjoy better sleep
- Regain appetites
- Increase alertness
- Lower the risk of falls and injuries (fewer broken hips)
- Improve strength, mobility, and circulation
- Improve skin tone
- Affect their bladder and bowel functioning
- Improve the workings of their liver, pancreas, and other organs
- Strengthen muscles, tendons, and ligaments (easing the pressure on old joints)

Pumping iron at 90

Enroll a group of frail, chronically ill elderly in their 80s and 90s in a weightlifting program (three days a week for six weeks) and wait. That's exactly what researchers from Tufts University did in 1989 at the Hebrew Rehabilitation Center for the Aged in Boston. The results were incredible. The elders increased their muscle strength an average of 180 percent and increased their walking speed an average of 48 percent. Two participants threw away their canes, and one participant was able to get up from a chair without using the arm rests to support himself. After the study, the participants resumed their sedentary lifestyles. When they were tested again four weeks later, they had lost 32 percent in maximum strength. If ever there was a case for "use it or lose it," this is it!

What exercise won't do (in the later years) is build the bulging biceps and sculpted physiques of youth. But if the result is that muscles work more efficiently and health improves, who cares!

 Many elders who suffer from congestive heart failure, diabetes, and arthritis can benefit tremendously from exercise, once their condition has been pronounced stable and under control. Check with the doctor before starting. When the doctor gives the go-ahead, engage a physical therapist to work with the older person to make sure that he or she follows the protocol and to train you to supervise the exercise at home.

For safety's sake, have your elders:

- ✔ Warm up with some gentle stretching exercises.
- ✔ Start slowly, building the amount of effort gradually.
- ✔ Drink plenty of fluids (unless the doctor says otherwise).
- ✔ Call it quits if there's any sign of shortness of breath, pain in the neck or jaw, palpitations, major muscle or joint pain, nausea, cramps, or excessive fatigue (in other words, discomfort).
- ✔ Exhale during muscle exertion and inhale during relaxation. For example, breathe out when lifting a weight and breathe in when they put it down.
- ✔ Avoid stopping abruptly. (Remind them to cool down slowly.)
- ✔ Avoid dizziness by getting up from a sitting or lying-down position slowly.
- ✔ Avoid light-headedness by not changing direction too fast.

 Breath-holding while straining (for example, lifting weights) is a no-no for people with high blood pressure.

Standing exercises

Many strengthening exercises can be done standing. I like this hip and lower abdomen exercise because your elder can do it by holding on to the back of a sturdy chair or a walker.

1. **Stand erect.**

2. **Raise one knee upward as far as possible keeping back straight.**

3. **Return to starting position.**

4. **Repeat with other leg.**

5. **Repeat five times for each leg.**

Your elder can do this next one either standing up or sitting down, using nothing heavier than a book or a can of soup.

1. **Stand or sit erect with arms at side, holding the book or can of soup.**

2. **Bend the arm, raising the object.**

3. **Lower the object.**

4. **Now switch arms.**

5. **Repeat 10 to 15 times for each arm.**

For more exercises, order *Exercise: A Guide from the National Institute on Aging,* a free illustrated 80-page booklet describing ways for older adults to exercise safely, by contacting the NIA Information Center, P.O. Box 8057, Gaithersburg, MD 20898-8057; 800-222-2225. The booklet is also online at www.nia.nih.gov/exercisebook/intro.htm.

Sitting exercises

A wheelchair-bound older person with upper body mobility can benefit from stretches. The one shown in Figure 7-1 relieves stiffness and tension in the neck and shoulders:

1. **Lift the shoulders up toward the earlobes.**

2. **Hold for 5 to 8 seconds.**

3. **Relax completely, letting the shoulders drop down naturally.**

4. **Repeat several times.**

The next exercise, shown in Figure 7-2, provides a nice stretch for an older person who uses a wheelchair.

1. **Pull one knee up toward your chest with both hands for an easy stretch.**

2. **Hold the knee near the chest until any tension disappears.**

3. **Pull the knee up just a wee more until you feel a mild comfortable tension again; release.**

4. **Repeat with the other leg.**

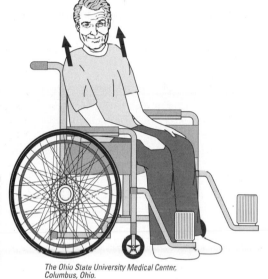

Figure 7-1:
The
shoulder
shrug.

*The Ohio State University Medical Center,
Columbus, Ohio.*

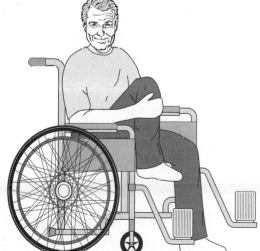

Figure 7-2:
The knee to
chest lift.

*The Ohio State University Medical Center,
Columbus, Ohio.*

Lock the wheelchair in place before exercising.

You can obtain the *Health for Life Stretching Exercises for Wheelchair Users,* which contains many other exercises for wheelchair users, free by contacting the Center For Health Information, 410 W. 10th Ave., Columbus, OH 43201; 614-293-3707.

Lying-down exercises

Bed-bound elderly need exercise, too. Range-of-motion exercises can prevent tight muscles and stiff joints. A full-body-range regimen starts with the shoulders and works toward the feet. Each joint is moved gently through its normal range of motion by the caregiver. A trained therapist, nurse, or doctor can train you to do range-of-motion exercises. The important thing is to do the exercises carefully and slowly and to stop if your older adult seems to be experiencing distress.

Giving a Hug a Day Keeps the Doctor Away

Older people don't get hugged nearly enough. Embracing infants, toddlers, and children is a national pastime. Teenagers smooch when they can. Adults get pleasure from affectionate relationships with their partners. Children grow up and move away, and life partners die, making oldsters vulnerable to still another hardship — *skin hunger.*

Proper nutrition, a good night's sleep, and plenty of fluids keep bodies healthy, but an unfulfilled longing for human touch (sometimes called skin hunger) leaves a hole in the heart and soul. Hug, hold, caress, and touch your elderly person often and firmly. Contact receptors are less sensitive with age, so a hug has to be firm to truly be appreciated.

A pet that likes to be stroked and snuggles up to his owner also helps to satisfy the longing for touch. If you can't keep a pet, try borrowing one.

Caregivers or bed-bound or wheelchair-bound elders who would like to receive visits from a pet therapist can call the Delta Society at: 425-226-7357 (8:30 a.m. to 5 p.m., PST, Monday through Friday). The Delta Society is a nationwide, free service that offers the Pet Partners Program. Callers will be

Rosie and Jack

Rosie and Jack met in a home for the elderly. One thing led to another until they were sneaking into each other's rooms to spend the night. The administration forbade it, but here was no halting their growing love and affection. Rosie, the more vocal of the pair, asked for a double bed to replace her single one. Time after time she was refused — until Jack fell out of her bed, landing and breaking his arm. The nursing home administrator pulled some strings and got a double bed for the lovebirds.

asked about the older person's level of frailty, preference for cats or dogs, and how long and how often visits should last. The Delta Society will then contact a pet therapy volunteer in the caller's area and facilitate a meeting time. The address for the Delta Society is: 580 Naches Ave. SW, Suite 101, Renton, WA 98055-2297. Information about the Delta Society is online at www.deltasociety.org.

The elderly's desire for human contact isn't limited to cuddling. Sexual interest and desire actually decline very little throughout life, despite the lack of a partner or other obstacles. A broken hip, for example, may compromise sexual functioning, but it doesn't necessarily dampen sexual interest or desire.

If Mom wants to hold hands with the man she met at the adult daycare center, rejoice. If the widow next door comes to call with a casserole in hand (and your elder doesn't mind), give the pair privacy and allow the relationship to flourish.

Enabling romance requires understanding and appreciating that sexual intimacy and affection are life-enhancing. Be an advocate, pressuring agencies that serve elders to promote and celebrate romance between their older consumers. Studies show that older people welcome questions from professionals about their sexual functioning or sexual problems even though most would never dream of bringing it up themselves. (See Chapter 18 for information on inappropriate sexual behavior.)

Enabling Romance is a wonderful book on love, sex, and relationships for people with disabilities and the people who love them. You can order it directly from New Mobility at 888-850-0344 or online at www.newmobility.com.

Together Again: Our Guide to Intimacy After Stroke is another well-written pamphlet. You can order it directly by calling the American Stroke Association family warmline at 800-553-6321.

Devoutly in love

Lucille, a confused older lady, resides in a nursing home because her husband Edward no longer can keep her safe at home. Her roommate Catherine reports to anyone who will listen that "Lucille's husband loves her so much. Every night he bends down to pray with her." Indeed, Edward does love Lucille a lot, but it's not praying that they do. Lucille's mattress is close to the floor, minimizing the risk of her falling out of bed. Edward goes on his knees nightly to put his arms around her, cover her face with kisses, and tuck her in. The nightly affection comforts the couple in a way that nothing else can.

Chapter 8

Sharing the Caring

• •

In This Chapter

▶ Recognizing caregiver stress

▶ Finding a way to "have a life" and be a caregiver at the same time

▶ Reaching out to professionals and community services for assistance

▶ Hiring in-home help

▶ Avoiding a "meltdown" when the help doesn't show up

• •

*F*amily members step up to the plate every day to pay bills, shop, cook, houseclean, and supervise medications. As their elderly person grows more frail, their tasks tend to become more time-consuming (and often more difficult). Helping Mom with the laundry may evolve into dressing Mom each morning and undressing her each night. A weekly telephone call to check up on Dad may develop into a daily visit to reassure yourself that he is safe and well.

Nearly seven million older Americans depend on others to help them carry out their daily tasks of living. This chapter is about the professionals and the community services equipped to help you provide care and — as a bonus — prevent you from falling victim to caregiver stress.

Identifying Caregiver Burnout

When a good night's sleep (or a great meal) fails to brighten your mood, you may be staring *caregiver stress* in the face. When nothing seems interesting, and the present and the future seem hopelessly bleak, you may be experiencing symptoms of *burnout*. Caregiving can be tremendously satisfying, but the unrelenting responsibilities, challenges, and demands of caregiving can also deplete you physically, emotionally, and spiritually over time, turning simple stress into burnout.

It doesn't seem to matter much whether you're doing the daily grunt work or managing and organizing care from a distance. Caregiver burnout occurs when the amount of work that needs doing outstrips your time and energy.

Providing care, day in and day out, and getting nothing in return (because your elderly person is too ill or too confused to do something for you) also adds to caregiver stress. Life is lovely when giving is balanced with getting. For example, when your best friend rolls up his sleeves to help with the Christmas cookie baking, and you reciprocate by lending your muscles to his yard work, both of you feel pleased with the relationship — and the labor involved is hardly noticed.

When caregiving brings you nothing in return — not even appreciation — seek other sources of satisfaction, such as a support group or the warmth of a sympathetic friend.

Answering the following questions can help you determine whether you're suffering from the effects of caregiver stress:

- ✔ Do you frequently feel blue (especially about having to give up your old activities and familiar social life)?
- ✔ Do you feel fatigued despite the amount of rest you get?
- ✔ Do you have trouble falling asleep or staying asleep?
- ✔ Have you lost interest in your work, hobbies, friends, children, or grandchildren?
- ✔ Have you let your grooming slip?
- ✔ Have you been careless about your own health and medical needs?
- ✔ Has a chronic health condition (for example, an ulcer or high blood pressure) flared up?
- ✔ Do you feel that you're losing touch with the world (and perhaps becoming less interesting to others)?
- ✔ Do people keep telling you that you look bad or that you should hire help?
- ✔ Are you smoking or drinking more?
- ✔ Are you abusing or misusing sleeping pills or other drugs?
- ✔ Has your appetite increased or decreased?
- ✔ Do you experience feelings of helplessness?
- ✔ Are your emotions reeling out of control? For example, are you more irritable, is your temper shorter, or are you more anxious?

A single "yes" answer may be a sign of caregiver stress. Two or more affirmative answers are an even greater indication that you may be suffering from stress. (See the next section, "Care for the caregiver," for help.)

Don't ignore such warning signs. Older caregivers who experience caregiver stress (and have chronic health conditions to boot) have a 63 percent higher chance of dying prematurely than people of a similar age and health who are not experiencing caregiver stress.

Caring for a parent who didn't care for you

The majority of parents do a pretty good job of parenting their children, which helps to ensure that most children will grow up honoring and loving their parents — and offering eldercare. But what happens when an abusive or absent parent, now up in years, turns to his or her resentful adult child for help? How in the world do you care for a mother or father who showed no love, compassion, or understanding to you when you were a child?

A sense of moral obligation and love motivates many people to take care of such neglectful parents — but no law says that you must provide financial, emotional, or physical assistance to a parent. Whatever you choose to do, be clear about your expectations. Providing care in the hopes of finally getting a parent's approval or love may be a setup for disappointment.

You can resolve deep-seated hurts and anger between parent and child (or spouses or siblings) as the end of life approaches, but it's still a rare occurrence. On the brighter side, the experience of forgiving a parent and expressing long-buried questions and feelings (and providing care) may be one of the most satisfying experiences of your life. (See Chapter 9 for tips on grower closer.)

Care for the caregiver

Accepting limitations — your own and your elder's — is a superb way to reduce stress. Look at the big picture; don't dwell on small annoyances. For example, don't sweat it because the house is dusty, and you haven't been able to get Mom out of her favorite pink blouse for three days. What's important is the bigger picture — your care has resulted in Mom's blood pressure being in control for the first time in years.

Try the following additional strategies to reduce or prevent caregiver stress:

- **Lighten up.** Seek situations and experiences that make you laugh (like reruns of TV situation comedies) and see the humor in the funny things your confused elder does. He may enjoy the laugh, too, even though he doesn't fully comprehend the humor.

- **Look for ways to save energy and time.** For example, shop by catalog or telephone. Some stores take phone orders and have your groceries ready for you to pick up. Shop during off-hours (early is great). Many markets deliver.

- **Avoid isolation.** Staying in the house day after day gets you down. (See Chapter 14 for tips on getting out and about easily with your older person in tow.)

- **Practice what you preach.** You provide nutritious meals for your elder. You get her up, see that she exercises, and are always on the lookout for things to entertain and relax her. Do the same for yourself.

✔ **Find out more about your elder's health conditions.** Knowing what to expect next helps reduce anxiety and increases your confidence. (See Chapters 10 and 11 for information about age-related illness and medications.)

✔ **Join a support group.** No one understands you better than someone who is going through a similar experience. Group members are famous for giving each other emotional support, imparting information, and discovering and sharing creative solutions to mutually shared problems. (See the section on support groups for more information.)

✔ **Use relaxation techniques.** Simply closing your eyes and visualizing comforting peaceful scenes, listening to music, or meditating may refresh you.

✔ **Discover a new hobby or re-establish an old one.** Scrapbooking, puttering at a workbench, sewing, or organizing old photographs are just a few of the creative pastimes that have stress-fighting restorative powers.

✔ **Rotate chores.** Ask family and friends to occasionally (or regularly) relieve you of some of the more mundane but time-consuming tasks. (See Chapter 3 for more about rotating tasks.)

✔ **Compartmentalize tasks.** Break up big jobs (like preparing Dad's home so that he can live independently after his stroke) into tiny parts (for example, installing grab bars and railings). Then break those parts into smaller components (for example, buying the supplies at the hardware store, arranging a convenient time for installation, deciding where to place the devices). Focus on one small component at a time so as not to be overwhelmed by the big job. That's how I write books — one small section at a time!

✔ **Avoid multitasking.** It's generally far better for your psyche to work on one thing at a time. Trying to figure out this month's medical bills while eating dinner makes for indigestion at worst and an unpleasant meal at best.

On rare occasions, multitasking does make sense. For example, you may want to reconcile your checkbook while waiting in the doctor's office. (Bring something for your elder to do, too!) Better yet, call before you leave the house to see whether the doctor is running late. You may be able to leave the house later, saving you and your elder from the tedium of a long wait.

✔ **Seek professional help if the stress seems overwhelming.** A short course of professional counseling can lead to a period of personal growth for you.

✔ **Take advantage of respite care.** Regular breaks in eldercare prevent burnout. (See the next section for more on respite care.)

Respite care

Respite care is an arrangement in which a substitute caregiver (bless his or her heart!) enters the scene to give you a break. For example, a relative or close friend of yours or your elder's drops by the house for three hours twice a week to keep your elder company while you to do whatever you please. This simple remedy prevents stress, burnout, and downright collapse.

Respite works best when your time off is spent on activities that refuel, relax, or energize you. *Regularly* scheduled time off, whether for a few hours, an entire day, a weekend, or a whole week, can boost your mental and physical well-being and postpone premature institutionalization for your elder! When family and friends are unavailable, the age-advantaged person can join a respite program in the community, or you can hire in-home or respite workers. (See the section "Hiring Help Wisely," later in this chapter.)

To locate respite care services, go online to www.chtop.com. Click Respite ☞ National Respite Locator Services ☞ *Your State* for a listing of organizations that provide respite care workers.

Where to find respite care

Finding respite care referrals takes energy, but it's worth every ounce of effort. The following are places to call for services or referrals:

✔ **Local area agencies on aging.** These agencies, which often can provide referrals of self-employed respite workers, have different names in different states. You can find your local agency by calling the Eldercare Locator at 800-677-1116.

✔ **Houses of worship.** Many churches, synagogues, and other religious institutions can refer you to services.

✔ **Adult daycare centers.** You can find the numbers of these agencies in telephone directories. A number of daycare programs have special respite programs that include overnight options.

✔ **Skilled nursing facilities.** These facilities are great if you need extended time off,

although they can be quite costly. Medicare typically pays for respite care only for hospice patients. (See Chapter 23 for more about hospice.)

✔ **Word-of-mouth recommendations.** Ask around. Someone you work with or a friend of a friend may have had a truly dedicated caring person look after his or her loved one.

✔ **Home-care agencies.** Call your elder's doctor or a hospital discharge worker. (Also see the sections "Going to an agency" and "Hiring independently," later in this chapter.)

✔ **Call your state Department of Aging.** You can find the number in your telephone directory. Ask whether your state is one of the few that offers funds to pay for respite care. If the answer is "yes," keep your fingers crossed when you ask about a waiting list.

Where to find a support group

The following suggestions can help you find a support group in your area:

- The **Alzheimer's Association** provides contact information for support groups for caregivers of sufferers of Alzheimer's disease and related disorders. Call 800-272-3900 or go online (www.alz.org) to find your local Alzheimer's Association chapter, which will refer you to a support group.

- The **American Stroke Association** operates the Stroke Family Warmline. Telephone counseling for stroke survivors and their caregivers is provided by caregivers themselves. (One staff member is also a stroke survivor.) Counselors can refer you to a support group in your area. Call 800-553-6321.

- **Senior centers, hospital social services or social work departments, YMCA or YWCA branches, and houses of worship** may also have support groups. Let your fingers do the walking in the telephone directory to locate these resources and keep your eyes peeled for announcements of caregiver meetings in local newspaper Community Calendars.

- The **Family Caregiver Alliance** provides callers with referrals for support groups in the caller's area by telephone (800-445-8106) or through its Web site (www.caregiver.org).

- The **National Self-Help Clearinghouse** can refer callers to support groups in their area or to local information clearinghouses. Call 212-817-1822 or reach the organization through e-mail (info@selfhelpweb.org) or through its Web site (www.selfhelpweb.org).

- The **Well Spouse Foundation** is a national group offering support to the wives, husbands, and partners of chronically ill or disabled people. Although it may not have a support group in your area, it's worth checking out because the membership fee ($25 a year) includes six issues of a bimonthly newsletter, lists of support groups, announcements of workshops and conferences, and the opportunity to join a "round robin" letter-writing support group. No one is turned away because of financial hardship. Call 800-838-0879 or e-mail info@wellspouse.org. Its Web site is www.wellspouse.org.

When the idea of respite first arose, my Dad was adamantly against it, saying, "I don't need no baby sitter!" After weeks of cajoling, Dad reluctantly agreed to allow the respite care worker to visit briefly. The second time Evie came, she stayed a little longer than the first visit, and Mom went out. By the third visit, Dad was having such a good time regaling the young woman with his boyhood escapades that he barely noticed Mom's departure or return. Evie's enthusiasm for Dad's oft-repeated stories endeared her to the entire family and provided Mom with precious personal time. (See Chapters 2 and 4 for helping elders accept help.)

Most respite workers are women, but agencies will try to provide a male worker when requested.

Introduce the respite worker as a friend. Always tell your elder where you're going and when you'll return. For good measure, write down the information on a reminder note that your elder can read.

Support groups

Support groups work! Decades of research show that that people benefit tremendously from support groups. A support group can give you a fresh perspective, tried-and-true ideas for solving caregiving dilemmas, and information about resources you never knew existed. Other benefits include experiencing less anxiety, less depression, and also feeling helpful to others in the "same boat."

For your own well-being, try to overcome any natural reluctance you may feel to joining a group. Caregivers who participate in support groups are less likely to need healthcare themselves than caregivers who don't participate.

You may find yourself in a group that is just not right for you. For example, your elder is at the beginning stages of Alzheimer's disease, while the other members are caring for elders in the late stage. Should that happen, don't be shy about bowing out and looking for another group.

Helping Hands Are Welcome Hands

Home healthcare is a broad term that covers a host of health and social services delivered in the home. The helping hands who deliver these services come with a baffling range of titles, levels of experience, education, and training. Some work for agencies; others can be hired independently. To complicate the picture even more, different helpers with the same title may not perform the same services, whereas helpers with different titles may carry out many of the same services.

About 8,000 home health-care agencies throughout the country are Medicare-certified, which means that they're authorized to provide services for Medicare-eligible elderly. Health-care agencies usually advertise the fact that they're certified in their ads (but not all agencies are certified or licensed).

Medicare will probably pay for some of the care if your elder requires skilled nursing service. Your elder must be Medicare-eligible, be under a physician's care, and require "medically necessary" skilled nursing care, therapeutic interventions, or hospice services. He must be *homebound* (meaning he can leave the home for medical reasons only and for occasional special events such as a family reunion, funeral, or graduation). The agency bills Medicare directly for the services in the same way that doctors do. (See Chapter 21 for more information on Medicare coverage.)

If your elder requires *only* nonskilled services, you'll probably have to hire an aide from an agency or registry or find someone on your own and pay for it yourself.

You can obtain a free booklet, *Medicare and Home Health Care,* published by The Centers for Medicare and Medicaid Services. Call 800-633-4227 and ask for publication #10969. You can also download or order this booklet online at www.medicare.gov (click Publications). The booklet describes the home health benefit and eligibility.

You can sort out the virtual army of potential helpers by those who mainly do household tasks, those who primarily perform personal care, and finally those who carry out skilled health and medical duties. (For more information about home health-care agencies, see the section "Going to an agency," later in this chapter.)

When medical expenses are tax deductible, the cost of in-home care is deductible only to the extent of nursing care, not homemaker services. In other words, when one person delivers both nursing care and homemaker services, only the hours spent on nursing care are deductible. Ask your tax preparer how to handle this deduction properly.

Chore workers

Chore workers mostly help with minor household repairs and maintenance (doing yard work, cleaning house, removing snow, and installing safety devices, such as ramps). They may also do grocery shopping, laundry, and meal preparation. Churches, senior centers, or other nonprofit groups in your community may offer such services for free (however, you may be asked to pay for materials) or on a sliding scale.

Homemakers

Homemakers tidy up, shop, do laundry, and prepare meals. They may do some paperwork and make phone calls. You can find these helpers through home-care agencies or your own resourcefulness.

Companions

Companions provide company or supervision for someone who can't be left alone. They may prepare lunch. Some may stay through the night. Like homemakers, you can find these helpers through home-care agencies or your own resourcefulness.

Home-health aides and personal attendants

Home-health aides and personal attendants assist with bathing, feeding, walking, toileting, and transferring the elder to and from a chair, bed, or toilet. *Home-health aides* who work for certified home-health agencies are trained and supervised by a registered nurse (or physical therapist) and may also take temperature, pulse, respiration, and blood pressure readings, change bandages, and assist with exercises prescribed by physical and occupational therapists. Medicare covers this cost only when these services are needed *in addition* to "medically necessary" in-home nursing care or therapy.

Personal attendants tend to work with people with disabilities and are most often hired independently. They assist with personal care and accompany clients to recreational activities and medical appointments. For example, thanks to his personal attendant José, Milton (a stroke survivor) continues to enjoy painting lessons at the community college. José drives Milton to the studio, sets up his paints, straps a brush to his hand, and cleans Milton and the art supplies when the class is over.

Physical therapists

Physical therapists use specialized equipment and massage to improve the muscle strength, flexibility, and mobility of people with disabilities or physical injuries. They also train caregivers in how to lift and bend with minimal strain. A physician usually prescribes physical therapy.

Occupational therapists

Occupational therapists help elderly cope with and compensate for their limitations. They train the caregiver and the older person in techniques aimed at improving the elder's muscle control and coordination. The goal is to make everyday tasks of living easier. For example, they teach the elder how to use a walker and cane properly, navigate stairs, and get up safely from chairs. A physician usually prescribes occupational therapy.

Speech therapists

Speech therapists assist individuals with communication disorders (resulting from disease, injury, surgical intervention, and stroke). They help elders regain lost speech and also teach techniques to aid in swallowing and breathing. A physician usually prescribes speech therapy.

Nutritionists

Nutritionists provide dietary guidance. They put together a diet compatible with the elder's medications, taking into account food restrictions determined by specific ailments (for example, diabetes or heart disease). Nutritionists can also instruct caregivers about food preparation (pureeing, portion control).

Nurses

Visiting registered nurses only work under a doctor's prescription. Their visits can be anywhere from half an hour to an hour once a week or every day (although daily visits are extremely rare). Medicare covers the cost when nursing services are deemed "medically necessary." Nurses' tasks include preparing a plan of care, taking blood and urine samples and delivering them to the lab, changing wound dressings, caring for ostomy openings and intravenous sites, inserting intravenous lines and catheters, and giving injections. They also train caregivers to perform some medical tasks and show them safe ways to transfer and lift their elder.

Care managers

Geriatric care managers (also called case managers) can carry out a thorough assessment of your elder's needs, line up all the required helpers, and monitor and evaluate their services, making adjustments as needed. Care managers are usually (but not always) social workers or nurses who are well schooled in the needs of frail older people. You pay a monthly fee to the care manager in addition to the individual services he or she procures and oversees. (See Chapter 2 to find out how to locate a geriatric care manager.)

Medicare doesn't cover care manager fees. The good news is that sometimes you can obtain a brief course of care management services for free from the local agency on aging or a senior center.

Hire a care manager to handle only the tasks you dread or aren't good at, such as arranging doctor's appointments, conferring with medical personnel, or managing banking and taxes.

Social workers

Because *social workers* are skilled at marshalling local community services for their clients, they make effective elder care managers. Many are also experienced counselors who can help your elder recover from depression, grief, and loss. They can assist you during crises, help you manage caregiver stress, and help relatives work out family conflicts. Many social workers specialize in death and dying issues. A professional social worker holds a master's degree in social work (MSW) and, in most states, must pass a licensing exam. Some institutions hire employees without an MSW, but still call them social workers. It's always best to inquire about professional qualifications. (See Chapter 2 to find out how to locate a qualified social worker.)

Community services

Most communities offer some sort of services to their elderly citizens. Sometimes these services are sponsored by local churches, synagogues, or civic groups. Businesses, nonprofit organizations, or public agencies also establish services for elders. Good places to hunt them down are the social service department at your local hospital, the yellow and blue pages of your phone book, and your state agency on aging.

Senior centers

Senior centers are gathering places for older people to socialize and enjoy educational and recreational activities. Centers vary in their offerings. One center may sponsor Senior Sundays, including transportation, lunch, and entertainment. Another center may focus on bus trips to tourist attractions and shopping malls. Some senior centers offer an impressive roster of classes on everything from yoga to ceramics to courses on learning a new language.

To get a list of senior centers, contact your local Area Agency on Aging. (You can get the telephone number of your state's Area Agency on Aging by calling the national Eldercare Locator at 800-677-1116.)

Adult daycare

Adult daycare is an away-from-home daytime program for frail or disabled elders. Clients are picked up at about 9 a.m. and dropped off at home at around 5 p.m. (although not all programs provide transportation). A solid activity program helps elders in adult daycare socialize with staff and clients, recall and sing old familiar tunes, and use their hands and minds in art, cooking, or gardening projects. Many facilities are designed so that elders can wander on a secure garden path. While some programs are mainly social, providing activities, a hot lunch, and minimal nursing services, other programs also offer intensive health and therapeutic services for elderly who have severe medical problems and are at high risk for nursing home care.

When adult daycare is good, it's very good! Your elder gets a meaningful place to go to, and you have peace of mind. About 4,000 adult daycare centers operate across the country. Half of the clients have Alzheimer's disease or other dementing illnesses; the rest have physical impairments. The right program care can ward off caregiver stress, keep your elder safe, and extend his or her involvement in life.

Unfortunately, not all adult daycare centers are good or appropriate for your elder. Investigate every one in your community and visit the ones you like two or three times before enrolling your loved one. Taste the food and observe the activities. Evaluate whether your elder's needs match their offerings. Look for an upbeat atmosphere and beware of understaffing. Staff members may be sweet and kind, but when they're in short supply, consistent quality care won't be delivered. (See Chapter 24 about how to assess nursing homes and apply the appropriate characteristics to adult daycare.) Very little is available in the way of public funding for adult daycare, so most families have to pay the daily rate of about $50 (plus transportation charges) out of their own pockets. But daycare is still a bargain compared to the costs of in-home care, nursing home care, or assisted-living arrangements.

Don't let your elder's resistance to adult daycare stop you in your tracks. It's a new concept to most people! Encourage your oldster to give it a go for a few days or a week and work closely with the staff to ease the adjustment period.

Meal programs

Meal programs come in basically two forms, *congregate meals* (inexpensive nutritious meals served in group settings) and *home-delivered meals*. About 1,600 or so congregate meal sites across the country offer hot lunches to seniors over 60 years old. The sites are often located in senior centers, churches and synagogues, schools, and apartment buildings. Many offer transportation and some activities along with lunch. Some places ask for a small donation.

Home-delivered meals (usually one hot meal a day on weekdays) are strictly for homebound seniors. Meals on Wheels isn't the only program, but it's certainly the most well-known. Unfortunately, the need in many communities is greater than the funding, so an elder who qualifies may have to go on a waiting list. The volunteers who deliver meals are usually trained to spot and report problems.

To locate a Meals on Wheels service in your older person's community, contact The Meals on Wheels Association of America online at: www.mowaa.org. Click Search For A Program ☞ *Your State* to get the address and phone number of every Meals on Wheels program in your area. To locate other home-delivered meals programs, contact your local Area Agency on Aging. (You can get the telephone number of your state's Area Agency on Aging by calling the National Eldercare Locator at 800-677-1116.)

Transportation services

Transportation services for frail older people differ tremendously — some rural areas have no systems for elders at all, whereas other communities may have vans that pick up your elder (by appointment) and deliver him or her door-to-door. Many services operate on set schedules with predetermined destinations (malls, shopping centers, medical centers, casinos). Some are free, some are not. Your area agency on aging, as always, is your first information resource. Then try the other usual spots — senior centers, volunteer organizations, and houses of worship. One small-town synagogue's van is used on Sundays to pick up elderly parishioners and take them to church.

Your local public transportation system is mandated by the Americans with Disabilities Act to provide transportation services to disabled people. Give them a call. Who knows? Perhaps your elder qualifies for their services.

Volunteers

After he lost his only friend to cancer, Irwin grew increasingly depressed and isolated. His health deteriorated. His daughter (a long-distance caregiver) called the senior center in her dad's community for help. The social worker suggested their "friendly visitor" program.

At first, Irwin refused. He grumbled that he didn't want any "do-gooder getting into my business." Finally, to get his daughter off his back, Irwin agreed to one (and only one) visit. During the brief introductory visit, Fred (the volunteer friendly visitor) got Irwin to agree to another visit. The next time Fred (who was also a senior) visited, he came bearing a flowering plant he had grown himself from a seedling. Irwin was touched by Fred's interest in him.

Like any relationship, this one had its ups and downs, but eventually the men grew closer. When Irwin's health improved, he volunteered to become a friendly visitor himself!

Faith in Action is a network of organizations that help chronically ill, frail, elderly, and disabled people with everyday activities. Services may include transportation, grocery shopping, assistance with bills and paperwork, friendly visiting, or reading aloud. Faith in Action volunteers provide respite to elder caregivers as long as the elderly person doesn't need assistance with toileting or any other type of hands-on nursing care. Visit the Web site at www.fiavolunteers.org and click Find A Local Program ☞ *Your State* to get a complete listing of organizations and contact information.

Hiring Help Wisely

Before you lift the phone to call an agency or to place an ad, decide what home-care skills your elder requires and what specific tasks have to be performed. (See Chapter 2 for how to figure out your elder's needs.)

Write the required skills and tasks down and, voila! You have a handy dandy job description that you can use to clearly communicate your elder's specific needs to an agency. For example, you may want someone skilled in managing the difficult behavior of a confused older adult or providing range-of-motion exercises to a stroke victim, or managing incontinence. Tasks may include lifting, bathing, or even driving to medical appointments.

Should you place an ad in the local newspaper and hire someone on your own, the job description becomes part of the contract between employer and employee. Both of you should have signed copies. (See Figure 8-1 for a typical job contract format.)

Going to an agency

The usual way to find a home-health agency is to ask your elder's doctor for suggestions, search through the yellow pages, ask a hospital discharge worker for referrals, or rely on word-of-mouth recommendations from friends who have faced similar situations. "Perfect" probably doesn't exist, but a high-quality agency would do the following:

- ✔ Keep up-to-date employee references
- ✔ Perform background checks
- ✔ Bond its workers (which protects you in case of theft)
- ✔ Carry workers' compensation (which covers on-the-job injuries)
- ✔ Train and supervise workers to create a plan for care with input from family members and the elder client
- ✔ Train employees in both general and specialized caregiving tasks
- ✔ Train employees to be culturally sensitive (for example, to accommodate to the elder's traditional practices, such as burning candles or not eating pork)
- ✔ Explain the training program to you without hesitation
- ✔ Send a few workers for you to interview
- ✔ Provide ongoing supervision
- ✔ Send a substitute should your regular aide be a no-show

Pros

Most agencies screen applicants, hire them, monitor them, and terminate them. This responsibility is great if the thought of firing someone leaves you weak in the knees. Agencies deal with taxes and payroll, provide backup, and assume liability. They usually supply help on very short notice. (See the characteristics of a high-quality agency earlier in this chapter for more "pros.")

Employment Contract

This contract is between [name of employer] _____ and

[name of employee] _____

[name of employee] _____ agrees to work as a [job

title] _____ for [name of elderly client] _____

_____ for the sum of $_____ an hour, for _____ hours per day, _____ days

per week, to be paid on [insert pay day (for example, every Friday or the 15th of each month)]

_____

Duties will include [insert the job description you have written]: _____

_____

_____

Additional agreements:[write in any other agreed-upon details — for example, withholding of

taxes and Social Security contributions, matching Social Security contributions, benefits (meals,

breaks, paid vacation days, paid and unpaid holidays); reasons for termination and amount of

notice that must be given] _____

_____

_____

_____

This contract has been agreed to by the parties below:

_____
Employer   date

_____
Employee   Social Security Number   date

Figure 8-1:
Sample job
contract for
in-home
workers.

1

Cons

The agency may send out several different people to care for your elder instead of one regular worker. (This practice can upset or confuse many elders.) You also may have little or no choice about the people they initially send. Agency workers usually cost more than independently hired aides, but there's no guarantee that a more expensive agency worker will be any better than a worker you hire independently.

Also, in-home workers may be limited in the kind of tasks they're permitted to do. For example, a worker may be able to cook and do laundry but not drive Mom to the beauty shop.

Check with your insurance carrier to be certain that your worker is covered adequately when driving your car.

Hiring independently

Careful phone screening saves time and eliminates obviously inappropriate applicants. Briefly describe the job (responsibilities and hours), some of your expectations (for example, no smoking), and wages. Ask the applicants about their past experience. Do they have references? Are they U.S. citizens? Do they have a green card? Follow your intuition. If you feel unsure about the person on the other end of the line, thank him or her and say goodbye.

During the face-to-face interview, give the applicant more details about your elder's needs, habits, preferences, and quirks. As a rule, you don't want to hire someone who bad-mouths previous employers and elderly clients. (See the sections "Holding out for warmth" and "Measuring character," later in this chapter.)

Pros

Your own good judgment is the deciding factor in the hire. Independent workers aren't constrained by agency rules, so they can perform a larger variety of tasks. (Be sure you agree upon all these tasks and put each one in the contract.) Lower cost gets you more hours for your home care dollar.

Cons

Checking references takes a time, and you also need to do a background check once you find a worker you feel comfortable with. Payroll and withholding taxes are your responsibility.

Unless you've done some amazing preplanning, you may be stuck for help when your aide is sick. (See the section "Coping When the Help Doesn't Show Up," later in this chapter.)

A little hiring means a little paperwork

The very idea of managing taxes, completing government forms, and calculating sums for employees makes my head swim and palms sweat. If I can do it, anyone can! Here are three things you need to complete:

✔ **Publication 926.** You complete this form to report home help workers you hire independently and obtain information about paying their federal taxes. You can order the form for free from the IRS Forms Distribution Center's automated phone system (800-TAX-FORM/800-829-3676). To download Publication 926, go online to www.irs.gov and click the link Forms And Publications.

✔ **Form SS4** is the form to request an employer identification number (FIN). You can order the form for free by phone (800-TAX-FORM) or download it at www.irs.gov; go to the link called Forms And Publications.

After completing the SS4 form, you can submit the information needed to request an EIN in one of three ways:

✔ Call the 866-816-2065 number and provide the information to the representative.

This method is the quickest way to receive the EIN. (You will receive it during the phone call.)

✔ Fax the SS4 form to the IRS.

The fax number is: 631-447-8960. It takes approximately five days to receive the EIN.

✔ Mail the SS4 form to the IRS.

Call the 866-816-2065 number to obtain the mailing address for the office that serves your area. Weeks may go by before you receive your EIN through the mail.

The **Employment Eligibility Verification Form I-9** verifies that the person you hire is legally entitled to work in the U.S. You can order this form from the INS Forms Request Line at 800-870-3676. The form should arrive in five to ten days. You can also request this form through the INS Web site: (www.immigration.gov; go to the Forms, Fees, And Fingerprinting link on the left side of the page). You can either download the form or order it to be mailed to you from the Web site.

Note that these forms are free of charge if you order them directly from the government. An unofficial Web site offers the same forms but charges for them.

Each state has its own regulations governing workers in your home. For specifics, call your state employment department listed in the government section of the telephone directory.

Check your household insurance (renter's or homeowner's) to see whether your household employee is covered in case he or she gets injured on the job.

Looking for skills and experience

Inquire about skills, experience, and training. Does the applicant have any certifications or licenses? Has he taken CPR courses? Expect to do some training yourself. Every elder is different, and every package of needs is unique. Aides can't know everything! I recall one woman who turned away a wonderful home health assistant because the worker didn't know how to do — in fact, had never heard of — range-of-motion exercises. Too bad, because these exercises are easy to learn.

A useful technique to gain an understanding of an aide's skills and experience is to recall a recent situation with your elder (perhaps a crisis — for example, the time she wandered away from the house). Ask the helper how she would handle the situation and what would she do to ensure Mom's safety in the future.

Be careful about assuming anything about the tasks you're asking her to perform or her feelings about these chores. For example, one daughter apologized to every applicant she interviewed that the job required colostomy care. She later discovered from the woman she hired that taking care of an elder in diapers was far more difficult. The worker was grateful to have only the colostomy care.

Holding out for warmth

It's the qualities that you can't teach someone that mean the most. Daily personal contact (often intimate care) calls for a good bedside manner (kindness, understanding, and warmth). Introduce possible hires to your elder and watch them interact. Does the worker have good eye contact? Does she listen to your elder? Does she speak with respect, or does she "talk down" to your elder? Look for an upbeat attitude and energetic style. You're looking for someone who is warm, not someone to warm your couch.

Sometimes an elder will be so abusive toward his or her home health assistants that no one will stay on the job for more than a few days. This behavior is not normal for old people! A medical evaluation and perhaps a psychiatric workup are in order to get to the root of the ill temper.

Measuring character

Character is one of those things that can best be determined in the face of a challenging dilemma or situation. Will your in-home worker be willing to stay with your loved one a little longer when you're stuck in traffic and she has an appointment she has to get to? Will he tell you if you overpaid him? Will she admit that she made an error in judgment?

After the aide has begun working, show an interest in her family life, goals, and dreams. Ask her opinion about news events. Find out what her interests are and share your own. At the very least, you'll get a grasp of the character of your employee. At the very best, the person who helps take care of your loved one will turn into a true family friend.

Checking references

Ask applicants for three references from jobs in which the needs of their clients were similar to your elder's needs. Ask former employers about lateness, reliability, and how well the worker communicated with the client and family members. How long was the person employed? Under what circumstances did he or she leave? What are the worker's strengths and weaknesses?

Home health registries (matching and referral services) maintain lists of home-care workers, but the workers the registry sends aren't employees of the registry. If you're dissatisfied, the service may send another worker within a specified time period, but check its brochures to be certain. Also, helpers from registries cost less than licensed home health-care agency employees (something to seriously consider when you pay out of pocket). On the other hand, registries aren't always licensed. Ask whether they screen, train, supervise, or check references for the people they send.

Coping When the Help Doesn't Show Up

Stuff happens! A day will come when your home-care assistant calls in sick or can't get to work because of a family emergency or car troubles. Agencies usually send a substitute, but when you've hired on your own, the only thing that saves the day is planning in advance for just such an emergency.

Keep a list of people who have offered to help you. When you get the original offer, ask whether you can put them on a list of people to call if your aide doesn't show up for her shift. Perhaps they can sit with your elder for a couple of hours. Save your own sick days or vacation days or family leave days (see Chapter 3 for information on the Family and Medical Leave Act) so that you can stay with your elder yourself. When you hire your helper, ask him whether he has someone he trusts to fill in for him should an emergency arise.

Your elder may not be entirely happy with these emergency plans, but her needs will not be neglected.

Chapter 9

Growing Closer and Dearer: Improving Relationships

Hearing "I love you" or I'm sorry" from a sick or dying parent is the stuff of Hollywood films, novels, and television mini-series. With music in the background, magical words reverse years of mutual misunderstanding, resentment, and disdain in a few moments. When such things happen in real life, the scene is seldom so dramatic or sudden. Intimacy and understanding between caregiver and elderly care-receiver grows slowly and often wordlessly over time. You may not even know it's happening at the time. The possibility for this kind of joyfulness (admittedly rare) lies under all the backbreaking work and despair involved in caring for a frail elder.

This chapter shows you ways to become closer to your elder. It gives you techniques for letting go of old resentments, forgiving the past, and accepting the reality that your elder may or may never change his or her ways. It's also about hope.

Working on the Relationship

Troubled relationships — business, marital, or family — share many characteristics. Usually, both sides believe it's the other party's responsibility or moral obligation to take the first step. Each person believes he or she was wronged and (as a wronged one) each waits for an apology, a confession, or remorse from the other person. Stalemates go on for decades.

You may find yourself caring for your elder with a mixture of love, hurt, disappointment, and hope about finally working out past difficulties. Opportunity exists. The physical and emotional contact involved in everyday caregiving tasks can possess the power to bring you closer and dearer to your older person.

Creating special moments

As the end of life draws near, elders usually reflect on the past. Their memories entertain them, serve as a pastime, and restore a sense of personal value and pride as they recall youth, adventures, and accomplishments. Stimulating such memories during meals or bedtime makes those times special — even anticipated. To help facilitate memories, try some of the following techniques:

- ✔ **Ask your elder about the old days.** For example, what foods and meals does she call to mind from celebrations, holidays, and country fairs?

- ✔ **Inquire about things related to night — like dreams and lullabies.** For example, ask the following questions: "How did your mother put you to bed?" "Did she sing a song or tell you a story?" "Did you have a favorite dream as a youngster?"

- ✔ **Be curious about the work Dad did at the mill or Mom did at home raising children.** What was a typical day like? (See Chapter 15 for more ideas to encourage reminiscence in older people.)

An interest in the elder's past helps you to connect with her. Creating special events that the two of you do together and that don't include others can also generate a feeling of intimacy. These events can be your *signature activities.* Here are some ideas:

- ✔ **Sip tea together every day at 4 p.m. while you discuss what happened during the day or on the afternoon news.** Do it once, it's lovely. Do it twice, it's nice. Do it three times, and it's a ritual!

- ✔ **Rub lotion on your elder's legs or brush her hair every night.** Personal acts like these carry meaningful messages.

- ✔ **Sit on the edge of the bed before turning out the lights and repeat familiar reassuring words, such as "You and I make a great team" or "Through thick or thin, it's good to be together."** Think of it as a mini-pep talk.

Special moments don't need words, they need only to be consistent and enjoyable. A late-afternoon backrub, humming his favorite old tune every evening, or taking a short morning walk down the same path can bond — no words necessary.

Being loving

Estelle and her daughter Barbara fought like dogs for decades. They really never liked one another. Estelle, a beautiful woman, seemed to be obsessed first with her own attractiveness and then with the attractiveness of her budding teenager. Barbara's teenage years were a harangue of criticisms. Feelings of being unloved unless she dieted and made herself up pushed her into escaping into an early marriage at 17 with the first young man who wanted her.

Fifty years later, 67-year-old Barbara — despite her resentment — found herself caring for her elderly mother, now a stroke survivor. Estelle, frail as she was, could still rub: "You really would look nicer if you wore foundation" or "Do you think that color does anything for you?"

One day, Barbara realized that she stopped obsessing about her own appearance years ago, but her poor mother continued to see physical beauty (including her own and her daughter's) as the only road to personal worth. This insight transformed Barbara's anger toward her mother into compassion.

Barbara couldn't change the past, so she decided to indulge her mother. She admired aloud Estelle's silver hair and engaged in the discussions she always hated — about glamour and fashion. The harsh edge between them softened.

Doing loving things makes you feel more loving. Performing acts of love (even when you don't feel loving) is a powerful tool. Acts of love include

- Affectionately stroking your elder's cheek for no reason
- Resting your hand on hers
- Going out of your way to bring your elder something hard to find, out of season, or rare but pleasing
- Being silent in the face of one of your elder's annoying habits

Listening like a pro

Listening requires so much more than a set of ears in working order! Listening is an art and — in my opinion — a healing art. When people hear each other — really *hear* each other — pathways to understanding and closeness open up. The following suggestions aren't guaranteed to get the wax out, but if you practice them, your enhanced listening will pay off:

- Refrain from thinking of a response before your elder has finished talking.
- Don't interrupt — and if you do, apologize.

✔ Nod to show you're involved.

✔ Ask for more details about what's being said.

✔ Summarize (occasionally) to demonstrate you've heard what's been said.

✔ Repeat the last few words once in a while to show your attentiveness.

✔ Ask questions.

When the dialogue is a complaint, find something to agree with. Even when complaints are exaggerated or unrealistic, you can always find a little kernel of truth or something to acknowledge. For example, Dad complains that a clothing label is itching him. You had cut out the label days ago and have checked his collar umpteen times since. Even though nothing's there, you're better off not arguing. Let him know that you hear how annoying it must be to have fabric next to sensitive skin. Acknowledging the problem and the discomfort are powerful tools to putting things at rest for now. People want to know that they're being understood even more than they want to be agreed with.

Experts say that the essential ingredient to letting go of anger is empathy for the other person's situation, motives, and feelings. Good listening enhances empathy.

Even the best listeners (including professional psychotherapists, attorneys, judges, clergy, and teachers) have limits. Decide how much time you have to listen and stick to it. Twenty to 30 minutes is the about the limit for even the saintly. Listening is hard work. Overdoing it backfires on the relationship.

Expressing your feelings

You're not just chopped liver! You have feelings, too. Emotional support from friends and professionals keeps you going, sure. But sharing your emotional life with your elder may enhance the intimacy between you.

Try trusting your older person with your own feelings and doubts (in very small doses). For example, "I had a bad moment this morning wondering who will take care of me when I'm old." Your feeling must be genuine and heartfelt. Don't expect any special reply. The magic is in the sharing, not the response. Test the waters. Sharing *positive* feelings is a good place to begin.

Focusing on their own troubles, disabilities, and symptoms is normal for frail or sick oldsters. They may hear every bowel sound, worry about new aches, and even obsess about their health. Illness-related depression can add to the self-centeredness.

Understanding How Resentment Happens

Resentment springs from hurt. In their book, *Forgiveness: How to Make Peace with Your Past and Get on with Your Life* (Warner Books), Sidney and Susan Simon name the top eight hurts on the "hurt parade." If any of these hit home, you have a handle on your feelings and the beginnings of making peace with yourself:

- ✔ Disappointment
- ✔ Rejection
- ✔ Abandonment
- ✔ Ridicule
- ✔ Humiliation
- ✔ Betrayal
- ✔ Deception
- ✔ Abuse

Its far easier to feel angry than hurt. Over time, the anger turns to resentment. Facing the hurt is the first step to letting the anger go and drawing closer.

Finishing unfinished business

Unfinished business only goes in two directions — getting finished or staying unfinished. There's no magic in closure. You can live without closure. The healing is in making the attempt to finish the business. Whether it works is less important.

A heart-to-heart talk with your older person may lead to new understanding for both of you. Or, perhaps, it will help you finally realize that nothing will change, no matter what you do. The following are some guidelines for your attempts at finishing unfinished business:

- ✔ Try to approach the talk understanding that you don't know everything, and your elder probably had very limited power to do better at the time.

- ✔ Don't approach your elder with anger. It may *feel* safer to express anger instead of hurt, but anger is usually met with an angry, defensive response.

- ✔ Voice your hurt instead. Once you show your tender spots, you become more vulnerable. Make it short.

- ✔ Don't expect a sea of change. Rejoice in the smallest acknowledgement.
- ✔ Acknowledge that the two of you will forever disagree on certain issues.
- ✔ Don't regret that you didn't or couldn't express exactly what you wanted. You tried.
- ✔ Consider forgiveness. You can forgive without reconciling.

Understanding why letting go is so hard

Holding on to anger and resentment actually has rewards. Enticing as those rewards may be, the benefits of letting go are greater — especially to your own health.

The following questions can help you expose the so-called rewards of resentment:

- ✔ Do I believe that by staying angry I am maintaining my principles and standards (thus not condoning what my parent did or did not do in the past)?
- ✔ Do I think that I must receive amends (apologies, special considerations) to compensate for the wrong I suffered and to stop feeling resentful?
- ✔ Does holding on to my resentment make me feel morally superior to my parent?
- ✔ Do I think I will be free of anger when my parent shows guilt?
- ✔ Do I think that anger is my only way to punish him or her?
- ✔ Do I believe that "letting go" of my anger means I am weak?

"Yes" to any of these questions indicates that the anger is performing a service you can do without. Letting go of your anger is courageous, loving, and good for your health and the health of your other relationships. (See the next section for ways to let go of resentment.)

Should the words "forgive me" or "I'm proud of you" not come as you hoped, you can say to yourself and your parent, "I regret that we have had our problems." It's true and it's tender, and most of all, it's nonblaming — a fact that may still open up possibilities in the days to come.

Accepting the Relationship as It Is

Letting go of years of anger and underlying hurt takes time. The following steps can help the speed the process:

✔ Share your feelings with your support group. You'll likely be surprised that others have similar experiences.

✔ See a professional counselor.

✔ Share your thoughts with someone who you know is understanding and a good listener.

✔ Seek religious guidance.

✔ Try to understand what shaped your parent to behave as he or she did. Inviting the opinions and viewpoints of others can give you a fresh perspective.

✔ Don't expect anything to change.

✔ Accept the fact that you'll never be close.

A spiritual guide from the East hits the "closeness conundrum" on the head

Warm and uncommonly engaging are descriptions of the 14th Dalai Lama, the exiled government ruler and highest priest of Tibetan Buddhism, who travels widely pleading his country's cause and gaining admiration for his simple but profound wisdom about human nature.

The Dalai Lama promotes human connection everywhere he speaks. The following are ideas gleaned from his philosophy about intimacy in general. Applying them to your relationship with your elder may draw you even closer if you're already close or make some inroads if you're distant:

✔ Approach your elder with a positive upbeat attitude, but don't expect him or her to respond to you in the same way. Anticipating or hoping your older person will react to you positively will throw up a barrier to the good feeling you're longing for.

✔ Suspend your current viewpoints about your elder. No doubt your elder had heartbreak, trauma, and disappointment, too. The Dalai Lama promotes trying to get in the other person's head, inserting yourself into his or her experience, imagining what he or she felt, feared, or thought in the past. Being able to crawl around in someone else's head even a little bit helps increase empathy. There's no one way to be closer to any one person because every situation is different, but *empathy* (the ability to appreciate another person's suffering) is one doozy of a place to start.

✔ Put aside — for the moment — the differences between you and think of the things you have in common. For example, you and your Mother both have blond hair, skin that burns easily in the sun, an affinity for dried fruit and car sickness, and a great talent for picking the wrong men. You may share the same gestures as your Dad, the same talent for fixing things, and the same tendency to rattle on a bit — or so you've been told.

✔ Don't get caught up in the goal of closeness with one person — in this case, your older person. Connecting with as many other people as possible affects the connection with an elderly parent.

For more ideas about enriching your relationships, read *The Art of Happiness: A Handbook in Living*, by His Holiness the Dalai Lama and Howard C. Cutler, M.D. (Riverhead Books, a member of Penguin Putnam, Inc.).

Part III

Keeping Elderly Folks Safe and Sound

The 5th Wave   By Rich Tennant

"If this is an assisted-living facility, then we'd like some assistance. How much do you know about driving a get-away car?"

In this part . . .

Imagine that you can take all the medical conditions and problems that plague older people and line them up like ducks in a shooting gallery. Now knock them over one by one. Wouldn't that be lovely? This part doesn't obliterate the chronic health problems of the elderly, but it does take away the mystery. You get crystal-clear explanations about the most common conditions and what can be done about them. A whole chapter also addresses taking drugs safely.

While I'm on the subject of safety, take a peek at the chapter on doohickeys and thingamajigs, which I could have titled "Everything You Need to Know to Keep Your Elder in One Piece" — a worthwhile endeavor, indeed!

Chapter 10

Living Well with Chronic Medical Conditions

Many people attend organ recitals when they reach middle age. I have been to a number of organ recitals myself. They go something like this: You're out with your friends. Toward the end of the evening, someone in the group provides an update on one of his medical ailments. The ice is broken. Before you know what has happened, everyone joins in talking about his or her own heart, kidney, bladder, and liver maladies — an organ recital!

Don't misunderstand. I am not bad-mouthing organ recitals. Sharing information about the latest drug therapies, surgical inventions, and symptoms is enlightening and — in a strange way — entertaining. Someone always has a funny anecdote to tell about a misdiagnosis or misunderstanding with a doctor. Even some of the scarier stories can get a laugh or two with hindsight.

Unfortunately, the older your elder gets, the more likely it is that she'll have several chronic medical conditions — and probably lots of organ recitals. Absorbing all that you can about these ailments helps tame the fear and prepares you for the unknown. This chapter presents down-to-earth information about the chronic diseases most often found in elderly people and what can be done about them.

Understanding Chronic Disease

Illnesses that last for a long time, show little or no change, or have a slow progression are considered *chronic*. Chronic illnesses, by definition, aren't curable. The goals are getting the condition under control, slowing the often-disabling progression, and relieving the symptoms. Your elder has a fair chance that he'll be devoting a good bit of time to visiting specialists and taking medicine.

When not attended to, chronic diseases cause serious damage to the body, affecting the quality of your older person's life and even hastening his or her death.

Heart disease

Heart disease is still the leading cause of death and disability in the United States for both men and women. At one time, it was commonly thought that heart disease was a man's disease. Not anymore. One quarter of women over age 65 have some form of heart disease. The American Heart Association reports that 475,000 Americans die of coronary heart disease every year. One of the most common types is *coronary artery disease*. Another common kind of heart disease is *congestive heart failure*.

What is it?

In coronary artery disease, the coronary arteries carry a constant supply of oxygen and nutrient-rich blood to the heart to enable it to do its work. Heart disease occurs when the coronary arteries are narrowed and clogged with a buildup of fatty deposits that prevent an adequate supply of oxygen from getting through to the heart.

When the heart muscle receives insufficient blood flow, the heart may respond with intense chest pain called *angina*. (*Silent angina* occurs when the blood supply to the heart is insufficient, but the person has no chest pain.)

A full-blown heart attack (called a *myocardial infarction*) occurs when blood supply to the heart is severely restricted or completely cut off. The lack of oxygen damages the heart muscle and, in some cases, causes sudden death.

In congestive heart failure, the amount of blood pumped out of the heart cannot satisfy the body's needs. Excess fluid accumulates, causing swelling in the ankles, feet, liver, and abdomen. In certain cases, victims experience extreme shortness of breath and fluid buildup in the lungs (a life-threatening situation). In the United States, about 400,000 new cases of heart failure are diagnosed each year. Heart failure is common among older people because they're most likely to suffer from the medical conditions that cause heart failure (including coronary artery disease, infection of the heart muscle, diabetes, overactive thyroid, extreme obesity, and heart valve disease).

What can be done about it?

You want to keep those coronary arteries clean as a whistle by whatever means possible — medicine, surgery, or alterations in habits. The heart medicine the doctor prescribes depends on the nature of your elder's heart disease. Surgery may be recommended for elders whose frequent or disabling angina cannot be remedied by medication or for patients who have severe blockages in their coronary arteries. Altering lifestyle habits is a powerful means for preventing heart disease — and, if it's too late to avoid it, stopping its progression.

Coronary artery disease and congestive heart failure have no cure. Doctors treat the underlying diseases and urge patients to adopt healthier lifestyles. (The advice for lowering blood pressure in the high blood pressure section later in this chapter is identical to the recommendations usually given to heart failure patients.) Treatment may also include prescribing diuretics to reduce fluid retention and additional medications to increase the power of each heartbeat, normalize the heart rate, or reduce the workload of the heart.

The American Heart Association has a free online service called Heart Profilers (www.americanheart.org). You complete an in-depth questionnaire (which you can do for or with your elder). Using the information you type, the program generates a personalized report that contains the key information to fully understand the treatment options your elder has for his heart disease. It includes a summary of those options, potential treatment side-effects, success rates, and a list of relevant medical journal articles and research studies. The whole process takes about 20 minutes.

Eliminating or reducing the following risk factors for coronary heart disease may help older adults avoid a heart attack (including a second heart attack if they've already had one):

- ✔ **High blood pressure.** See the section on high blood pressure later in this chapter for nonmedical ways to lower it.

- ✔ **High levels of cholesterol.** A reduced-cholesterol diet and cholesterol-lowering drugs can help prevent narrowed clogged arteries.

- ✔ **Cigarette smoking.** Smoking injures blood-vessel walls, speeds hardening of the arteries, forces the heart to work harder, and raises blood pressure.

- ✔ **Obesity.** Being overweight increases the risk of high cholesterol and high blood pressure, both of which increase the risk for heart disease.

- ✔ **Physical inactivity.** Studies have shown that even moderate amounts of physical activity are associated with lower death rates from coronary heart disease.
- ✔ **Diabetes.** Poorly controlled, it damages the heart.
- ✔ **Stress.** Many scientists agree that stress may be a risk factor, but they don't know exactly how stress is involved in heart disease.

When improved habits result in improved health, your elder's heart medication needs to be reevaluated.

The following symptoms require immediate medical attention:

- ✔ Chest discomfort (ranging from a sudden tight ache to intense crushing pain)
- ✔ Pain that starts in the chest and spreads to the shoulders, neck, or jaw or down the inner arm
- ✔ Pain associated with shortness of breath
- ✔ A feeling of pressure or squeezing on the chest
- ✔ An irregular pulse
- ✔ Dizziness, fainting, or sudden weakness
- ✔ Confusion or loss of consciousness
- ✔ *Palpitations* (a forceful, rapid, or irregular heartbeat that occurs with other symptoms in this list)
- ✔ Nausea, vomiting, or sweating (if it occurs with other symptoms in this list)

The sooner your older person gets medical attention, the better the chances for survival. The goal is to establish whether or not your elder's symptoms are due to heart disease or some other cause.

Mended Hearts, Inc. is a nationwide organization that offers educational resources and support (including groups) for people with heart disease, their families, and their caregivers. To locate the nearest Mended Hearts chapter, call the American Heart Association (800-AHA-USA1). If you or your elder would like to talk to another heart patient in your area, call 888-HEART99. You can find useful information online at www.mendedhearts.org.

High blood pressure

High blood pressure (also called *hypertension*) is the most common chronic illness in America. It's not curable, but it is treatable. Because high blood pressure has no symptoms, about a third of those who have it don't know it.

Your elder may feel great, while all along high blood pressure silently damages his organs. Untreated high blood pressure can lead to stroke, heart disease, an enlarged heart, kidney failure, scarred or hardened arteries, blindness, and a type of dementia called *vascular dementia*.

What is it?

Each time your heart beats, blood is forced through the arteries that deliver oxygen and nutrients to your organs. As the blood flows through the vessels, it pushes against the artery walls. The force exerted on the walls is called *blood pressure*. When the force becomes excessive, you have high blood pressure.

In about 80 to 90 percent of the people who have high blood pressure, the cause is unknown. High blood pressure probably has more than one cause. Obesity, a couch-potato lifestyle, stress, and excessive alcohol and salt intake contribute to the development of high blood pressure in people who are already vulnerable. (It runs in the family.)

Your elder should have his blood pressure taken every time he visits the doctor. Ideally, measurements are taken when the person is at rest — not after having run up a flight of stairs or when feeling excited or nervous. One reading indicates nothing! Blood pressure varies. If the first reading is elevated, you need to have several more readings done while your elder has been sitting or lying down for five minutes. One-third of the people who have high first readings have normal readings when checked again.

A blood-pressure reading produces two measurements. The top number (*systolic* pressure) is the pressure while the heart beats. The second number (*diastolic* pressure) is the pressure while the heart relaxes between the beats. Blood pressure is measured in millimeters of mercury (mmHg) — normal is considered 130/85 mmHg or lower. As people age, their blood pressure tends to rise. You have high blood pressure when your first number is 140 mmHg or more, or your second number is 90 mmHg or more or when both readings are high. The most common type of high blood pressure in older folks is called *isolated systolic hypertension*. In this reading, the top number is high, but the bottom number is normal.

What can be done about it?

Every case is unique. Fortunately, a large number of blood-pressure medications are available — and new ones are constantly being developed. So don't be alarmed if the doctor changes medicines more than once while searching for the right fit.

Your older person will probably have to take blood-pressure medication for the rest of his life — even when he feels fine. Try to make sure that your elder takes his medicine exactly as prescribed and that he doesn't run out of pills even for a single day. Ask the doctor whether it makes sense to buy a blood-pressure kit so that you or your elder can take readings at home.

White Coat Syndrome

Getting a high blood pressure reading while at the doctor's office may not be cause for alarm. Your elder may simply have *White Coat Syndrome* — the common phenomenon of a person's blood pressure being elevated from the anxiety of going to see the doctor. (Many members of the medical profession wear white coats.) When this elevation happens, it's wise to have a second measurement taken at the end of the visit or to drop by for an unscheduled blood-pressure check. Other possibilities are to check your elder's blood pressure at the machines available in some pharmacies. Keep in mind that blood pressure varies during the day. It's usually highest in the morning and lowest during the night while sleeping.

The best thing you can do as a caregiver is to help your elder alter the habits that contribute to his high blood pressure. Changing habits isn't easy, but the rewards are tremendous. Healthier habits can reduce the risk of developing heart disease and stroke and may even reduce the amount of medication needed to control blood pressure.

To lower high blood pressure, encourage your elder to heed the following advice:

- **Cut down on salt intake.** The doctor can set the appropriate salt intake for your elder. Avoid prepared foods (such as canned goods and frozen dinners) that are high in salt — especially soups.

- **Eat healthy.** Try to include more low-fat dairy products, fruits, vegetables, whole grains, and fish in the diet.

- **Lose weight.** Being overweight makes you two to six times more likely to develop high blood pressure. As little as a ten-pound weight loss can have an effect on blood pressure.

- **Exercise.** As long as the doctor says it's okay, urge your elder to engage in at least 30 minutes of moderate exercise five times a week. A daily walk can make a difference. Mall walking is the rage! Many shopping malls open early and close late to accommodate people who prefer walking in well-lit, climate-controlled secure locations with level floors rather than taking their chances in the unpredictable outdoors.

   Call your elder's local mall to find out whether it sponsors a mall walkers group.

- **Limit alcohol intake.** The generally recommended amount is no more than two drinks a day for men and one drink a day for lighter weight men or women. Be aware that alcohol has other negative effects. (See Chapter 5 about how alcohol interferes with sleep and Chapter 11 about how alcohol interferes with medication.)

✔ **Stop smoking.** Smoking may reduce the effectiveness of blood-pressure medication. Quitting smoking also lowers the risk for heart disease and stroke.

Check with the doctor before your older person takes any over-the-counter medications. Certain cold, cough, and flu medications can be dangerous for elders with high blood pressure. For example, decongestants have been reported to increase blood pressure and may interfere with blood-pressure medications.

Schering-Plough HealthCare Products has developed a free wallet card that lists types and specific examples of over-the-counter medications that people with high blood pressure should generally avoid. To order the wallet card, write to Schering-Plough HealthCare Products, 3 Connell Dr., Berkeley Heights, NJ 07922-0603.

Stroke

According to the National Stroke Association, stroke strikes about 750,000 Americans every year. Stroke is the third most common cause of death in the United States. It's also the leading cause of adult disability. The risk of having a stroke increases with age — about 72 percent of all stroke victims are over age 65.

What is it?

A *stroke* — sometimes called a brain attack — occurs when the brain doesn't get sufficient oxygen. If brain tissue is deprived of oxygen — even for a few minutes — it dies. The resulting disability depends on what region of the brain is affected. Every case is different. Damage on the right side of the brain may impair movement and sensation on the left side of the body. Damage on the left

Why does the doctor keep changing Mom's high-blood-pressure medicine?

Different drugs lower blood pressure in different ways. For example, many doctors begin drug treatment with a *diuretic* (a drug that lowers the blood pressure by helping the kidney get rid of salt and water in the body). After a while, the doctor may find that it becomes necessary to add another drug to the diuretic.

Sometimes the doctor prescribes one drug, finds it ineffective, and then tries another — repeating the process until he finds the right one or the right combination. Drug decisions are also based on your elder's age, his or her other health problems, and the potential side effects of the medication.

side of the brain may affect movement on the right side. Vision loss can occur with either right- or left-side brain damage. Speech and language, breathing, swallowing, balance, hearing, and bladder and bowel function may be affected. Mood changes, including depression, are frequent. Some survivors have emotional episodes (for example, uncontrollable crying, anger, or laughter) that don't seem to be connected to anything that is going on at the moment.

In 80 percent of strokes, either fatty deposits build up in the arteries, narrowing the walls and blocking blood flow to the brain, or a blood clot lodges in an artery, cutting off the blood flow to the brain. These types of strokes are called *ischemic* strokes. In a second type of stroke, *hemorrhagic,* a blood vessel in the brain bursts, and the blood leaks into the brain, destroying brain cells.

A *transient ischemic attack* (TIA) is a temporary interruption of blood flow to the brain that doesn't appear to cause any permanent damage. The warning signs can be the same as the ones for a stroke. But with a TIA, the symptoms appear for as little as a few minutes or for as long as 24 hours. Then they disappear. Even though the symptoms may vanish, consider the event a medical emergency. There's no way to know for sure whether it's a stroke or a TIA until you get to the hospital!

Although TIA symptoms don't last, be sure to get a medical evaluation. One-third of the people who suffer a TIA go on to have a stroke in the following five years. Medical attention now may prevent a full-blown stroke later.

What can be done about it?

If it appears that your older person is having a stroke, call 911 (or whatever the emergency number is in your area) for transport to the hospital emergency room. The doctor has to quickly determine which kind of stroke it is and where the damage is located before initiating treatment. If it's an ischemic stroke, a clot-busting drug has to be administered within a three-hour window in order to increase chances for survival and prevent or reverse brain damage. You don't have a minute to lose! On the other hand, if it's a hemorrhagic stroke, a clot-busting drug can worsen the situation. Surgery may be necessary to remove blood that has accumulated in the brain and to relieve increased pressure. You can see why a prompt and accurate diagnosis is important!

If any of the following warning signs appear in your elderly person, get emergency medical help:

- ✔ Sudden numbness or weakness of the face, arm, or leg (especially on only one side of the body)
- ✔ Sudden difficulty speaking or understanding what is said
- ✔ Sudden trouble seeing out of one or both eyes
- ✔ Sudden trouble walking

✔ Sudden dizziness, loss of balance, or impaired coordination

✔ Sudden onset of severe headache with unknown cause

Rehabilitation begins as soon as the elder's condition stabilizes. Rehabilitation can help about 80 percent of the deficits, but retraining can be grueling and frustrating, especially if there are communication problems.

Preventing stroke

Medical attention for the following conditions can lower the risk of getting a second stroke (or a first one):

✔ **High blood pressure.** This condition is the leading cause of stroke. (See the tips for lowering high blood pressure in the section on high blood pressure, earlier in this chapter.)

✔ **Atherosclerosis.** In this condition, the arteries have become narrowed or partially blocked. (See the section later in this chapter on atherosclerosis.)

✔ **Heart disease.** Several conditions increase the risk of stroke (including a previous heart attack, an infection in the heart valve, or irregular or rapid heartbeats).

✔ **Diabetes.** This chronic illness may interfere with the body's ability to break down dangerous blood clots.

✔ **Stress.** Experts believe that stress may increase the blood's tendency to clot, increasing the risk for stroke.

If your elder is at risk for stroke, ask her primary care physician whether ACE inhibitors and anticholesterol agents for stroke prevention would help her.

Communicating with a stroke survivor who has language problems

Imagine how frustrating it is to know what you want to say but be unable to form the words or find yourself blurting out the wrong words. The technical name for language problems caused by an injury to the brain is *aphasia.* About 25 percent of stroke survivors suffer from aphasia. Some are unable to speak at all or only with great effort. Others have trouble understanding what's being said to them. Language difficulties may improve, but often they become permanent disabilities.

If your elder suffers from aphasia, keep the following strategies in mind:

✔ **Don't talk down to her.** There's a tendency to talk to people with language problems in the same way you would talk to a young child.

✔ **Don't speak about your elder when she's in earshot.** Your oldster may have communication problems, but she can still overhear you and understand.

- ✔ **Don't speak loudly.** Unless your elder has a hearing loss, speak in a natural voice.

- ✔ **Give your elder plenty of time to respond.** She may need extra time for her brain to process what you said and to formulate her response.

- ✔ **Speak about one topic at a time and use short sentences.** Give your elder time to grasp one idea before introducing another.

- ✔ **Reduce background distraction from television and radios.** If other conversations are nearby, move to a better spot or wait until things quiet down before talking.

- ✔ **Try to have one-on-one conversations.** Conversations with three or more people interacting tend to create confusion.

- ✔ **Try adding gestures and facial expressions when your words aren't readily understood.**

- ✔ **Ask the doctor for a referral to a speech therapist who can pinpoint the specific communication problems and work toward improvement.**

The American Stroke Association operates the Stroke Family Warmline. The staff are all caregivers, with the exception of one stroke survivor. To take advantage of the free telephone counseling service and referrals to local support groups, call 800-553-6321.

Atherosclerosis

I heard about atherosclerosis from my Grandma Sally, only she called it hardening of the arteries. Atherosclerosis is the leading cause of illness and death in the United States. It took my grandma away from me when I was 12 years old.

Atherosclerosis is a general term for several diseases that share a common and deadly characteristic — an artery wall becomes thicker, harder, and less elastic. The hardening can develop in the arteries of the brain, heart, kidneys, and other vital organs. It can also develop in the arms and legs.

What is it?

Atherosclerosis is another one of those conditions like high blood pressure or diabetes that usually doesn't cause any symptoms until the damage is done. Fatty deposits build up in regions of the artery wall, creating thickened areas called plaques. The plaques may grow so large that blood flow through the artery is reduced, resulting in less oxygen to the part of the body that the artery feeds. The plaques can rupture — blocking blood flow — or they can travel to another part of the body. When it happens in the heart, a heart attack may occur. (See the section on heart disease, earlier in this chapter.) When it happens in the brain, a stroke may occur. (See the section on stroke, earlier in this chapter.) When the blood flow in the legs is reduced, the elder may get leg cramps and have difficulty walking.

What can be done about it?

The disease itself is not curable. Controlling the risk factors (high cholesterol, high blood pressure, cigarette smoking, obesity, and lack of exercise) helps prevent the development of atherosclerosis. Once the disease has developed and is severe, the best that can be done is to treat the complications (for example, angina, kidney failure, or abnormal heart rhythms).

To find a support group, call the American Heart Association (800-242-8721) or go online (www.americanheart.org).

Diabetes

One of every five Americans over age 65 has diabetes. Do the arithmetic — that's seven million diabetic seniors! If your elder has diabetes, he probably has type 2 diabetes. Type 1 represents only 10 percent of the cases and is usually diagnosed in childhood. Type 2 is more widespread (90 percent of all cases) and is far and away the most common type of diabetes in older people. In this section, I focus on type 2 diabetes.

What is it?

When everything is working according to design, *insulin* (which is manufactured in the pancreas) acts as a key to open the cells and allow sugar to enter. Once inside the cells, the sugar is available to fuel your body's functions.

When your body doesn't produce enough insulin to perform this job (or the cells resist the insulin), sugar builds up in the blood — exactly what the diabetic needs to avoid. The cells immediately become energy-starved. Untreated, over time, this condition contributes to numerous problems, including heart disease, stroke, high blood pressure, blindness, kidney disease, nervous system disease (such as impaired sensation in the feet), and gum disease. Diabetics are especially prone to serious foot problems. For example, damaged nerves can reduce sensation in the foot to such an extent that when the person injures his foot, he may not even realize it until infection sets in. The wounds may heal so slowly that eventually the skin and other tissues in the affected area die, making amputation of part of the leg necessary.

What can be done about it?

Many oldsters have diabetes and don't even know it. They may not have symptoms for years or even decades — about 40 percent of type 2 diabetics experience no symptoms at all. As a result, diabetes may not be diagnosed until serious complications develop. The doctor can diagnose diabetes with a simple test. (Blood-sugar levels are measured after an eight-hour fast.)

Beware of the sugar police

Wanting to help your elder control her blood sugar is only natural. But best wishes and good intentions frequently transform caregivers into "diabetes police." Scolding or shaming your elder because she fell off the wagon (that is, ate in an unhealthy way) hurts her feelings and damages your relationship. Be loving, not offensive. Your reproaches may initiate an argument, angry silence, or withdrawal. Even worse, your elder may start to hide her lapses instead of confiding in you about her struggle.

The following symptoms may indicate diabetes:

- Abnormal thirst
- Increased hunger
- Blurred vision
- Drowsiness
- Decreased endurance
- Excessive frequent urination
- Recurring infections
- Slow healing of sores and cuts

The person with diabetes must test his blood glucose frequently with a device called a *glucose meter*. Sometimes treatment overshoots the goal, and blood levels become dangerously low. Low blood sugar *(hypoglycemia)* can occur from not eating enough or exercising strenuously without eating. Symptoms are hunger, anxiety, shakiness, headache, and sweating. Hypoglycemia must be treated immediately, because in minutes it can lead to increasing confusion and coma. A quick dose of candy, a sugar cube, or glucose tablets (purchased in a pharmacy) is the remedy.

The focus is always on keeping the blood sugar within normal range so that there's no excessive blood sugar running amok, silently damaging organs, and no dangerous hypoglycemia to worry about. Some people gain control by achieving and maintaining their ideal weight (80 percent of those with type 2 diabetes are overweight). In some cases, losing 10 or 20 pounds can bring diabetes under control. When diet and exercise don't work, the next steps are pills and then insulin shots — or both.

The following ideas can help you assist your older person with his diabetes:

- Encourage exercise by offering to exercise along with your elder.

✔ Find out about the proper foods to prepare and offer your elder. (See *Diabetes For Dummies* [Wiley Publishing], by Alan L. Rubin, M.D., for more information.)

✔ Eat the same foods as your elder when dining together.

✔ Don't bring home foods that he can't eat.

✔ Inquire about your elder's blood glucose if you're present when he takes a reading. If the reading is low, offer a snack. When the reading is high, offer to go on a walk together.

✔ Develop a signal if your elder wants a reminder in a public place. No one wants to be told in public that the food he is about to dig into is forbidden. Decide beforehand on a way to get the message across unobtrusively (for example, a squeezed hand or a gentle nudge under the table means that the item he's about to put in his mouth is sugar-laden).

✔ Make sure that your elder has an emergency supply of candy, sugar cubes, or glucose tablets on his person in case of hypoglycemia. (It's always a good idea for the caregiver to carry a stash as well.)

To find a diabetes support group in your area, call the American Diabetes Association (800-232-3472). You can also go online for a listing of local information (www.diabetes.org).

Arthritis

The term arthritis covers more than 100 different kinds of disorders. According to the Arthritis Foundation, 70 million Americans have arthritis. Osteoarthritis and rheumatoid arthritis are the most common types.

What is it?

More than half of 65-year-olds have x-ray evidence of *osteoarthritis* in at least one joint. The characteristic symptoms are stiffness and mild-to-severe joint pain in the hands, knees, and hips that comes and goes. It's been called the "wear-and-tear" disease because cartilage in the joints (which allows the bones to glide easily to and fro without friction) wears down, becoming thin, frayed, and cracked. The shock-absorbing capabilities are lost, and the sufferer may end up with bone rubbing against bone. Osteoarthritis can run in families and can also result from injuries and overuse. Being overweight contributes to the problem.

The second type of arthritis, called *rheumatoid arthritis,* can be even more disabling. In this case, the immune system attacks the tissue that lines and cushions the joints. The exact cause isn't known. This illness affects about 1 percent of the population. Swelling usually occurs equally on both sides of the body in a symmetrical manner. Typically, the small joints in the fingers, toes, hands, feet, wrists, elbows, and ankles become inflamed first. In about 30 to 40 percent of the cases, nodules or bumps grow under the skin, deforming the joints.

What can be done about it?

Although most types of arthritis cannot be cured, treatment can help prevent and relieve pain, increase mobility, and reduce the joint damage that can lead to deformities. The earlier you go to the doctor for an evaluation, the better you can control the symptoms. The physician may refer your elder to a *rheumatologist* (a specialist who has expertise in treating arthritis).

The following are common symptoms of arthritis:

✔ Swelling in one or more joints

✔ Morning stiffness in the joints that lasts for about one hour

✔ Persistent or recurring pain or tenderness in a joint

✔ Difficulty moving or using a joint in the normal way

✔ Warmth and redness in a joint

Usually the doctor will recommend the following treatments, moving from the most conservative to the most aggressive. (The doctor may also recommend several strategies at the same time.)

✔ **Rest.** Resting when feeling pain or fatigue is helpful. But be aware that too much rest may have the opposite effect — more pain and fatigue — because too much inactivity makes muscles and joints stiff.

✔ **Exercise.** Increasing flexibility, muscle strength, and stamina can decrease joint pain and stiffness. Aquatic programs are especially useful because exercising in water takes some of the weight off painful joints, making it easier to exercise and also helping muscles to relax. Consult with the doctor before starting an exercise program.

✔ **Healthy diet.** Because extra weight puts pressure on joints, weight control should be a priority.

✔ **Assistive devices.** Splints and braces support weakened joints, allowing the elder to be more mobile. (See Chapter 12 about other assistive devices.)

✔ **Medication.** Arthritis has no cure. Pain-killers and anti-inflammatory medications manage or control the symptoms. Doctors often suggest over-the-counter medications like aspirin, ibuprofen, and acetaminophen to relieve the aches, graduating to prescription anti-inflammatory drugs when the over-the-counter drugs aren't sufficient.

Should you apply cold or hot packs to achy joints?

Both hot and cold therapies can reduce pain and inflammation. Warm towels or hot packs can increase blood flow, pain tolerance, and flexibility. Applying cold packs, soaking the joint in ice water, and using cooling over-the-counter sprays and ointments can relieve inflammations and reduce the pain by numbing the nerves around the joints. A frozen pack of corn or peas wrapped in a towel and molded around the joint may be just the ticket.

✔ **Surgery.** Sometime surgery is necessary to repair damage to the joints, restore function, and relieve pain (for example, fusing the bones in the joint or total hip and knee replacement).

The Arthritis Foundation can direct you to local support groups, aquatic programs, and exercise classes. It can also provide referrals to physicians who specialize in treating arthritis (rheumatologists). To find your local chapter and local programs, call (800-283-7800) or visit online (www.arthritis.org).

Osteoporosis

Half of all the women over age 50 will suffer a fracture — usually in the wrist, hip, or backbone — due to osteoporosis. Men develop osteoporosis, too, but less commonly. All in all, osteoporosis leads to 1.5 million bone fractures or breaks per year.

What is it?

Osteoporosis is a condition that thins and weakens bones (making them brittle and porous). A mere misstep off of a curb, bending down to pick up the newspaper in the driveway, or even sneezing can snap a bone. Osteoporosis can also cause the spinal cord to collapse and compress, producing a stooped posture, a "dowager's hump," and debilitating back pain.

Scientists don't fully understand how osteoporosis does its nasty work. But they do know that your bone mass is greatest at about age 30. Then your bones begin to lose minerals (especially calcium). Osteoporosis occurs when the loss of bone mass is fast and extensive, and your body doesn't have enough calcium to compensate for the loss.

If your elder had relatives who were stooped or suffered fractures in late life, she's more likely to develop osteoporosis than an elder without the same family history. In addition to hereditary factors, a diet low in calcium, hormonal loss from menopause, and lifestyle factors like smoking and meager physical activity contribute to the development of the disease. If your older person is Caucasian or Asian-American, has a petite body frame, or had an early menopause, she has a high risk for being a victim of this bone thief.

Anyone who has one or more of these risk characteristics (including a family history) should ask the doctor about getting a bone density test to find out whether indeed she has osteoporosis.

What can be done about it?

If the disease is present, the doctor may prescribe one of several medications to manage it. The doctor will also surely encourage your elder to follow the following recommendations to slow the progression of the disease or — for those who don't have the disease — to help prevent them from developing it:

✔ **Get enough calcium.** An elder needs to drink a quart of milk a day to get the calcium she needs. Most doctors recommend that women over 50 should take about 1,200 mg of calcium in supplement form.

✔ **Take vitamin D supplements.** Twenty minutes of sunlight every single day supplies enough vitamin D to help your body absorb the calcium it needs. Because lots of elders don't get that much sunlight, doctors usually recommend taking 600 to 800 units of vitamin D a day in tablet form. You can buy also calcium tablets with vitamin D.

✔ **Quit smoking.** Smoking causes the body to make less bone-protecting estrogen.

✔ **Drink alcohol in moderation.** Alcohol interferes with the body's absorption of calcium.

✔ **Engage in regular physical exercise such as walking.** Besides helping build and maintain strong bones, exercise increases good balance, muscle strength, and agility, making falls less likely.

The National Osteoporosis Foundation sponsors support groups. If a support group doesn't currently exist in your area, you can start a group (the foundation will provide all of the materials necessary), or your elder can join an online support group. For more information, call 202-223-2226 or send an e-mail (supgroup@nof.org) to Michelle Horton at the National Osteoporosis Foundation or write to her at *Building Strength Together,* 1232 22nd St., Washington, DC 20037-1232. The phone number for general information only is 800-223-9994.

Chronic Obstructive Pulmonary Disease (COPD)

The term *Chronic Obstructive Pulmonary Disease* (COPD) refers mainly to two diseases — emphysema and chronic bronchitis. Both conditions damage the lungs, resulting in persistently obstructed airways. About 16 million Americans suffer from COPD. It's the fourth leading cause of death in the United States.

What is it?

Emphysema causes the air sacs in the lungs to weaken and break, compromising the ability of the lungs to expand and contract. Sufferers have to breathe harder in order to get enough oxygen and eliminate carbon dioxide.

Chronic bronchitis is an *inflammatory* illness. In this case, the obstruction is caused by scarring of lung tissue, swelling of the lining, spasms, an excess production of mucus, and a decrease in the lungs' ability to take in oxygen and eliminate carbon dioxide.

Long-term smoking is the underlying cause of COPD in 80 to 90 percent of the cases. Elders with COPD may have a chronic cough, chest tightness, shortness of breath, difficulty breathing, and frequent throat clearing. They also have increased production of mucus. Typically, COPD takes hold after about ten years of smoking; at that time the symptoms are mild and hardly noticeable. By the time the person is 50 or 60 (the typical age at diagnosis), the symptoms have increased, and the person's quality of life has deteriorated.

What can be done about it?

As with all of the chronic conditions described in this chapter, elders with COPD should eat a healthy diet. A sensible exercise program (okayed by the doctor) helps maintain or improve functioning, but it won't reverse the lung damage. The main treatment for COPD is quitting smoking. Giving up cigarettes at any point in the progression of the disease slows the process down. Flu shots and pneumonia shots are a necessity; contracting either illness can worsen COPD because patients with COPD are at higher risk of serious consequences from these diseases. For the same reason, antibiotics are often given at the first signs of a respiratory infection in patients with COPD. Doctors may prescribe various medications to cut down the inflammation, reduce muscle spasms, and help loosen and expel mucus. Long-term oxygen therapy can prolong the lives of elders with severe COPD.

To find a COPD support group, call the American Lung Association (800-586-4872). You will automatically be connected to the American Lung Association in your county. Your county office can refer you to support groups for COPD that are sponsored by local hospitals.

Gastroesophageal Reflux Disease

Gastroesophageal Reflux Disease (GERD) is frequent and persistent heartburn. *Consumer Reports* magazine reported in September 2002 that nearly half the adults in America suffer from at least one attack of heartburn a month.

Quit smoking and live longer!

According to the American Lung Association, close to 13 million Americans over age 50 smoke. Almost every chronic illness improves by quitting cigarette smoking. For example, circulation improves immediately, and lungs begin to repair damage. But anyone who has ever tried knows how difficult it is to quit. Research shows that going "cold turkey" is often a setup for repeated failure. Experts agree that success is more likely when as many elements as possible are included in the effort to quit. This advice is especially true for heavy smokers. You need to hit your habit with everything you can — willpower, nicotine replacement products (patch, gum, nasal spray, or inhaler), and behavioral changes.

QuitNet (www.quitnet.com) is a Web site devoted to helping people give up tobacco. It's loaded with general information, advice, and product information and can help you locate a cessation program in your older person's area.

Another excellent resource packed with cessation advice and guidance is The Office on Smoking and Health National Center for Chronic Disease Prevention and Health Promotion. Visit online at www.cdc.gov/tobacco.

The American Lung Association can provide a referral to a Freedom From Smoking Clinic in your older person's community. To connect to your local chapter, call the American Lung Association (800-LUNG-USA).

One attack a month is unpleasant, but it isn't serious. On the other hand, chronic heartburn (two or more attacks per week) can lead to asthma, bronchitis, pneumonia, and even cancer of the esophagus.

What is it?

The esophagus is a muscular tube that carries food from the mouth to the stomach (where acids digest the food). These stomach acids aren't supposed to back up into the esophagus, but in some people, the ringlike muscle at the bottom of the esophagus that's meant to block the stomach juices from backing up doesn't function properly, and stomach acids flow back into the esophagus. The result is a burning sensation in the chest, inflammation, and — in some cases — serious damage (esophageal ulcers, scars, and a precancerous cell growth in the esophagus).

What can be done about it?

You may be able to help your elder control heartburn by encouraging the following lifestyle changes:

- ✔ **Avoid certain foods and beverages.** Common culprits are fatty and fried foods, peppermint, chocolate, alcohol, coffee, and orange juice.

- ✔ **Eat smaller portions.** Eating less food avoids the bloating that may contribute to heartburn.

- ✔ **Eat slower.** Take your time to avoid getting bloated.

✔ **Lose weight.** A belly that overhangs the belt probably presses on the abdomen, increasing the pressure in the stomach.

✔ **Avoid tight belts and waistbands.** Cinched-in waists may press on the abdomen, increasing the pressure in the stomach.

✔ **Quit smoking.** Nicotine is known to relax the muscle at the bottom of the esophagus (something you don't want) and increase the production of stomach acid.

✔ **Sit upright for two to three hours after eating.** In this position, gravity keeps the stomach acids down in the belly where they belong.

✔ **Elevate your head when sleeping or resting.** This position makes it more difficult (but not impossible) for the stomach acid to flow back into the esophagus.

✔ **Consider trying an over-the-counter antacid.** These products help neutralize the stomach acids.

GERD shouldn't be brushed off as simply heartburn and nothing to worry about. The doctor needs to know about it — what you think is heartburn may be angina (a symptom of coronary artery disease). Occasional heartburn for which you take an antacid isn't a serious problem, but frequent heartburn demands attention. The doctor may prescribe medications that may make the muscle at the bottom of the esophagus close more tightly, reduce the acidity of the stomach, or both.

Being Observant Can Save a Precious Life

Elders taking medication for chronic medical conditions and oldsters who have difficulty carrying out their daily living activities need to be looked in on frequently. Don't wait for your older person to tell you that something's amiss. Use your own senses to detect trouble signs and ask the folks who see your elder most often (home-health aides, friends, family members, and neighbors) to note and report any changes to you. Lives have been saved and disability avoided by eagle-eyed caregivers.

Tracking changes

Keep a record of changes that are more than passing, including increased or decreased appetite, sleep problems, or changes in functioning and mood. Report the changes to the doctor if they persist. Also track symptoms such as rashes, nausea, headaches, constipation, and pain and report them to the doctor, especially if your elder is on medication or has a chronic illness.

The A, B, C, D's of skin cancer

Because skin cancer is frequently seen in older adults (most cases appear after age 50), caregivers need to be on the lookout for it. It's estimated that 40 to 50 percent of those who live to age 65 will have a bout of skin cancer at least once. This number sounds alarming, but if the cancer is discovered early and treated promptly, it's almost 100 percent curable.

The most common warning sign is a change in the skin (a new growth or a sore that doesn't heal). The cancer may start off as a small shiny, pale, or waxy lump, but it can also be a hard red lump or a flat, rough dry spot.

Your elder's skin needs to be inspected regularly. Urge your independent older person to check her skin often. Be on the watch for suspicious spots when you help bathe and dress your frail elder. Ask the doctor to inspect your elder's skin as well.

Make an appointment with a dermatologist if your elder has moles or pigmented spots with the following characteristics:

✔ **A**symmetrical dark spots or moles

✔ **B**orders that are irregular or ragged

✔ **C**olor that varies from one area to another

✔ **D**iameter that's larger than a pencil eraser

Always read the inserts packed with prescription medicines. New medications often have adverse side effects. Notify the doctor if symptoms appear early in the course of a new medication. (See Chapter 11 for more information about medication.)

Elders who suffer from Alzheimer's disease or other dementias may not be able to tell you that they're experiencing pain. They may get irritable or pace the floor. They may withdraw and refuse to eat. If this behavior isn't usual, they may indicate that the confused elder is in pain.

Knowing when to call for emergency help

If your elder has symptoms of a heart attack or stroke (see sections on heart disease and stroke, earlier in this chapter), is unconscious, or has fallen and is obviously injured or in severe pain, call 911 immediately. If vomiting occurs, turn her head to the side to prevent choking. If breathing stops, begin CPR. (See Chapter 6 to find out how to get CPR training.) Contact your elder's physician as soon as possible (while waiting for the ambulance to arrive or when you get to the hospital's emergency room) so that the doctor can inform the medical staff about your elder's needs, background, and medical condition.

Make it easy for the police or ambulance driver to find you. House numbers should be clearly visible from the street. To save precious time when the emergency occurs after dark, buy a small battery-operated flasher that you can place outside to identify the home for emergency rescuers.

Be prepared for an emergency by keeping a written list of all the medicines your elder is taking (see Chapter 11 for advice on how best to organize this information), as well as his medical conditions and the name and phone number of his primary physician.

Elders who go out and about in the community on their own should always carry identification and important medical information on their person. In the event of an emergency, urgent-care personnel would then have the information to act appropriately. A MedicAlert bracelet or necklace is another effective method. During a crisis, the bracelet or necklace is spotted. The medical personnel radios the emergency department of the hospital. A hospital staff member calls MedicAlert. MedicAlert in turn transmits the patient's medical file to the hospital ER and notifies the family. The cost of MedicAlert is $35 for the first year and $20 each year after that. For more information, write MedicAlert, Box 1009, Turlock, CA 95381. You can sign up for MedicAlert by calling (800-344-3226) or going online (www.medicalert.com).

Communicating with the Doctor

Visiting the doctor can be intimidating, especially when he spouts unfamiliar medical terms. Your elder may end up not fully understanding her health problems or her treatment options. She may forget to ask important questions and come away feeling frustrated and confused.

Generally, doctors today are under much more pressure than they were a decade ago. They have to see more patients than ever before and are required to spend less time with each person. Pair that with the fact that many older people (in awe of the medical profession) are reluctant to demand more time, and you have a dreadful doctor-patient relationship.

Making the most out of doctor appointments

In the old days, the doctor took the lead, and the patient did what she was told. Nowadays, many doctors tend to be rushed because of the demands of managed care. Doctors typically schedule 45 minutes for a first visit and 15 to 20 minutes for follow-up visits. This appointment includes time to get a history of current symptoms, perform a physical exam, explain his findings, and write a note and prescriptions.

Patients must be assertive — presenting their concerns precisely and well, asking questions, and requesting clarification about medical conditions, medications, and treatment choices. If more time is needed for additional concerns, ask to schedule a longer visit or another follow-up to go over additional concerns.

The following advice can make your elder's visit to the doctor's office more productive and more satisfying. (If your elder is frail, she may need your assistance in carrying out the tips.)

- ✔ **Take a notepad or tape recorder.** Remembering everything the doctor says is nearly impossible, especially if you're anxious or ill. Write down as much as you can. Better yet, ask whether it's okay for you to tape-record the physician's comments and instructions.

- ✔ **Remember to take your hearing aid or eyeglasses.** Don't be shy about asking the doctor to slow down or speak up.

- ✔ **Have someone accompany you to serve as an extra set of ears, take notes, and advocate for your well-being.**

- ✔ **Put your medicines in a bag and bring them with you (or take a written list).** Include nonprescription drugs, vitamins, herbal remedies, even cough medicines, and laxatives. Everything needs to be reported!

- ✔ **Have a list of your questions and concerns in order of importance.** Make the questions precise and to the point. Have a copy for the doctor in case he wants to follow along. Keep it to one page. Include details (when symptoms started, how frequent, and anything that triggers or relieves symptoms). The physician is more likely to be interested in new symptoms or problems than in reviewing chronic problems extensively at each visit.

- ✔ **Talk openly.** Disclose your diet, alcohol consumption, smoking habits, and any other healthcare you're receiving elsewhere. Also mention important changes in your life (moving in with children, the passing of a loved one).

- ✔ **Make sure that you understand his recommendations and treatment.** Ask him to repeat or say something you don't understand in another way to help your comprehension. Such a request isn't a reflection of your IQ; it's a reflection of the lack of sensitivity of the doctor. Ask for a summary at the end of the visit or repeat back to him the main points, as you understand them.

- ✔ **Be willing to seek a second opinion on any serious health matter, especially when surgery is recommended.**

It's often difficult for an older person who was accustomed to the old model of doctoring to speak up. The National Institute on Aging has a wonderful booklet written to help older people get the most out of their visits to the doctor. For a free copy of *Talking with Your Doctor: A Guide for Older People,* call 800-222-2225.

Knowing when to call the doctor

Although you certainly don't want to be calling the doctor needlessly, telephone conversations with the physician or her nurse may help avoid unnecessary visits. Most doctors see telephone advice as part of their jobs and are willing to chat briefly, as long as you don't abuse this service. But when every single call you make results in the doctor advising you to bring your elder in, the doctor is sending you a message that she doesn't provide telephone advice. If that policy doesn't work for you and your elder, you may be better off finding a doctor with a different policy.

Determining whether your physician has the right stuff

Not every aged person needs to be treated by a *geriatrician,* but every physician who treats older people should have had at least some training in geriatrics. Asking about geriatric training should be the first question when deciding whether a doctor is right for your elder.

The following are additional questions to keep in mind when your age-advantaged person is looking for a doctor or deciding whether the current physician is right for the job:

- Is the doctor board certified in internal medicine by the American Board of Internal Medicine?

- Does the doctor have a Certificate of Added Qualification in Geriatric Medicine?

- Is the doctor someone she can talk to and feel comfortable with? Does he welcome her questions, show an interest in her, and have obvious concern for her well-being?

- Does the doctor seek underlying causes for her complaints and prescribe treatments, or does he attribute many of her ailments to "age"? (When a doctor frequently dismisses complaints as just being the result of "old age," the only thing that should be dismissed is the doctor.)

- Are the doctor's services covered by her health insurance plan? If not, can she afford to go to him?

- Does the doctor have privileges in the hospital she prefers to use?

- Are the doctor's visiting hours and location convenient for you?

- Does he have competent backup when he's on vacation?

✔ Will she have to wait many weeks or even months to get an appointment?

✔ Will the doctor or his nurse or assistant handle routine questions on the phone?

Finding a geriatrician

The average 75-year-old has three chronic conditions and takes four to five prescription drugs as well as over-the-counter medications. Symptoms of illness also present themselves differently in older people than they do in younger people. Pair this discrepancy with the fact that older people metabolize, absorb, and clear these drugs from their bodies differently than younger people, and you begin to see how complex medical care for the aged can be.

Primary care physicians care for most older adults. But when frail elderly people have complicated medical problems and their caregivers are at a loss for what to do, geriatricians are occasionally consulted.

Geriatricians are primary care physicians who have been board certified in either family practice or internal medicine and have passed an exam certifying them in the specialty of geriatric medicine. They must take continuing medical courses to stay certified. Only about 9,000 geriatricians are in the United States. This number is about 11,000 short of what is needed to take care of 35 million older people.

For a list of geriatricians in your elder's area, call 800-563-4916 or write to: The AGS Foundation for Health in Aging, The Empire State Building, 350 Fifth Ave., Suite 801, New York, NY 10118. You can find additional sources of information online. Start by visiting The American Medical Association at `www.ama-assn.org`. Clicking the Doctor Finder tab leads you to the names and addresses of local geriatricians. Click a particular doctor to get an office phone number, office address, gender, primary practice specialty, medical school, year of graduation, place of residency training, major professional activities, and board certifications. Another "must-visit" site in your search for a geriatrician is the American Board of Internal Medicine (`www.abim.org`). Click Online Diplomat Directory for an impressively detailed list of geriatricians.

Chapter 11

Just Say "Yes" to Health-Giving Drugs

Most people over 65 take about four or five prescription drugs and two over-the-counter drugs each day. Some medications are taken with food, a few may be taken at bedtime, some twice a day, others every four hours. It's enough to make anyone's head spin! Keeping track can be daunting, but that's only part of the problem. Older people are more than twice as likely as younger adults to suffer from adverse drug reactions.

Overseeing your elder's medication (or at least helping out with it) may be your most important caregiving task. Your vigilance can protect your older person from unnecessary discomfort — and even save his life.

This chapter assists you in making sure that your oldster's medicines help (not hurt) him. It alerts you to possible adverse drug reactions and shows you how to safely organize and supervise drug-taking. It also discusses the risks of alternative therapies and warns about health scams.

Making the Most of Medications

The best way to get a grip on your elder's medications is to first find out what prescription medicines, over-the-counter drugs, herbs, vitamins, minerals, and other dietary supplements your elder is using. This job may be as simple as reading the labels on bottles lined up next to the kitchen sink or as difficult as weeding through dozens of medications in several different spots throughout the house.

Once you have gathered all the medications, create a chart documenting everything you or your elder needs to know about the drugs he is taking. (See Table 11-1 for a sample medication chart.)

Arrange an appointment with your elder's primary physician to review all the medications and help you fill in the missing information on the medication chart you've created. The primary physician may be unaware of medications prescribed by other doctors, over-the-counter drugs, and dietary supplements used by your elder — a potentially dangerous situation!

When you go to your appointment, ask your elder's doctor the following questions:

- Do my records match your records?
- Can any of these medications be reduced or eliminated?
- Can mixing any of these drugs cause adverse drug interactions?
- Is it safe to drink alcohol (also a drug) with these medications?
- Are any of these drugs habit-forming?
- Are generics or less expensive alternatives in the same class of drugs available for any of these medications, and would they be good for my loved one?

Update the medication chart every time a new remedy is introduced and take it along to every medical appointment (specialists included). If a specialist prescribes a new medicine, inform the primary physician.

Keep the medication chart in a place where emergency personnel can see it (for example, on the refrigerator door held with a magnet).

Once the medications are organized and reviewed, it doesn't matter whether the pill-taker or the caretaker is in charge of the medication schedule — as long as the following strategies are heeded.

Table 11-1

My Medication Chart

Name of Drug*	What It's For	What It Looks Like	Date Started	Doctor	Dosage (Should Be on the Label)	When to Take It (e.g., on an Empty Stomach, with Meals, Bedtime, etc.)	How Long to Take It (e.g., Until Further Notice, Until Pills Are Used Up)	Special Instructions (e.g., Avoid Sun, What to Do if a Dose Is Missed)
Prandin	Diabetes	Small round pink pill		Davis	2-4 mg	15 min. before meals	Indefinitely	
Insulin	"	Clear liquid		Davis	Take as directed	At bedtime	"	Keep refrigerated
Toprol XL	Heart	White, medium, round pill		Gold	50 mg	Once a day	"	
Altace	Heart	Small orange capsule		Gold	2.5 mg	"	"	
Prevacid	Indigestion	Large pink & black capsule		Jones	30 mg	"	"	
Vitamin C	Prevent colds	Medium round beige tablet			500 mg	"	"	

Things your elder should do:

- ✔ Frequent a pharmacist who keeps a "drug profile" for customers and will alert you about interaction problems. Continue to compare prices at other pharmacies. Your pharmacist may match a cheaper price at another drugstore if you're a regular customer.

- ✔ Ask the doctor to write the medication's purpose on the prescription (for example, "for arthritis pain"). The pharmacist can then type it on the label, helping to reduce the chance of accidental mix-ups. If asked, most pharmacists will put the expiration date on the label, too.

- ✔ Ask the pharmacist for easy-open caps, large-print labels, and oversized bottles if needed.

- ✔ Check prescriptions before leaving the pharmacy. Make sure that the correct patient's name is on the bottle and that the directions match what the doctor said.

- ✔ Ask your pharmacist whether your pillbox or pill organizer will affect the stability of the medication.

- ✔ Talk to your doctor and your pharmacist to find out whether crushing pills and putting them in liquid or applesauce degrades the medicine, making it less effective.

- ✔ Read the medicine-bottle labels before each dose.

- ✔ Take prescriptions exactly as prescribed. A recent reported stated that nearly 25 percent of nursing home admissions were due to elders not following the prescribed medication therapy (on time, every time, the correct amount).

Things your elder should *not* do:

- ✔ Put drugs in a different bottle. Without the original label, it's easy to forget what the medicine is for or how much to take. Also, the original bottle is opaque or tinted to keep out damaging light.

- ✔ Split pills in advance. When the doctor says take half a pill, ask the pharmacist whether splitting in advance will affect the medication. (Most large pharmacies or medical-supply stores sell tablet cutters, which split unscored pills.)

- ✔ Chew or break pills unless directed.

- ✔ Take anyone else's medication.

- ✔ Drive when the warning on the bottle says "may cause drowsiness or fatigue."

- ✔ Tinker with doses (for example, taking a little more or less depending on how you feel).

- ✔ Discontinue prescribed medicine even if he's feeling chipper. This is especially true for antibiotics. Quitting before all the pills are taken, contributes to an increase in antibiotic-resistant strains of bacteria. Quitting abruptly may also cause unpleasant withdrawal symptoms. The doctor needs to be informed anytime a medication is stopped before the prescribed time.

✔ Accumulate old medicines. Unused medicines make medication management more confusing and difficult. The best way to dispose of medications is by flushing them down the toilet, ensuring that children, pets, or others will not find them in the trash and possibly be harmed by them.

Once the medications are all organized and charted, you can easily dispense them to your frail elder. You can lay out the pills the night before or set them out a week ahead of time. In some cases, egg cartons (with each egg pocket labeled for a different day of the week) can serve just as well as fancy organizers. (Again, check with the pharmacist to find out whether exposure to the air will have a negative effect on any of the pills.)

Creating a chart that lists all of the medications and when and how they should be taken simplifies even the most complicated schedule. (See Table 11-2 for a sample medication schedule.)

To assist more independent elders, you can choose from a wide assortment of pill organizers in many sizes and styles in pharmacies and medical-supply houses. Pillboxes with alarms and buzzers help with forgetfulness. I know one family that hired a telephone service to call and remind Pop to take his medicine.

Some elders manage their medications well, except for the occasional distraction — for example, answering the telephone and then, after saying goodbye, not remembering whether the pill was taken. One strategy is to turn the bottle upside down after taking the medicine. The upside-down bottle then becomes a signal that the pill has been taken. Another idea is to place the day's medicine bottles on the counter each morning. As soon as a pill is taken, the bottle is returned to the cabinet or drawer where it lives. Bottles on the counter mean that the pills have yet to be taken.

AARP has a free consumer guide, "How to be Drug Smart," which provides expert advice on drug taking from leading experts. Call 800-424-3410 and ask for publication D17698.

Where's the worst place to keep medicine?

Bathroom medicine cabinets are probably the worst places for keeping drugs. Like kitchens, they tend to have too much moisture. Medications need to be kept cool, dry, and out of direct sunlight. Medications in a purse, dresser drawer, or anywhere within a grandchild's reach should have child-resistant caps. Consider placing medicine on a high shelf in the linen closet. It's close to the bathroom, but out of small children's sight and reach.

Table 11-2   **Elsa's Medication Schedule**

Time of Day	Drug	What It Looks Like	How Many?	How Often?	How to Take It	Special Instructions
Upon arising	Fosamax	Oval white pill	1	Once a week	On an empty stomach, with at least 8 oz of water	Don't lie down for half an hour afterwards. Don't eat anything (including coffee or juice) for at least half an hour.
Upon arising	Metamucil (psyllium)	Orange powder	1 Tbsp	Daily, except on Fosamax day	With at least 8 oz of water	Bulk fiber supplement — label says it may interfere with other medications, so take at least 2 hours before or after other medicine
With dinner	Baby aspirin	Tiny round pill	1	Daily	Decided to do this on my own, because many health articles recommend a baby aspirin a day; must ask doctor about this on my next visit	
With dinner	Calcium + D	Big oval off-white pill	1	Daily	Works better if taken with food, but sometimes take it later or earlier if it's more convenient	
Before bedtime	Prempro	Small beige pill in dispenser	1	One daily	On the 1st through 25th of each month	Could take this in the morning and Metamucil at night, but that would mean more trips to the bathroom at night

Avoiding hospital faux pas

To avoid mix-ups in the hospital, urge your elder to follow these guidelines:

✔ Check to be sure that the medicine looks the same as always (size, shape, color, and dose). If it doesn't, ask why.

✔ Ask for the name, dose, possible side effects, and reason it's given before taking any new medicine.

✔ Make sure that the dispensing nurse checks your identification bracelet before she gives you that little paper cup of drugs.

✔ Don't take any medicine if you think it's wrong. Ask the nurse to call the doctor.

Recognizing and Preventing Adverse Drug Reactions

Reactions to medications can range from the mild and moderate (nausea, fatigue, constipation, headache, joint pain) to the severe (internal bleeding, liver damage).

Adverse drug reactions are bad enough on their own, but they can also lead to psychological distress, making elders miserable. For example, many years ago, my mom's doctor (in an attempt to get her runaway high blood pressure under control) prescribed a drug called Minoxidil. The new medicine did the job, all right. But as Mom's blood pressure dropped, lush dark hair sprouted on her cheeks, upper lip, and chin. The reaction was not life-threatening or painful, but Mom wept for weeks. Fortunately, the unwanted hair fell away when the minoxidil was discontinued, and Mom's happy-go-lucky nature returned. (Since then, a form of minoxidil applied directly to the scalp has been developed and approved by the Federal Drug Administration to promote hair growth in people with thinning hair.)

Because of their slower metabolism, oldsters are more prone to adverse drug reactions than younger adults. The liver and kidneys, for example, slow down, becoming less efficient at breaking down medication. This slowdown causes a higher blood concentration of the drug. In addition, because people lose water and muscle and gain fat as they age, drugs that are stored in fat cells hang around in the older body longer than they would in a younger body. This lingering effect is why older people, in some cases, get along just fine (and have fewer side effects) on lower than the standard adult dose Doctors who are aware of these differences in drug metabolism tend to start low and go slow when prescribing new medications, increasing the dose until the desired effect is achieved with the minimum amount of medication. (This practice doesn't apply when treating acute or severe conditions.)

The following sections categorize adverse drug reactions into four separate categories for convenience, but in reality, the lines between them are often blurred. You don't need to figure out which category your elder's symptoms fall into — leave that to the physician. What is important is to prevent an adverse reaction in your elder from happening in the first place and to recognize when medication is at the root of the problem.

Allergies

The patient (or caregiver) is 100 percent responsible for informing the doctor of allergies to certain drugs, and the older person's doctor is 100 percent responsible for asking and noting whether the elder has any drug allergies. This overlapping responsibility is especially important when the doctor is getting ready to write a new prescription.

A drug allergy is different than a side effect or a reaction caused by mixing drugs. The allergic reaction occurs when the immune system, having been exposed to the drug before (one or more times with no reaction), creates antibodies to it. Then, after a subsequent exposure to the drug, the antibodies cause a release of histamines. Antihistimines are used to treat mild allergic reactions (itching, rash, headache, nausea).

A more severe and potentially life-threatening allergic reaction is known as *anaphylactic shock.* (Symptoms include itchiness on the soles of the feet and palms, dificulty breathing because of throat swelling, wheezing, erratic heart beat, a rapid dangerous drop in blood pressure, and possible shock.) Emergency treatment usually consists of an injection of epinephrine (adrenaline), which opens the blood vessels and airways. Additional treatments with antihistamines and sometimes steroids may be required. Anaphylactic shock can't occur on the first exposure. Many people don't even remember the first time they were exposed to the substance.

Older adults who have had serious allergic reactions to medications and are well enough to be out and about on their own should consider wearing a MedicAlert bracelet or necklace. (See Chapter 10 for information on how these items can help and how to obtain them.)

Side effects

Side effects from medication include confusion, nausea, poor balance, change in bowel patterns, and sleep changes. When these effects are mistaken for symptoms of another illness, additional medicines may be prescribed. For example, if your elder complains of sleeplessness and the doctor is unaware that your elder has been taking over-the-counter cold medicines, the doctor

Are generics the same as brand-name drugs?

The answer is yes, generics are the same as brand-name medications. The Federal Drug Administration (FDA) requires that a generic drug deliver the same amount of active ingredients into the bloodstream at the same rate as its brand-name equivalent. They're very strict about this requirement.

The only differences between a brand name and generic drug are the inactive ingredients (preservatives, food coloring, and compounds that hold the medicine together) and price.

When a generic drug enters the market, it's usually about 30 percent cheaper than the brand name. If other competing generic drugs are on the market, you may find a generic as much as 75 percent cheaper than the brand name.

But if you switch from a brand name to a generic, be alert for reactions or side effects, on the extraordinarily rare chance that your elder is having an allergic reaction to one of the inactive ingredients or a change in the way her body is absorbing the medication.

may prescribe a sleeping pill for insomnia. The drugs in the sleep aid and the cold medicine may combine and accumulate in your elder's body (see the section on overdoses, later in this chapter, to understand how such overdosing occurs), causing grogginess. The grogginess can cause a fall and a broken hip. Now you have a situation in which the senior may never be able to live independently again, and the family begins to consider nursing home placement. All this tragedy from a harmless side effect!

To protect your elder from side effects, observe the following guidelines:

- ✔ Read and save the information inserts that come with the medication.

- ✔ Ask the doctor to introduce one new medication at a time. Then, if a side effect occurs, the doctor can easily identify which new drug is the culprit.

- ✔ Be aware of the side effects for every new drug. Find out as much as possible about the drugs your elder is taking.

- ✔ Be aware that your elder's chronic medical conditions may make him more vulnerable to adverse reactions.

- ✔ Ask the doctor to try reducing the drug or changing prescriptions. Most of the time, side effects go away when the drug is stopped or the dose is reduced, and no real harm is done.

When an elder becomes confused, withdraws from contact, and is clearly not himself, review his medications with his primary physician or geriatrician before jumping to the conclusion that the elder is demented.

Drug interactions

When one drug interferes with another drug, the way one or both of them act in the body can be altered, resulting in nausea, stomach upset, headache, heartburn, and dizziness. These reactions are relatively minor, but other drug interactions (fortunately less common) can cause a drop in blood pressure, a fast or irregular heart beat, or damage to the heart or liver.

Sometimes when various drugs are combined (including prescription drugs and over-the-counter medications), an *increase* in the overall desired effect occurs. For example, if you take aspirin (which can thin the blood) with certain blood thinners (used to prevent blood clots from forming), the result may be excessive bleeding.

Other interactions can cause *less* of an effect than desired. For example, certain over-the-counter antacids — if taken with antibiotics, blood thinners, and heart medications — prevent the medications from being absorbed into the bloodstream. The medicines may not work as well, or may not work at all.

Or the combination of two drugs may produce an entirely different effect. Again, the danger is that not knowing what's causing the new problems may make a doctor inclined to prescribe more medicine, creating a real confusion of symptoms and causes.

A good general rule is to ask the doctor and pharmacist whether certain foods should be restricted with certain medications. For example, calcium-rich foods (milk, cheese, ice cream), antacids, and vitamins containing iron can reduce the effectiveness of antibiotics. Asparagus, spinach, and broccoli can neutralize anticoagulants because these vegetables have vitamin K, which promotes blood clotting. Grapefruit juice increases the risk of side effects when taken with most statin drugs (prescribed for lowering cholesterol).

Risky prescriptions

The American Medical Association says that nearly 7 million seniors a year are routinely prescribed drugs that are too risky for them. AARP recently warned its older adult members to heed expert advice and avoid certain drugs (or take them in carefully calculated and monitored doses). Included in their list of highly risky drugs are the analgesic propoxyphene, the anti-inflammatory indomethacin, the antidepressant amitriptyline, and over-the-counter drugs containing diphenhydramine (Benadryl), chlorpheniramine (Chlor-Trimeton), and most other nonprescription antihistamines. Among the negative effects of these drugs is confusion. Unfortunately, confusion in older people can lead to accidents and increased disability.

When it's all Greek (oops — Latin) to you!

The following abbreviations of Latin terms come in handy when you're trying to decipher a prescription or a medicine bottle label:

p.r.n. — as needed

q.d. — every day

b.i.d. — twice a day

t.i.d. — three times a day

q.i.d. — four times a day

Overdoses

Each year, 17 percent of elderly Americans end up in the hospital as a result of a dangerous drug interaction or of taking incorrect dosages.

Ask the doctor how age, weight, gender, and ethnicity may affect the dosage. For example, Prilosec, an ulcer remedy, accumulates in the blood of Asian-Americans four times as much as it does with Caucasians. In elderly people, the same amount of Prilosec lasts 50 percent longer than it lasts in younger people.

The dose for a 200-pound man may be too much for a woman weighing 108 pounds. Women may also be more sensitive to drugs than men. Ask your doctor whether the stature and gender of your elder may affect the dosage.

More is not better when it comes to medications. Sometimes people take an extra swig of over-the-counter medicine, for example. Just because you can buy it without a prescription doesn't mean it's harmless. Too much can be harmful. (See more about over-the-counter medication in the section "Using Over-the-Counter Drugs," later in this chapter.)

Cutting Costs

A 2002 survey of nearly 11,000 seniors reported that because of high costs, one out of every four people age 65 and over did not fill their prescriptions or skipped doses of medicine to make the prescription last longer. Nearly 25 percent of those surveyed said they spent a minimum of $100 a month on drugs. Some elders even take half a dose of medicine to stretch it out. Not taking the medication the way it's supposed to be taken leads to increased illness, deterioration, medical emergencies, and hospitalizations.

The following ideas can stretch your senior's medication dollars:

- ✔ Investigate prescription programs for low-income elders.
- ✔ Ask the druggist for a senior discount.
- ✔ Ask your druggist to recommend a store brand or discount brand over-the-counter drug with the same active ingredients as the more expensive brand.
- ✔ Find out whether your prescription insurance plan offers a mail-order option. Some plans allow considerable discounts when you buy in quantity — great for medications for chronic conditions.

Using Over-the-Counter Drugs

Over 700 of the over-the-counter drugs used today were prescription drugs 30 years ago. To avoid the drug interactions, side effects, and even overdoses that may be caused by over-the-counter drugs, consult with your elder's doctor (and pharmacist) before using these preparations.

One way to avoid an overdose is to note the active ingredient on the back of the box or bottle of a nonprescription medication. If your elder is taking more than one medication with the same active ingredient, he may ingest more than the recommended dose of that chemical compound, which can lead to a serious health problem. This situation occurs most often with over the-counter pain relievers. For example, acetaminophen is in a variety of over-the-counter

Medicine for all occasions

Jerome, 80, and Annie, 75, are excited about their upcoming marriage. While going for a stroll to discuss their wedding plans, they notice that a new drugstore has opened in their neighborhood. Jerome suggests that they go in. He addresses the gentleman behind the counter:

"Are you the owner?"

The pharmacist answers, "Yes."

Jerome: "Do you sell heart medication?"

Pharmacist: "All kinds."

Jerome: "Do have medicine for rheumatism?"

Pharmacist: "Definitely."

Jerome: "How about Viagra?"

Pharmacist: "Of course."

Jerome: "Do you carry medications for memory?"

Pharmacist: "Yes, several."

Jerome: "What about vitamins and sleeping pills?"

Pharmacist: "Absolutely."

Jerome: "Perfect! We'd like to register here for our wedding gifts."

WORLD WIDE WEB

Deep drug discounts for low-income seniors

The following programs can knock hundreds of dollars off of prescription drugs costs each year:

✔ **Together Rx.** This prescription-savings program, which can save approximately 20 to 40 percent off the usual amount paid right at the pharmacy counter, covers products from a number of major drug companies. Your elder must have an annual income of less than $28,000 (or $38,000 for couples), be a Medicare enrollee, and have no drug coverage. There's no membership fee. Obtain an application by calling 800-865-7211 or download an application online (www.Together-Rx.com).

✔ **Pfizer for Living Share Card.** This program is for seniors with incomes less than $18,000 ($24,000 for couples). They must be Medicare enrollees and have no other drug coverage. Members pay $15 for a 30-day supply of their Pfizer drugs at pharmacies that take the card. Obtain an application by calling 800-717-6005 or download an application online (www.pfizerforliving.com).

✔ **Lilly Answer Card.** This program is for seniors with incomes less than $18,000 ($24,000 for couples). They must be Medicare enrollees and have no other drug coverage. Members pay $12 for a 30-day supply of their prescription Lilly drug at participating pharmacies. Obtain an application by calling 877-795-4559 or download an application online (www.lillyanswers.com).

✔ **AARP's Member Choice.** This program charges a $15-per-year membership fee, which allows you to save up to 47 percent on top-selling prescriptions. You can use the membership card at over 48,000 participating neighborhood pharmacies, or you can order prescriptions through the mail. To take advantage of the mail-order prescription program, you must be an AARP member; membership is $12.50 per year. Call 800-439-4457 or visit online (www.aarppharmacy.com)

and prescription medicines, including headache remedies, pain relievers, and sleeping aids. Add alcohol, and you increase your risk for liver damage.

TIP

Cold medicines and cough medicines can increase blood-sugar levels. If your elder is diabetic, ask the pharmacist for cough medicine without sugar in it.

Considering Alternative and Complementary Treatments

Complementary treatments are therapies that are outside of conventional medicine (as practiced in the United States), but that may be used in addition to traditional therapies. For example, *aromatherapy* (the use of extracts and essences from flowers and herbs) may be used to help relax a patient after surgery.

An *alternative* therapy, on the other hand, is a treatment that's also outside of conventional medicine (as practiced in the United States), but it is used instead of traditional therapies — for example, fighting cancer with a special diet instead of undergoing chemotherapy, radiation, or surgery.

Acupuncture, biofeedback, hypnosis, guided imagery, and various forms of massage and therapeutic touch are a few complementary and alternative treatments. Dozens more techniques also exist. (See Chapter 16 about the mental health benefits of the arts.)

Using dietary supplements (including vitamins, minerals, and herbs) to treat illness has become more commonplace in recent years. The popularity of herbs, in particular, can be attributed, in part, to advertisements extolling exaggerated bits of scientific information and disenchantment with conventional medicine. The main criticism of dietary supplements — especially herbal remedies (made from plants or plant parts) — is that they haven't undergone rigorous scientific scrutiny to determine whether they're safe to use for certain maladies and, if so, how much and for how long they should be used. "If it's natural, it must be okay" is not necessarily true. Without testing, you have only individual personal success stories to go on. These stories can be exaggerations, or the apparent cures can simply be due to a placebo effect (if a person thinks something helps, it often does) or remissions in the illness. For example, arthritis is a condition in which the pain comes and goes. A person may take an herbal remedy, improve, and then mistakenly believe that the herbal remedy cured him.

Using dietary supplements (including herbal remedies) without consulting the doctor about their safety, effectiveness, and possible interactions with prescription medications or over-the-counter preparations is a prescription for trouble. For example, Ginkgo biloba extract has been touted as a means to prevent or delay dementia in the elderly, but little evidence supports that claim. Ginkgo, which inhibits blood clotting, may cause a problem if it's taken with medicines used to thin the blood. Some researchers have reported that Ginkgo extract used with aspirin can cause internal bleeding. Kava is a popular herbal taken to reduce stress and anxiety and treat insomnia; when taken with muscle relaxers, sedatives, or antidepressants, it may increase the effects of those drugs — increasing the chance of falls. St. John's Wort, taken for depression, may weaken the effectiveness of some prescription drugs.

Surely some of these therapies are benign. Some may possibly be helpful, but until scientists can distinguish between the helpful, the useless, and the harmful, tell your elder to hold on to her money and focus on adopting a healthy lifestyle and adhering to her doctor's orders.

Steering Clear of Treatment Scams

Older people are popular targets for unscrupulous con artists who say that they're offering miraculous cures and scientific breakthroughs. What they really offer is false hope — a hope that is quickly dashed. Symptoms are no better, maybe worse, and money is wasted. The worst part is that these char-latans keep elders from seeking and getting appropriate medical treatment. Quacks and swindlers market over the telephone, with bogus advertising in newspapers and magazines, by e-mail, and even at the front door. (See Chapter 21 to determine whether your elder is already a victim and has been profiled as a good candidate for fraud by other con operations.)

Anti-aging preparations, products that promise that you can eat everything you want and still lose weight, and cures for serious or chronic ailments like Alzheimer's disease, diabetes, or arthritis are among the most common fraud-ulent claims.

When something sounds too good to be true, it usually is. The following words and phrases are typically used in fraudulent marketing schemes:

- ✔ "Extremely beneficial in the treatment of arthritis, infection, prostate problems, ulcers, heart trouble, hardening of the arteries, and more." (Cure-all medicines don't exist.)

- ✔ "This product shrinks tumors," or "This treatment cures cancer." (These promises are false.)

- ✔ "Scientific breakthrough," "miraculous cure," "exclusive product," "secret ingredient," and "ancient remedy." (All are ploys to separate you from your money.)

- ✔ "Hurry — this offer won't last. Send a check now to reserve your order." (Limited offers and advanced payments are designed to promote impul-sive buying.)

- ✔ "My husband was riddled with cancer, and now he is cancer-free after 30 days." (Undocumented case histories are worthless. Reputable treatments undergo many years of scientific study involving many individuals.)

- ✔ "No-risk money-back guarantee if not completely satisfied." (These slick salespeople are not always easy to find, and when they can be located, they often use small-print loopholes to refuse a refund.)

If you or your senior has been misled or deceived by such claims, call the Federal Trade Commission (877-382-4357), write to Consumer Response Center, Federal Trade Commission, Washington, DC 20580, or go online (www.ftc.gov, click File A Complaint). Your state attorney also wants to know about these crooks. Look for your state attorney general's office in the blue pages of your telephone directory. You can also get the name, address, and telephone number of your state attorney general by visiting the National Association of State Attorneys General Web site (www.naag.org).

Buying medication from an unfamiliar Web site opens the door for more problems than you may already have. The Web site may be selling drugs illegally. You may receive a counterfeit or contaminated product, the wrong product, or nothing at all. Beware of getting a prescription online by simply filling out a questionnaire about your health. Filling out a questionnaire about your health in order to get a prescription online is not part of legitimate medical practice. To check whether a Web site is a pharmacy in good standing, call the National Association of Boards of Pharmacy at 847-698-6227 or visit online (www.nabp.net). Beware of purchasing medications from foreign Web sites, because it's generally illegal to import drugs bought from these sites. Not only will the United States be unable to help you if you're ripped off, but the health risks are great.

Chapter 12

Protective Doohickeys and Thingamajigs

Step into 78-year-old Agnes's shoes — or her bedroom slippers — because that's what she wears every day along with her tired housecoat. Agnes doesn't have a reason to get dressed. She says, "Why bother? I don't go anywhere." Getting herself out of bed is ingenious but dangerous. Before she retires, she pulls out two drawers from the six drawer dresser next to her bed. In the morning, she grabs on to them with her left hand and struggles to lift herself upright. From there, leaning on the wall, holding on to doorways and furniture, she makes her way through the darkened apartment to the bathroom and kitchen. An old tabby rubs against her leg as she moves down the darkened corridor. Agnes skirts around a never-put-away artificial Christmas tree and boxes of photos she intends to sort through. In the tiny kitchen, she makes a cup of tea and carries it with her strong hand, the cup shaking on its saucer, the tea threatening to spill out.

Agnes makes a mental note to ask Joey (the neighbor boy who brings in her mail and picks up groceries) to get her some more jelly donuts for breakfast. She looks around the kitchen. All her medicine bottles are lined up on the counter without their lids. Tabby lurks dangerously close. Tea, coffee, plates, bowls, and glasses fill up the surfaces, along with anything else she may need during the day. She wishes she could keep things tidier, but leaving dishes on the counter is easier than having to reach and bend to retrieve and put stuff away.

Better safe than sorry

This chapter begins with the all-too-common example of an older frail lady struggling vainly to live on her own — or an accident waiting to happen! If you haven't read it already, you may want to take a peek at it and then test yourself by seeing how many safety suggestions you can propose for Agnes. I list a few in this sidebar. You can probably think of even more.

The following suggestions may make your frail elder's living space safer:

✔ Raise the height of a low bed to make it easier to get out of.

✔ Install grab bars next to the bed and in other strategic places throughout the living space.

✔ Improve lighting throughout the home to lower the risk of stumbling.

✔ Decide with the elder about the fate of pets (weighing companionship against safety).

✔ Remove obstacles on floors and counters.

✔ Put an automatic pill dispenser into service.

✔ Install turntable shelves in her cabinets or set up plastic turntables on existing shelves.

✔ Buy a reaching device for getting items on and off shelves.

Agnes lives on the edge. Thousands of elderly people live like Agnes, putting their lives in jeopardy. This chapter sheds light on specific things to do to make your elder's life safer, more independent, more functional, and certainly filled with less frustration.

Elder-Proofing the Home

Experts maintain that you can prevent one-third to one-half of all home accidents with home modifications and repair. Some elbow grease, an eagle eye for potential hazards, and the drive to pursue dollar-stretching home repair and modification programs can keep your older person safe.

You can double and triple your chances of keeping your elder out of harm's way by also systematically taking a troubleshooting survey, from the outside of the house or apartment to the inside, and then going room to room from big structures like stairwells to potential problems like loose bathroom tiles. Have you ever observed an accident (for example, something falling off the edge of a table or someone tripping on a bump in the rug) and practically kicked yourself because you had a feeling before it happened that it *would* happen? The feeling is your intuition. Trust it. When you think something could happen, there's a high likelihood that it will.

Adding a ramp

Ramps rule! Well-designed ramps erase barriers to the outside world for elders living by themselves as well as elders who have home-care help. A ramp may allow a frail elder to independently enter and exit his homes, use transportation, and gain access to public buildings — not to mention how much easier it makes life for caregivers and personal attendants.

Ramps built to help elders avoid steps should have handrails on both sides.

Makeshift ramps are dangerous. One with too steep an incline or an uneven platform can tip a wheelchair. Unanchored planks can collapse.

Before buying or building any sort of ramp, consult with the elder's physicians, therapists, or other rehabilitation professionals for an evaluation to determine whether ramps are the best access option for your elder. Sometimes a portable ramp fills the bill. Such ramps are cheaper and can be moved to different situations, but you need to be sure that they're suitable for your elder. Lots of situations demand a permanent ramp connected with bolts and clamps and other doodads.

Depending upon the terms of the policy, some medical insurance providers may cover a portion of the cost of a ramp, provided that you have a doctor's prescription and justification of medical need. Additional funding sources include community agencies, community organizations, and churches.

ABLEDATA is a federally funded project that provides consumers, organizations, professionals, and caregivers with information about assistive technology. The ABLEDATA database contains detailed descriptions of 19,000 products (including price, manufacturer contact information, and product reviews from current owners). The database also covers threshold ramps, building ramps, and vehicle ramps currently available in the United States, as well as information about ramp manufacturers and local distributors. You can reach ABLEDATA by phone (800-227-0216 or 301-608-8998) or visit online (www.ABLEDATA.com).

Home repair, especially door-to-door solicitation, is especially risky. The unscrupulous love to target elderly people. When deciding to use a contractor, check his or her references. Hire only bonded licensed contractors and ask to see the license (issued by the state). Check the individual's driver's license to make sure that the name matches the name on the contractor's license. Check the contractor's performance record with your local Better Business Bureau or City or County's Consumer Affairs Office. Get everything in writing. Only agree to a small down payment, with the final payment due only after project has been completed. Contractors usually have 30- to 45-day payment terms with their suppliers so that they don't have to get money for materials from you in advance. Make sure that the contractor has workers' compensation insurance — otherwise, your elder can be held financially liable for an injury on the job. (See Chapter 21 about ways to avoid scams and con artists who prey on seniors.)

For tips about choosing a contractor to perform home safety modifications, log on to the Administration on Aging Web site (`www.aoa.dhhs.gov/aoa/eldractn/homemodf.html`). An excellent resource for finding assistance with home modification is the National Resource Center on Supportive Housing and Home Modification Web site (`www.usc.edu/dept/gero/nrcshhm`); go to the Resources link and click the last listing, Who Will Help With Ramps And Home Modifications?. This link provides a list of national organizations that can help you with financial assistance for building ramps and making home modifications for a safer home.

A landlord who refuses to allow your elder to make reasonable home modifications (providing your elder pays for it) is acting illegally. If your elder's landlord gives you any mouth, give it right back to him or her, citing The Fair Housing Act of 1988 Section 6(a).

Dealing with stairs

Although stairwells can seem as intimidating as the Grand Canyon to a shaky elder, they can be elder-proofed. Here are a few ideas:

- ✔ Put up a second railing to reduce chances of stumbling.
- ✔ Mark the edges of steps with brightly colored tape to compensate for failing eyesight and faulty depth perception.
- ✔ Paint outdoor steps with a rough-texture paint or trim the steps with abrasive strips.
- ✔ Make sure that your elder wears shoes with soles that grip the floor. Socks or smooth-soled slippers are hazardous.
- ✔ Consider moving your elder to the first floor if possible.
- ✔ Install a *stair-lift* (a motorized chair appointed with safety belts and a swivel seat that rides up and down a rail attached to a stairwell).

Motion detectors can signal that your elder is near a dangerous situation, such as approaching the top of the stairs or slipping out the front door in the middle of the night. Some models emit a soft chime that sounds near where the caregiver is sleeping, rather than setting off a loud alarm that could scare the dickens out of the elder. Call The Alzheimer Store for more information (800-752-3238) or visit online (`www.alzstore.com`). (See Chapter 18 for more advice on keeping the confused elder out of harm's way.)

Expanding doorways

A 32-inch threshold accommodates most wheelchairs and walkers. Sometimes removing a door, its hinges, and the door molding or threshold will make the opening large enough and save the cost of paying for a new doorway to be cut out and built. Power-driven or extra-wide wheelchairs may require 36 inches to pass.

Most of the home modifications necessary for wheelchair accessibility (such as adding ramps or widening doorways) don't require a permit. But you need to be certain that you don't need one in your little part of the world. Before you start construction, call your local housing inspector (found in the front of your phone book under "City Government").

You can find typical accessibility problems, home-modification solutions, and suggestions for locating financial assistance for home modifications on the Administration on Aging Web site, called "Elder Action: Action Ideas for Older Persons and Their Families" (www.aoa.dhhs.gov/aoa/eldractn/homemodf.html).

Neighborhood senior centers and local Area Agencies on Aging (which may be located through the Eldercare Locator) are other sources of information about free or low-cost home modification and repair programs in your area.

Elders suffering from confusion can literally walk into walls. When walls, floors, and doorways are the same color, bewildered elders simply can't tell where one ends and another begins. Painting a dark line where the wall meets the floor or painting the woodwork a bright color helps. Turn this oddity into an advantage by purposely coloring the door the same as the walls when you want to prevent your elder from wandering out a door. But do not even think of doing this trick for an elder who lives alone. The elder should be reminded of where the exits are situated and what to do in emergencies.

Avoiding bathroom booby traps

Inch by inch, bathrooms are more perilous than any other room. Surfaces are hard and slippery, and space is tight. Consider the following adjustments for elder-proofing bathrooms:

- ✔ Install grab bars in the shower alongside the tub.
- ✔ Apply skid mats or strips on the shower and tub floors.
- ✔ Add a hand-held shower head (so that the bather is in control of the water stream and not the other way around).

- Check to make sure that all the faucets turn off easily and completely so that they don't drip.

- Install gauges that regulate the pressure and temperature to prevent scalding, or set the water heater below 120 degrees. Thinner older skin reacts slowly to temperature change, placing the elder at risk for scalding.

- Raise the toilet seat. (Possibilities include molded seats attached to sturdy height-adjustable steel frames that fit over standard toilet units, and solid bases that you can install under toilet units, making the whole fixture higher.)

With the right shower bench, bathing returns to being pleasurable instead of frightening. Take into account your elder's shape, size, and physical limitations:

- Will the bench support my overweight older person without danger of collapsing?

- Is the stool too awkward or heavy for me to maneuver into and out of the shower or tub?

- Does my elder need a shower chair with a back and armrest?

- Would a horseshoe-shaped seat make cleaning his or her private parts easier for my elder?

- Will the surface of the bench get slippery from soapy water, creating a hazard for my elder with impaired balance? (Avoid vinyl seats.)

- Will a *tub-board* (a lightweight portable board that locks onto the side of a tub so that the bather doesn't have sit on the tub floor) be stable enough and provide sufficient support for my older person?

Creating Safe Surroundings for a Live-Alone Older Person

At least 60 percent of the elders in the United States have been living in the same home for 20 years. In so many cases, the structure of the home remains as it was when the elder was younger and more agile. Now the furniture has grown shaky, stairs have worn down to slipperiness, and edges of carpets have turned up. No one tends to notice these sorts of things until they cause falls and injuries. (See the section "Preventing Falls," later in this chapter, for more information on preventing falls that come from internal sources.)

Be a sleuth. Roam through your age-advantaged person's home, peering, peeking, and peeping around, using the following questions as a guide:

Lily's battle with the toilet

Eighty-four-year-old Lily's feistiness is enviable. She hides her limitations, ingeniously trying to overcome them. Unfortunately, her remedies sometimes put her life and limbs in jeopardy. Unable to lift herself off the toilet seat, Lily raises her cane over her head, swings it forward, hooks the curved end onto the towel bar on the opposite wall, and pulls herself up. Clever? Yes. Dangerous? Absolutely. By the time her son figured out what was going on, the chrome bar was already separating from the wall. He installed grab bars and a simple device to raise the height of the toilet seat.

✔ Is an emergency list of numbers by the phone in large, easy-to-read type? Include 911 and numbers for the primary care physician, fire and police departments, the landlord, and a neighbor (or whoever can get to the elder fastest).

911 remains the best number for emergency help. Available in only some cities, 311 is a number for non-emergency related questions or reports to the police or fire department.

✔ Is the home warm enough in winter and cool enough in summer?

The U.S. Department of Energy (www.energy.gov) sponsors two programs for low-income persons for "weatherization" of the home or assistance with energy bills. From the home page of the Web site, click the red bubble titled House and link to the Weatherization Assistance Program. You can also go directly to the Weatherization Assistance Program (www.eren.doe.gov/buildings/weatherization_assistance). On this page, you find more information about weatherization and a link called Am I Eligible? That page contains eligibility criteria and answers to commonly asked questions about the program. From the Weatherization Assistance Program, you can also link to State Activities, which gives you state-by-state programs.

✔ Is there a way to tell who is at the door before opening it (for example, a peephole, a window that has a clear view of any visitors, or an intercom system for the front door)?

✔ Can the lock on the outside door be operated without resorting to special wiggles or multiple attempts?

✔ Is your elder able to put on outer garments (hats or umbrellas or boots)?

✔ Are there obstacles to getting the mail (for example, a sticky latch or a letter receptacle that requires painful bending)?

✔ Are the smoke detectors working? (Each floor of the house should have a smoke detector. Fire departments recommend that smoke detectors be tested twice a year, when clocks are re-set for daylight saving time.)

- ✔ Can you spot any spaghetti-like clumps of electrical cords?

- ✔ Do electrical cords run under carpets?

- ✔ Are there any overloaded electrical outlets that could overheat and cause a fire — for example, outlets stuffed with "octopus" plugs (sometimes called cube taps) and multiple extension cords?

- ✔ Are doorways, stairs, and hallways clear of plants, storage containers, and general clutter?

- ✔ Can your elder benefit from a few more portable telephones?

- ✔ Is existing furniture stable enough to support your elder should he lose balance and reach out for something solid?

- ✔ Have all rugs (room size and throw rugs) been tacked at corners and secured with rubber nonslip backings?

- ✔ Is the linoleum or other flooring showing any tiny breaks, buckling, or warping?

- ✔ Is your elder able to reach pots and pans?

- ✔ Are drapes, aprons, rags, or dishcloths dangling near a stove?

- ✔ Are hotplates, teapots, lamps, and heaters away from bedding?

Encourage elders to switch from cooking in a conventional oven and stovetop (which pose safety hazards) to a microwave or a toaster oven. Remind them not to put paper plates in the toaster oven and not to put metal containers in the microwave.

Local fire departments offer home inspections, but the extent of the inspection varies from fire department to fire department. Don't call 911 about home inspections. Instead, contact your local fire department using the non-emergency phone number in your telephone directory (or dial 411 for telephone number information) to find out about local home inspections.

Creating Safe Surroundings for the Older Person Who Lives with You

Living with your elder doesn't ensure security. You can't be with him or her every second, but you can make the environment safer with or without your presence. Ask yourself the following questions. (The list of questions in the preceding section, designed for oldsters who live alone, may also alert you to safety concerns for the elder who lives with you.)

- ✔ Can your older person easily get your attention from another room with a bell, buzzer, or his or her voice?

- ✔ Are the doorways, stairwells, and areas between rooms clearly lit?

- ✔ Are the staircase and room entrances marked in some way so that the elder can anticipate that she is coming to one?

TIP

Painting the transition between rooms or the start of a staircase a bright and different color alerts the elder of the change in terrain. Periodically change the color of the paint or the tacked-down rug or tape because eyes get oblivious to the same color after awhile.

- ✔ Are there obstacles that could lead to a fall, such as pets, magazine racks, and unstable items like pole lamps that could tumble if bumped the wrong way?

FOR CONFUSED ELDERLY

Childproof locks and doorknobs (found in stores that sell merchandise for infants and children) keep your confused older person away from cabinets that have dangerous substances in them or drawers where knives and scissors are kept. Remove bathroom locks that can be locked from inside and not unlocked from outside.

Finding the Right Assistive Devices

Watching your elder take so much time to do the simple tasks he used to do so easily can be painful. Your elder may begin to woefully think of himself as an invalid or cripple. Resist doing things for your elder (you have a lot of other things to do!) and help him devise ways to be more independent. Point out that most older people have some difficulties, but that today is a wonderful time in which many gizmos and gadgets can extend independence and preserve personhood.

These gadgets are known as *assistive devices*. Most of the devices commonly found in medical-supply stores and in some large pharmacies focus on walking, incontinence, and modifications to bathrooms. You can use your imagination, ingenuity, and shopping skills to come up with other devices that help in your elder's particular situation.

Don't be impulsive and believe every advertisement you see. Investigate whether the device will actually improve your elder's ability to perform daily activities. Godsends like *reachers* (long tools with retractable hooks controlled by hand) allow a person to reach into a cabinet and pluck items out of arm's length off shelves. Some reachers handle objects weighing up to two pounds, but can also pick up a dime or hold a paper cup without crushing it. Many fold for easy carrying. Reachers furnish a sense of independence.

You can create many assistive devices at home. For example, you can tape cut-up tennis balls to the legs of aluminum walkers so that the metal doesn't damage floors or make a racket. Another trick is to wrap foam rubber around the handles of toothbrushes, hairbrushes, and kitchen utensils to improve the grip.

On the other hand, a "press-the-photo" telephone with small frames into which you place pictures of frequently called family and friends may be a wise purchase. An elder with less-than-nimble fingers or who has problems remembering phone numbers (even with speed dialing) merely has to press the photo of the person she wants to talk to. Oversized knobs that fit over standard cabinet knobs are another example of a small adjustment that can make a big difference in the life of an older person with some weaknesses living alone.

The National Center for the Blind has an online store that features assistive devices for people with low vision. Items include talking clocks, watches, and tape measures, as well as an "Oh no!" talking scale. Call (410-659-9314, ext. 216), e-mail (materials@nfb.org) or visit online (www.kifwebe.com). (See Chapter 2 for more safety tips and assistive suggestions for low-vision elderly.)

Finding solutions to dressing difficulties

Sock donners, dressing sticks, zipper pulls, long-handled shoehorns, and thousands of low-tech, sturdy but lightweight gadgets facilitate self-dressing despite painful joints, stiff backs, and limited range of motion or weakness in shoulders and elbows. An elder with the right devices can reach clothing in a closet, pull it toward himself, hold the items, insert his legs and arms without strain, and even button and zip.

You can solve many obstacles with a little help and ingenuity from your friends. You can ask family and friends who once offered to help to now offer suggestions and do a little work. For example, ask people who sew to replace difficult clothing fasteners with Velcro. Swapping regular shoelaces with elastic ones solves the shoelace-tying problem.

If your senior can cross his legs safely, have him do just that to put his shoes on. Crossing one leg over the other brings the foot higher and makes putting on footwear easier.

Renting and buying wheelchairs, walkers, and canes

Determining what kind of wheelchair, walker, or cane your elder needs requires an evaluation by an expert (usually a physical therapist or occupational therapist). A garage-sale bargain or a hand-me-down from the next-door neighbor or Cousin Charlie may seem like an economic blessing, but an improper fit can cause bruises and sores — problems your elder doesn't need.

Wheelchairs

When you care for an older person who requires a wheelchair, refer to her as a "wheelchair user." Terms like "confined to a wheelchair" or "wheelchair-bound" make the wheelchair user sound like a captive — not an attitude you want to promote. Users are *in charge* of the chair. The wheelchair works for him or her — not the other way around.

Wheelchairs come in hundreds of different models and with countless options. Can your elder use a manual model? Will a power-operated model be necessary? Your elder may want to rent different models to try out before buying a wheelchair.

Wheelchairs aren't just for seniors who can't walk. Folded and kept in the trunk of the car, a wheelchair enables some elders who can walk but tire easily to enjoy long excursions to shopping malls, outdoor events, and theme parks.

 Charge battery-operated wheelchairs on a regular schedule. Recharging them every night before bedtime is a good habit. You don't want your loved one to get in a jam like the woman who was lax about recharging and found herself with a dead battery — holding up rush-hour traffic in the middle of one of Cleveland's busiest intersections.

Walkers

Walkers (which support up to 50 percent of an older person's body weight) are ideal for weak knees or ankles, severe balance problems, or when bearing weight on one leg is painful. Selecting a walker demands expert advice. Rigid ones (usually aluminum) must be lifted to move forward, which takes practice. Walkers with wheels (usually pushed along) may be better when lifting causes strain on arms, wrists, and shoulders. Older folks with one strong arm may be able to use a one-handed small walker with four legs. My friend's Aunt Carmine, who lives in a retirement village, has a jazzy little number with a black metal frame and a blue seat. When she wants to stop between her apartment and the dining room, she can sit down. She also uses the seat as a carrier for small items. She says it was expensive but worth every penny!

Canes

Canes come in a variety of styles, with different support structures, handle shapes, and fashion features. They support up to 25 percent of a senior's weight. Single-point canes work for slight balance problems or weakness or a painful leg. Quad canes (which have four feet) give more stability and support. Aluminum canes adjust to your elder's height. Folding canes that snap to full length can be packed in a tote bag or suitcase ready for emergencies or

Guess who owns a scooter?

Remember the legendary Evel Knievel, the motorcycle daredevil who broke 35 different bones in his body and had 20 major surgeries to put him back together? Evel is 65 years old now and is as spirited as ever. Although he's had a liver transplant, diabetes, and a full hip replacement, he's still talking and dreaming about a comeback jump. Browsing through a catalog for scooters, who should one see but the legendary Knievel atop his high-performance stylish luxury scooter with mag wheels and a metallic jazzy color!

just a tiring day. Choosing a grip can't be rushed. A walking stick with a croc-odile head on top may be charming, but a handle molded to your elder's grip or a pistol handle may make more sense (especially when arthritis is the problem).

Colorful stylish designs and fancy handles may make a cane more acceptable to some folks. Time, patience, and understanding are good strategies when your older person isn't dazzled by the technology alone.

Scooters

A battery-operated scooter offers an alternative — albeit a pricey one — to a wheelchair. Models come with front-wheel drive (less powerful, more man-ageable) and rear-wheel drive (outdoor drive is better). Scooters need to be recharged frequently. Many scooter owners live independently and can walk short distances around the house, but they may have health conditions that limit stamina and make walking long distances impossible.

Deciding on a "hospital" bed

I remember when caregivers got cranky cranking their older person up and down on old-fashioned hospital beds. (Manually operated ones are still around, but I don't recommend them.) Basically, an electrically powered hos-pital bed makes care easier for the caregiver and rest more manageable for the elder. No special electrical capacity is needed for the operation of the electric beds in the home.

When faced with the decision about whether to obtain a hospital bed, con-sider the following pros:

- You can raise and lower the head, foot, or entire bed to increase your elder's comfort.
- You can manage personal care with less physical strain.

- Elders recovering from illness (for example, hip or back surgery) who can't move well by themselves can move up and down by merely pushing a button.

- Bed linens are easier to change because you can raise the mattress to a more convenient height.

- Special hospital bed mattresses (such as a low air-loss mattress or one containing a pad that changes the air flow in the mattress) protect the elder from developing bedsores.

- Hospital beds that raise or lower help the older person who has trouble transferring into or out of a wheelchair.

- You can attach rails or trapeze bars (to assist the elder who's transferring him or herself out of bed) to a hospital bed for even greater safety.

Consider the following cons:

- Costs of hospital beds range from around $1,500 to more than $10,000, depending on the model.

    You can find hospital beds for purchase or rent in the yellow pages under Medical Equipment. If a person is being released from a hospital, he or she may get referrals from the hospital about reputable companies. Insurance often covers the purchase or rental of a hospital bed. (Rentals are in the neighborhood of $110 per month.)

- Breakdowns require more effort than simply replacing an old mattress. Repairs on rentals should be free, while repairs to purchased beds may be costly.

- Using a hospital bed may trigger sadness and depression because home seems less homelike. On the other hand, comfort and convenience may override any psychological issues.

- Most rental companies will deliver a hospital bed to a ground floor only. Moving furniture to make room for the bed or moving the old bed out of the room will mostly likely be your responsibility. Here's a time to cash in on those offers of help from sturdy relatives and friends.

Figuring out who pays

Medicare helps cover what is known as "durable medical equipment." There's no guarantee that items covered today will be covered tomorrow because rampant Medicare fraud and abuse have caused difficulties. Regulations change periodically.

To be eligible for coverage, durable medical equipment must meet the following criteria:

- ✔ Be reasonable and necessary for an individual elder
- ✔ Be able to withstand repeated use
- ✔ Be used primarily for a medical purpose
- ✔ Be useless to elders who aren't sick or injured
- ✔ Be appropriate for home use

A doctor needs to prescribe many, if not most, covered items (for example, electric hospital beds, special mattresses, and even lamb's wool bed pads). (See Chapter 21 for guidance in understanding and accessing the Medicare Program.)

Local Area Agencies on Aging and local senior centers (located through the Eldercare Locator at 800-677-1116) are good resources for finding programs in your area that provide free or low-cost assistive devices. Check with your local Lion's Club, Kiwanis Club, or religious institutions. Some provide free equipment or equipment loans. Veterans (regardless of the degree of service-connected disability) may be eligible to receive assistive devices at no cost. See your primary physician at your VA facility who will submit a request for a consultation with an occupational or physical therapist for the appropriate device.

Many Easter Seals offices provide financial assistance for the purchase of assistive devices or have a "loan closet" containing devices such as wheelchairs, walkers, and shower transfer benches that you can borrow at no cost. Offices that don't have these programs can refer you to local organizations that do. To find the telephone number and address of your state office, go online to `www.easter-seals.org`.

Preventing Falls

The consequences of falls are devastating — hip fractures (about 340,000 people age 65 and over break a hip each year), vertebral fractures, head injuries, and fear of walking. Approximately 10,000 seniors die each year from injuries sustained in falls. External changes, such as installing safety devices and taking care of repairs, are effective and fairly easy to do. Of course, that's easy for me to say!

Internal causes for falls (mental confusion, blood pressure that doesn't adjust as quickly as it should when your elder goes from sitting to walking, balance and gait problems, medications, diseases, low vision, and muscular weakness) are another matter and are much more difficult — but not impossible — to lessen.

Don't ignore complaints of lightheadedness. Dizziness is a common side effect of medication. Prescribing for elders is often tricky. The doctor may have to change medications and dosages more than once until he or she gets the exact drug treatment to fit your elder's needs and metabolism. (See Chapter 11 about recognizing drug side effects and watching for potential signs of overdose and negative drug interactions.)

The following ideas can help you prevent your elder from falling:

- **Don't allow your elder to become sedentary.** Inactivity causes muscles to become even weaker. Walking less does not mean one will fall less. The opposite is true — the more sedentary a person is, the higher the risk of falling.

- **When your elder rises from a sitting position, remind him or her to stand still for a few minutes before taking a first step.** This pause gives your elder's blood pressure a chance to adjust to the change in position and lessen the chance of falling from dizziness.

- **Check your elder's feet regularly.** Neglected toenails curling around the toes can impair the elder's ability to walk and increase the chance of a fall. Healthy feet grip the floor better than feet with skin problems and sores. Consider having toenails trimmed professionally by a podiatrist. (*Chiropodist* is the old name for a podiatrist. They do the very same thing.)

- **Light up your elder's path.** Nightlights that switch on automatically at twilight and lamps with sensors that automatically go on when lights go low can accommodate to your elder's age-related need for more light. (See Chapter 2 for more ways to assist an age-advantaged person who has low vision.)

- **Make sure that your elder keeps the nighttime temperature in the home above 65 degrees.** Hours in a cold bedroom may cause his or her body temperature to drop, leading to dizziness and a fall when he or she tries to get out of bed.

Ask the doctor about prescribing a course of occupational therapy to help your elder learn to compensate for impairments that may make him more vulnerable to falls.

Fear of falling haunts many older adults, especially when they've had a tumble or two. Occupational and physical therapy, maintaining a regular schedule of walking, and learning techniques for falling and getting up safely help diminish the fear.

An older person may get out of her chair by putting extra pressure on her heel and hip — a common occurrence when the chair doesn't have adequate arm supports. The result may be a hip fracture. The odd part of this scenario is that the hip breaks first, and then the fall happens.

Falling 101

Showing your elder how to fall may be the best thing you can do. Elders — and everyone else — tense when they sense they're falling. But with a little practice, your older person can learn to fall like a rag doll — get loose and let it happen. Demonstrate by falling into a chair or a bed, letting your muscles go limp as you drop into the chair or bed. Then have your elder practice it himself.

If your elder is willing, show her how to roll onto her hands (from a position on the floor) and crawl to a phone, using a solid piece of furniture to raise herself for support. Practicing this way may help her have the presence of mind to help herself, rather than panic, in an emergency.

What if a fall occurs when you're present? Check for severe pain or difficulty with moving. Offer support by bending your legs and keeping your own body straight. Don't twist. Or bring a table or solid chair to her so that she can lift herself up on the item, with your assistance.

Don't take a chance of injuring yourself or your loved one. If you can't get him up, get help.

After any fall, a doctor needs to check for injuries and investigate the cause. Falls can indicate illnesses, stroke, infection, and medication problems.

Investigate a medical alert system (sometimes called an emergency or personal response system) for your elder who lives alone and has a condition that leaves her at risk for falling. A necklace or bracelet with a call button puts her a push away from help should a fall or other serious problem occur. The button sends a signal to a receiver next to the telephone, which dials a response center. The caller is identified by a code. The operator on the receiving end calls the elder on the telephone or on a two-way voice intercom system to determine the extent of the emergency and then summons the appropriate help. If the operator gets no response or if the elder verifies that trouble's at hand, emergency assistance (usually an ambulance) is sent, and prearranged contacts (for example, family members) are called. Look under the yellow pages under medical alarms or call a medical-supply store. Some sell the systems and charge monthly service fees. Other companies may lease the services after installation. Try to get a money-back guarantee if you or your elder isn't satisfied. On the first day, try it from several locations in the house and yard. (The device has a limited range so that it can't be used in the car or at the next door neighbor's house.) Ask how long the average response time is. Check the batteries often.

When walking with your unsteady elder, try what I call the "Gimme five" method. Walking side by side, your elder holds her arm parallel to the floor with her palm down. You support her arm with your arm under hers, parallel to the floor with your palm up — sort of a palm sandwich. Should your senior stumble, your upturned palm offers the most support.

Caring for Delicate Skin

Skin protects the body from the sun, bacteria, and infection. It regulates temperature, stores fat and water, and synthesizes vitamin D (from the sun). Keeping your older person's skin whole and healthy is the first line of defense from all sorts of perils.

The skin of an elder who uses a wheelchair or is confined to bed must be checked frequently for reddened areas and open sores (known as pressure sores, bedsores, and decubitis ulcers). A bedsore begins with a reddened area (just like the sore spot you get from a too-tight shoe). In advanced cases, the bedsore is down to the bone, the flesh surrounding it is dead, and a strong odor may be present. Untreated bedsore wounds can result in amputation or death.

Elders confined to a bed should be repositioned every two hours to prevent bedsores. The same goes for sedentary older folks. Get them up off the couch and moving as much as possible. Strategically placed foot and elbow pads and air pressure mattresses are standard precautions for those at risk.

Very old people have very thin skin that bruises easily, leaving large purplish skin discolorations (which look more troubling than they are).

Have suspicious skin problems examined by the doctor. Skin cancer is one of the most common problems in the elderly. Be especially watchful of moles that grow rapidly, have uneven coloring, are irregularly shaped, or bleed. Also look for any other marks that look odd, like gritty red patches. Anything that wasn't there before and doesn't look right needs to be medically checked. (See Chapter 10 for more about skin cancer.)

The right chair may save your elder from a tumble

Frail elders utilize chairs in every room for support. A rickety chair is an accident waiting to happen. A chair without armrests to push up on is a hazard (especially for those with muscle weakness) and may result in excess weight-bearing on a hip or other fragile, breakable bone. Elders who are weak in the trunk need raised seats. In fact, higher seats may help ease lots of problems.

One of the best inventions since sliced bread is the electrically powered reclining chair that lifts an age-advantaged person to a standing position. Some models have trays for eating, vibrators, reading lights, pockets for magazines, and emergency backup systems should the power fail in the home. Urge your older person to slide to the end of seat before getting up. Chant "Nose to the toes" to encourage a little helpful rocking motion.

Dry itchy skin can drive your elder nuts and presents a major caregiving challenge for you. Try the following

- ✔ Apply lotion right after bathing to coat the skin and hold in moisture.

- ✔ Lower the water temperature for showers and suggest that lingering is not good. The hotter the water, the dryer the skin becomes.

- ✔ Avoid perfumed soaps and lotions.

- ✔ Encourage more drinking. (See Chapter 6 for ways to prevent dehydration.)

- ✔ Use a room humidifier to get moisture back into the air, especially during winter when heating turns everything to the texture of a corn husk.

- ✔ Avoid alcohol and caffeine.

- ✔ Guard against the sun with hats and sunscreen (SPF 30 or higher) and limit exposure.

Dryness and itching can be side effects of medications.

Chapter 13

Dealing with Leaky Plumbing and Other Incontinence Problems

*W*etting and soiling your pants is *not* part of normal aging.

Many elders and their caregivers mistakenly assume that losing control of one's bladder *(urinary incontinence)* or bowels *(bowel incontinence)* is a distressing but usual part of growing old. Seniors who have this trouble often withdraw from friends and family because they fear having an accident in a public place. Incontinence can evoke embarrassment and all sorts of other disturbing emotions in the elder and her caregiver.

Many elders hide the problem, refusing to even discuss it with the doctor. Incontinence is one of the major reasons families place their loved ones in institutions. In this chapter, I take a frank nuts-and-bolts approach to incontinence, providing strategies to deal with it so that premature institutionalization may be avoided.

Coping with Urinary Incontinence

Urinary incontinence is a fancy name for wetting yourself. Approximately 15 to 30 percent of older adults (over age 60) who live at home experience this condition. And at least half of the 1.5 million Americans who live in nursing homes are incontinent. Women are twice as likely as men to be affected.

The good news is that urinary incontinence can be cured or improved in about 80 percent of the people who have it. Despite such a high success rate, only 40 percent of affected people actually seek medical help. The remainder suffer in silence.

Recognizing the different types

The doctor (with a little help from diagnostic tests) will be able to tell your elder which type of incontinence she has.

Temporary incontinence

When bladder control is lost suddenly only to return just as mysteriously, the situation is usually labeled *transient incontinence,* but I think the word "temporary" is more comforting. Constipation, changes in medication, a recent injury (such as a hip fracture), or an infection of the bladder or urinary tract can cause these bouts of incontinence.

Because women have a shorter *urethra* (the thin tube that carries urine from the bladder out of the body) than men, bacteria travel through the urethra to the bladder more easily, making women more prone to bladder infections.

Stress incontinence

In the case of *stress incontinence,* urine leaks out of the bladder when the person laughs, sneezes, coughs, lifts a heavy object, or gets up from a chair. In women, this condition occurs because the ring of muscles around the urethra has lost tone (from childbirth or hormonal changes). The bladder and the weak muscles are unable to hold back the urine when these fairly mild activities cause pressure on the bladder. Stress incontinence is the most common type of incontinence in women under 75, and it's nearly always curable.

Encourage your elder with stress incontinence to cross her legs whenever she feels a sneeze, laugh, or cough coming on. It may prevent leakage.

Urge incontinence

Better known as *overactive bladder,* this condition is common in women over 75. In this situation, the bladder contracts and releases urine involuntarily (often without warning). The elder feels an uncontrollable urge to urinate but can't reach the bathroom in time. This event happens even when the bladder is not full. Causes include infection, stroke, and early stages of bladder cancer.

Overflow incontinence

Overflow incontinence is mainly found in older men with enlarged prostates. The prostate gland blocks the passageway for the urine, making complete emptying of the bladder impossible. Urine eventually overflows from the very full bladder, causing dribbling and spotting on pants fronts throughout the day. This buildup of urine in the bladder may lead to bladder and kidney infections. Causes include infection, weak bladder muscles, and conditions that affect the nerves, such as neuropathy associated with diabetes.

Functional incontinence

In functional incontinence, physical disabilities or mental impairment prevent your elder from getting to the bathroom in time or communicating to you that she's gotta go. In other cases, the older person's brain no longer gets the message from her bladder that it's full and needs emptying. Without the brain's participation, the bladder spills over, and a puddle results. Causes include dementia, stroke, head injury, or physical limitations such as arthritis.

A combination of stress and urge incontinence, called *mixed incontinence,* is more common in women than men.

Seeking treatment

Your elder's primary physician will take a medical history and conduct a thorough physical examination. Remember to bring along your elder's medications or a list of the medicines she takes. (See Chapter 11 for a sample medication chart.) The doctor most often (but not always) orders diagnostic tests. After she's received the test results, she outlines treatment options or provides a referral to a *urologist* (specialist in disorders of urinary tract) or a *gynecologist* (specialist in the female reproductive system).

Behavioral treatments

Treatment usually starts with the most gentle, progressing to the more aggressive if needed. The following remedies are typical of the kinds of things your elder's doctor may suggest:

- Eliminating or reducing alcohol, carbonated beverages, and other bladder-irritating products, such as citrus juice and fruits, tomatoes and tomato-based foods, artificial sweeteners, and spicy foods.

- Trimming down. (Obesity contributes to incontinence.)

- Prompting. Ask "Do you need to use the toilet?" every two hours.

- Scheduling. Take the elder to the bathroom every two to four hours and help unfasten clothing when necessary.

- Training the bladder. (Helpful in cases of urge incontinence, this process consists of extending the time between bathroom visits to train the bladder to delay for longer intervals.)

- Initiating biofeedback. (Includes using a device that helps your elder learn how to do Kegels, an exercise to strengthen pelvic muscles.)

Kegels — the exercise no one can see

In 1948, a young surgeon named Arnold Kegel promoted the Kegel exercise. Since then, women have been squeezing their pelvic muscles in line at the supermarket, while waiting for a bus, while sitting in traffic, and while watching television. The exercise, often recommended to help treat stress incontinence, strengthens the ring of muscles around the urethra — the sphincter that stops and starts the flow of urine. Basically, you squeeze these muscles, hold for 4 to 10 seconds and relax for 4 to 10 seconds, increasing the repetitions over several weeks. The doctor will tell you how many to do and how often (commonly ten repetitions ten times a day). Biofeedback is useful for helping women find the spot and the proper squeeze technique. This regimen of Kegel exercises will take about a month to be effective and should be kept up to maintain the sphincter improvement.

Identifying the bathroom with a picture of a toilet on the door or a sign that says "bathroom" may shave precious minutes off the journey to the toilet for the confused older person.

Medications

A variety of drugs can relieve urge and stress incontinence. But — as with most medications — one has to be aware of possible side effects. You may have heard that hormone replacement therapy for women is good for urinary incontinence because it improves pelvic muscle tone. The latest reports cast a shadow of doubt and highlight the risks of hormone treatment. Review your elder's medications with the doctor — one or more may be contributing to the problem.

Collection and compression devices

When urinary incontinence can't be cured, external devices to collect the urine or obstruction devices that compress the urethra and prevent the flow of urine are other options. For example, a *catheter* (a flexible tube) can be inserted into the urethra to collect urine and direct it into a container. Another external device for men is a catheter attached to a condom that fits over the penis. It, too, collects urine and is connected to a collection bag. Compression devices include urethra plugs for women. When inserted into the urethra, they prevent leakage; they're removed when the woman wants to urinate and then should be replaced with a fresh one. Such devices are only good for people with good manual dexterity, and they require meticulous care to avoid skin irritation and serious skin breakdown.

Surgical treatment

Doctors can use more than 100 types of surgery to treat urinary incontinence. The nature of the procedure depends on the type of incontinence and the reason for it. The surgeon may clear obstructions (such as an enlarged prostate), reposition a bladder that is bumping against another body part, make weak muscles stronger, implant devices to control urine flow, or inject collagen to support weak sphincter muscles. When all the noninvasive treatments have failed, a surgical procedure may or may not make sense for your elder.

One of the best sources of information about urinary incontinence is the American Foundation for Urologic Disease. Call 800-242-2383 for a free brochure on overactive bladder. The Web site `www.incontinence.org` is loaded with useful information and links.

Dealing with Bowel Incontinence

Bowel incontinence is less common than bladder incontinence. But it, too, can be reversed — or, if not cured, at least managed efficiently. Nothing stirs emotions quite like the odors and damage to carpets, upholstery, bed linens, and clothing that results from bowel incontinence. Cleaning and diapering your elder's bottom (especially when it's your father or mother) can arouse embarrassment, disgust, sadness, anger, and frustration — and may foretell the end of home care and the beginning of institutional care.

Understanding the causes

Before you resign yourself to diapers, diaper pails, pads, liners, and scented sanitizing sprays — or nursing home placement — take your elder to the doctor. By figuring out what's causing the incontinence, the doctor may be able to eliminate it.

Not all doctors are willing or able to address bowel problems. A doctor who shrugs off your concern with "It's just part of growing old" is not the doctor to help with this problem. Ask for a referral to a *proctologist* (doctor who specializes in diseases of the colon, rectum, and anus) or a geriatrician.

Constipation

Oddly enough, *constipation* (difficult, incomplete, or infrequent evacuation of dry, hardened feces) is the most common cause of bowel incontinence. What happens is that the hard stool blocks the bowel, and liquid stool leaks around the obstruction.

Seniors can become obsessed with their bowel movements — especially if they don't have a bowel movement every day. If your elder is one of these worriers but has no symptoms, reassure her that she has nothing to fret about. (Normal bowel patterns range from two to three bowel movements a day to two to three times a week.) On the other hand, the following symptoms may indicate constipation:

✔ Decreased appetite

✔ Abdominal bloating

✔ Painful bowel movements

✔ General malaise

✔ A feeling of pressure or fullness in the rectal area

✔ Small frequent smears of stool on underwear

✔ Rectal bleeding

✔ Tiny amounts of dry, hard stool (pebbles)

✔ Small amounts of loose stool, leaking, or diarrhea

A chart that tracks your elder's bowel movements is extremely useful to the doctor who's trying to diagnose the problem or evaluate the effectiveness of treatment for constipation. Tacking a chart on the back of the bathroom door and hanging a pencil from a string may be all your elder needs to record her bowel movements. (See Table 13-1 for a sample chart.)

Table 13-1:		Bathroom Chart for Week of _____					
Time of Day	*Sunday*	*Monday*	*Tuesday*	*Wednesday*	*Thursday*	*Friday*	*Saturday*

Don't forget to record what the stool looked like (for example, small lumps, loose, dry, dark, and watery) and any comments about difficulty (for example, painful, took a long time, explosive, gassy). Note times when stool softeners, laxatives, suppositories, or enemas were used.

Many confused elders can't remember whether they moved their bowels. When asked, they may say "yes," but the truth may be "no." Constipation sometimes increases confusion in an already confused elder. In this case, ask your elder not to flush and then do the charting for her. Should that plan fail, perform a "sniff test" in the bathroom to determine whether your elder has indeed had a bowel movement.

When good medicines do bad things

Perfectly good medications may contribute to leaky plumbing. If your elder has trouble holding her urine, ask the doctor or pharmacist whether any of her medicines are responsible. The following drugs are a sample of the medicines that may contribute to incontinence.

✔ **For the heart:** enalapril (Vasotec), propranolol (Inderal)

✔ **For anxiety, depression, or insomnia:** alprazolam (Xanax), olanzapine (Zyprexia), paroxetine (Paxil), hydroxyzine (Atarax)

✔ **For inflammation:** naproxen (Naprosyn), ibuprofen (Advil)

✔ **For sinus trouble:** chlorpheniramine (Chlor-Trimenton), diphenhydramine (Benadryl)

✔ **For relief of muscle spasms or pain:** codeine

Confused elders have been known to get carried away with the toilet tissue roll, stuffing up the toilet with excess paper. You may try giving them an appropriate amount of paper each time. Above all, have a plunger handy and find out where the water shut-off to the toilet is located.

The following situations may contribute to the development of constipation:

✔ A recent change in diet (for example, eating more processed foods and fewer fiber-rich foods like fresh fruits and vegetables when traveling).

✔ A decrease in physical activity (for example, being bedridden because of illness).

✔ Use of certain medications (for example, antihypertensives, antidepressants, narcotics, sedatives, and aluminum hydroxide, which is common in over-the-counter antacids).

✔ Hemorrhoids and anal fissures (tears in the lining of the anus) from repeated straining. (This situation leads to chronic constipation when the elder withholds his stool to avoid pain.)

✔ Certain medical conditions (for example, Parkinson's disease, underactive thyroid, and high blood levels of calcium).

✔ Recent surgery (for example, an abdominal operation).

✔ Reduction in fluid intake (for example, intentionally cutting down on fluids to avoid frequent bathroom trips). (See Chapter 6 about preventing dehydration.)

Call the doctor immediately when severe abdominal pain or vomiting occurs along with the constipation. Pain may indicate a serious disorder, and vomiting may be a sign of a bowel obstruction.

Seriously debilitated or bedridden elders may develop *fecal impaction* (a condition in which the stool in the last part of the large intestine and rectum hardens, causing a blockage). The blockage leads to cramps and rectal pain. Toxins leaking into the bloodstream can produce a grave health threat. When suppositories and enemas fail to bring relief, the doctor or nurse may have to *disimpact* the feces manually with a gloved finger. In rare cases, surgery may be necessary.

Diarrhea

Most people suffer from occasional bouts of *diarrhea* (loose, watery bowel movements) without even knowing the cause. It's annoying and uncomfortable but is usually over in a day or two. Diarrhea may trigger incontinence in a frail older person.

Severe or chronic diarrhea (and blood in the stool) demands medical attention. It may be a symptom of colon cancer, diabetes, infection, fecal blockage, or other serious problems. Loss of fluids can lead to life-threatening dehydration.

When the diarrhea is frequent and accompanied by stomach cramps or high fever (generally a sign of infection), call the doctor immediately.

The following situations may contribute to the development of diarrhea:

- Eating dietetic candy and chewing dietetic gum. (Some of these products contain sorbitol or mannitol, sugar substitutes that linger in the intestine, causing excessive amounts of water to remain in the stool.)

- Eating or drinking certain foods (for example, apple and pear juice, grapes, dates, figs, nuts).

- Consuming caffeinated products (coffee, tea, and colas as well as over-the-counter headache remedies) and antacids containing magnesium.

- Using certain medications. (For example, antibiotics may disturb the usual balance of "good" bacteria in the intestines.)

- Consuming milk and other dairy products. (Avoiding dairy products is advice that applies to *lactose-intolerant* people whose bodies can't convert milk sugar into a form that can be absorbed into the bloodstream.)

- Having certain medical conditions (for example, ulcerative colitis, Crohn's disease, overactive thyroid).

Investigating the remedies for bowel problems

A medical evaluation usually includes a host of questions about your elder's bowel patterns (bring the Bathroom Chart with you — refer to Table 13-1) and

The laxative lexicon

If you ever doubt that constipation is a common problem, go to your local pharmacy. You'll face an amazingly large array of products to "make you go." The following explanations for each type of laxative should help:

Bulking agents (better known as *fiber*). Fiber is the indigestible part of a plant. When consumed, it sits in your tummy, soaking up fluids and making stools bigger, softer, and easier to pass. Many doctors suggest store-bought fiber products (such as Metamucil) to prevent constipation in people with that tendency. But you can get fiber naturally by eating fresh vegetables and fruits, dried fruits, and wheat bran. Among the favorite fiber-rich foods are apples, figs, prunes, dried apricots, peas, carrots, and 100-percent bran cereal. Adding fiber to the diet is one of the best ways to prevent constipation. It's even safe for long-term use, but your elder must drink plenty of fluids when taking these bulking agents (at least four to six glasses of liquid a day). Caffeinated drinks don't count — they're diuretics that actually take water out of the body. Add fiber to your elder's diet slowly; otherwise, you're going to have one gassy, crampy, bloated elder on your hands.

Stool softeners. Doctors recommend a number of over-the-counter drugs (such as Colace) that draw water into the stool. The increased bulk stimulates the large intestine to contract and move the stool out of the body with greater ease and comfort.

Mineral oil. This stool-softening method comes with a number of warnings. Mineral oil may pre-vent certain vitamins from being absorbed into the body, and the oil may also seep from the rectum.

Enemas. The injection of liquid into the rectum relieves occasional constipation and is used to cleanse the bowel before rectal examinations and diagnostic tests. The fluid stretches the walls of the large intestine and stimulates evacuation. You can prepare enemas at home with warm tap water and an enema bag, but ready-to-use ones (such as Fleet) make the whole process simpler and more efficient. Never give an enema without a doctor's instruction. It can be dangerous for elders with kidney problems or heart failure.

Suppositories. Laxative products (such as Dulcolax) are inserted into the rectum to stimulate the lower bowel. Like enemas, they work quickly but can be safely used only for occasional constipation. Check with the doctor for advice about how often suppositories should be used.

Oral laxatives. These products (such as Milk of Magnesia) contain substances that stimulate the walls of the large intestine to contract, moving the stool out of the body. They work well as an occasional constipation remedy and for emptying the large intestine before diagnostic tests. Sometimes they give rise to cramps. Prolonged use may cause dependence and may damage the large intestine.

current medications (bring the My Medication Chart with you — see Chapter 11). The doctor uses examination and diagnostic tests to look for structural or neurological abnormalities. Your oldster may undergo a *sigmoidoscopy* (an examination of the lower part of the bowel using a flexible viewing tube).

What can be done about constipation?

Generally, the treatment of constipation includes the following strategies:

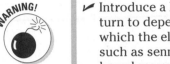

- ✔ Diagnose and treat underlying diseases (for example, *hypothyroidism* which is an underactive thyroid).

- ✔ Increase physical activity (see Chapter 7 about getting your age-advantaged person to exercise).

- ✔ Introduce a laxative (but only with doctor's blessing). Habitual use can turn to dependence and a condition called *lazy bowel syndrome,* in which the elder loses the ability to go on her own. Also, home remedies such as senna tea and castor oil are irritants that produce a semisolid bowel movement in six to eight hours but often cause cramping.

What can be done about diarrhea?

Generally, the treatment of diarrhea includes the following strategies:

- ✔ Diagnose and treat underlying diseases (for example, ulcerative colitis or Crohn's disease).

- ✔ Introduce antidiarrheal medication. The doctor or pharmacist may suggest an over-the-counter medication to slow bowel movements.

- ✔ Encourage the elder to drink chicken broth, tea, ginger ale, or apple or cranberry juice to replace lost fluids.

- ✔ Replace lost potassium with high-potassium foods (for example, bananas, mashed potatoes).

- ✔ Serve low-fiber, easy-to-digest foods (for example, bananas, rice, applesauce, toast, crackers, chicken, eggs, fish, cottage cheese).

- ✔ Avoid spicy foods, citrus juices, fatty meats, and fried foods.

- ✔ Limit bowel-stimulating caffeine products.

- ✔ Avoid milk and diary products, which can worsen diarrhea and stomach cramps.

What can be done to prevent bowel incontinence?

Normal evacuation should resume after the bout of constipation or diarrhea has been treated. If it doesn't, then try additional strategies to prevent the condition from becoming chronic.

Biofeedback can be helpful in increasing the elder's sensitivity to the presence of stools in her bowel. One method is to place a balloon inside the patient's rectum. The patient practices contracting muscles while observing a monitor that feeds back information about her efforts.

Demented elders may soil themselves because they don't recognize the urge to go, they forget where the bathroom is, or they forget how to use it. However, once seated on the throne, they may produce a bowel movement. Escorting a confused older person to the bathroom every two hours and assisting her onto the toilet helps. You may also want to streamline the process with easy-to-maneuver clothing (elastic waists, Velcro closures) or place a portable commode nearby.

Realize your elder isn't doing it out of spite. Except in rare instances of mental illness, elders don't soil themselves on purpose.

Saying Goodbye to Embarrassment

Diapers should be used with caution, because once your elder learns to rely on them, she'll probably stop exercising her bladder muscles. Diapers also carry an emotional stigma. A healthy friend recently commented that she would rather die than be in a condition where someone had to diaper her. She didn't say if it would make a difference whether that someone was a professional healthcare worker or a family member. This situation can be excruciatingly painful for your frail, incontinent older adult. It's not pretty work for you either — all the more difficult when the older person was once the self-sufficient individual who parented you or who is your life partner. In addition, viewing and touching a parent's genitals makes many people uncomfortable.

Adopting the following strategies can help you and your elder cope with the situation (especially with the diapering part):

✔ **Avoid using the word "diaper" in front of your elder.** It conjures up images of helplessness and infancy. No matter how impaired your elder is, she is not a child. When you must refer to these products, use terms like pads, guards, shields, or underwear.

✔ **Change and clean your older person in the bathroom (if possible) while he holds on to the sink for support.** Avoid facing the elder.

✔ **Adopt a nonchalant, nonjudgmental attitude.** Practice telling yourself that cleaning your elder's bottom is just another chore — nothing less, nothing more. Tell an embarrassed senior that this task is no different than cooking a meal for her or helping her walk — in other words, no big deal!

✔ **Demonstrate a casual attitude (even before you have achieved one).** Should your elder show shame or embarrassment, you can say, "I don't mind the smell" (or whatever she seems concerned about). Then regard what you've said to be a small kindness rather than a white lie.

✔ **Offer support to your elder if she continues to feel embarrassment despite your casual attitude.** Acknowledging how uncomfortable it must be to have someone else help her in this way can be a comfort.

✔ **Provide as much privacy as possible.** If others share the home, close the doors and make sure that the shades are down and curtains are drawn. Sound travels, so speak in a soft voice that won't carry into other rooms.

✔ **Preserve the privacy and dignity of your elder even when dementia has robbed her of her inhibitions.** (For example, don't talk about her incontinence in front of her.)

✔ **Get emotional support for yourself.** See Chapter 8 about joining a caregiver support group.

✔ **Cultivate a sense of humor.** (For example, chuckling at the realization that after 16 years of education or 4 years of military service or raising 3 children, you still can't figure out how to stop your elder's diaper from falling to her knees.)

✔ **Bag the guilt.** If adult diapers are more than you can handle — and you're all out of options — placement may be your only choice. Recognize that you did the best that you could do for as long as you could do it.

Obtaining Incontinence Supplies and Equipment

Medical-supply houses and many pharmacies carry a tremendous variety of incontinence products, including rustle-free, absorbent, clothlike protective undergarments that are no more bulky than underwear. I've even seen ones in tartan plaid. Pads that adhere to underwear or protect the mattress are available as well. Most of these items have a gel core that absorbs urine and cuts down on odors and skin breakdown.

An inexpensive plastic shower curtain liner or tablecloth placed under a bed sheet or other washable fabric can protect a mattress, car seat, or favorite chair just as well as more expensive store-bought liners.

North Shore Care's Web site (www.northshorecare.com) has descriptions and photographs of various supplies such as pads, pull-on protective underwear, adult diapers, belted and washable undergarments, underpads, wipes, and gloves. The company ships its products via FedEx in plain brown boxes and accepts major credit cards. (Free samples are available.) You can get answers to your product-related questions by calling at 800-563-0161.

Store Brand, a manufacturer of store-brand incontinence products (products that carry the name of the store or the store's brand name on the package) sponsors an excellent Web site (www.incontinent.com). The articles and general information are worthwhile, but the best feature is the chart of photos and information about the various types of absorbent products, the capacity of each product for light, moderate, or heavy incontinence, and recommendations to fit the needs of gender and life style (active or sedentary lifestyle).

Maintaining Health and Cleanliness

Incontinence can lead to nasty skin infections and rashes. Sitting in urine for a long time opens the way for nitrogen in the urine to damage the skin.

If your incontinent elder takes care of her own toileting, make sure that all her supplies are handy and well-stocked. Many folks with urinary incontinence don't realize that the genital area must be cleansed with every change. It may not be easy for you to do, but gently reminding your elder to wash the area can save a lot of discomfort later. This advice is especially important if your elder is a little forgetful.

You can purchase soft, moist, flushable wipes in little plastic tubs in the toilet-paper section of the grocery store. Because they're wet, they do a nice job of cleaning. (They're especially handy after a bout of diarrhea.)

If your elder needs you to change her, agree on a schedule to help make the task more routine. (About every two hours may be right.) Also impress upon your elder that she needs to tell you right away if she's wet or soiled. You can casually say, "Be sure to tell me right away so that we can take care of it. That way, your skin will remain nice and soft, and you can have as little disruption to your life as possible."

For bowel incontinence, gently clean the rectal area with diaper wipes or a soft washcloth and warm water. Allow the skin to air dry if possible.

It's a good idea to apply a diaper-rash ointment, which acts as a barrier to the constant moisture, protecting against chapping (which provides a breeding ground for infection) and rehydrating the skin at the same time. A variety of these ointments are sold in the baby section of drugstores and supermarkets. Alert the doctor if your elder's skin becomes sore and red. (See Chapter 12 for more about protecting delicate skin.)

Chapter 14

Getting Out and About

. . . .

In This Chapter

▶ Overcoming the obstacles to eating out and going to the theatre

▶ Facilitating travel — in the air, on the rails, on the sea, and on the road

▶ Taking advantage of senior discounts

. . . .

*L*osing a spouse, giving up the car keys, and contending with chronic illness all shrink your elder's world. As the outside world grows smaller, your older person may naturally spend more time in his or her inner world. Self-reflection — recalling the past and coming to terms with a life lived — isn't a bad thing. In fact, many experts consider it one of the most important tasks of old age.

On the other hand, when inner attention is focused on aches, ailments, and losses, the result may be depression, anxiety, and a reduced quality of life (for your elder *and* you).

This chapter is about stopping the shrinking — and even enlarging your elder's world — by overcoming the obstacles to getting out and about. With a little planning, a lot of patience, and the willingness to try, you and the elder you care for can come out ahead in the duel with formidable limitations — and have a good time while you're at it. The tips in this chapter are designed to smooth the way, whether the way is a car ride in the countryside or a cruise to a foreign country.

Planning Goes a Long Way

Most parents of infants and toddlers lug around diaper bags, bottles, changes of clothing, toys, and car seats. Extended trips require even more equipment — portable cribs and the like. Most families don't make a big deal out of it. The paraphernalia simply comes with the territory! And so it is when traveling with an elder, especially a frail older adult. In addition to carrying extra stuff, the following ideas may help make outings go more smoothly:

✔ Anticipate what items you'll need to keep your elder comfortable while you're out (for example, medications, a pillow or cushion, snacks).

✔ Be aware of your elder's limitations and your own capabilities. Over- or underestimating either one can turn a much anticipated outing into a disappointment.

✔ Call ahead to your destination to ask questions about accessibility (for example, location, and size of bathrooms, drop-off area, stairs, and wheelchair access).

✔ Go over brochures and videos with your elder about the place you plan to visit (whether a downtown art museum or a foreign country) to increase the excitement and take away some of the unknowns.

✔ Invite a third person to go along. The more the merrier — and the more help on hand.

✔ Don't push, coax, or cajole your elder to travel near, far, or in between when he's been a lifelong homebody.

✔ Return to the sites of successful outings. New experiences mean unfamiliar terrain and unexpected barriers. Going back to the same places at different times for different meals, shows, and events can provide more than enough novelty.

✔ Get to know by name the ticket-takers, ushers, clerks, and workers you frequently encounter. Once your elder's face and needs become familiar to them, acquiring the needed seat location, for example, becomes automatic.

Unfamiliar places and strangers may trigger fear, anxiety, and confusion in elders with severe memory loss. Stick to the familiar.

If you're a long-distance caregiver and your loved one has no one nearby to take her out for a pleasant jaunt, a geriatric care manager in your elder's town can schedule regular outings with a qualified companion. For a listing of geriatric care managers in your elder's area, contact the National Association of Professional Geriatric Care Managers, 1604 N. Country Club Road, Tucson, AZ 85716-3102 (520-881-8008, Fax 520-325-7925; www.caremanager.org/gcm/ProfCareManagers.htm).

Calling ahead about wheelchair and bathroom accessibility is a great idea. Unisex bathrooms (sometimes called family bathrooms) are ideal if your opposite-sex parent needs help with the toileting. Locate bathrooms before you need them.

Restaurants

Living in Hong Kong and Taiwan for a time, I gained — among many other things — a deep appreciation for going out to lunch and dinner. Business is conducted, people's achievements are recognized, and family milestones are honored in restaurants. Celebratory meals and Sunday dinners include the youngest and the very oldest. The dining rooms are noisy, and the decor is usually red. Everyone seems to know everyone else, and meals go on for hours. Most of all, restaurants (anywhere in the world) are where people partake in life! If your elder has always enjoyed dining away from home, chances are she still does.

You can enrich dining-out experiences with your elder by doing the following:

- ✔ Request a table on the street level to avoid the extra strain of taking the stairs to reach lower and upper dining rooms.

- ✔ Make sure that no uneven thresholds are between dining areas, requiring difficult navigation for your elder.

- ✔ Ask for a well-lit table.

- ✔ Find out whether the entry is protected by a canopy or awnings (important in inclement weather).

- ✔ Take advantage of "early bird" dinner specials, senior discounts, and offerings of senior-size portions. (See the upcoming section "Discovering Senior Discounts and Freebies" for more ideas for pursuing discounts.)

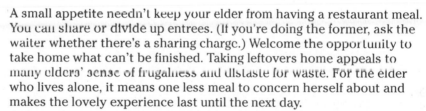

A small appetite needn't keep your elder from having a restaurant meal. You can share or divide up entrees. (If you're doing the former, ask the waiter whether there's a sharing charge.) Welcome the opportunity to take home what can't be finished. Taking leftovers home appeals to many elders' sense of frugalness and distaste for waste. For the elder who lives alone, it means one less meal to concern herself about and makes the lovely experience last until the next day.

- ✔ Create new reasons for restaurant gatherings with family members and friends — for example, a child visiting from out-of-town, an improvement in the elder's functioning, or finishing some home modification.

Theaters

With some preparation, live plays and feature films are doable. Try the following:

- ✔ Order movie and theater tickets in advance to avoid a line at the box office.

- ✔ Ask management what accommodations they can make for guests with mobility, hearing, or vision problems.

- ✔ Ask about the bathroom location and stick to theaters with first-floor restrooms or easy-access elevators to lavatories.

✔ Request curbside assistance for wheelchair users (for example, help getting the wheelchair out of the trunk and pushing the elder into the lobby while you park the car).

✔ Don't expect courtesy ushers to take on unreasonable responsibilities. (Many ushers are reluctant to lift a disabled person into a wheelchair or theater seat — as well they should be, for fear of dropping the person.)

✔ Arrive early and ask to be let into the house or auditorium before it's open to the rest of the audience.

✔ Seat your elder strategically. (For example, a seat in the middle of a row reduces the number of people who have to slide by your elder on the way to their seats or the bathroom, while a seat at the end of the row makes more sense if your elder needs easy access to the bathroom.)

✔ Exit the theater after the auditorium empties.

InSight Cinema (a nonprofit organization dedicated to bringing the big screen to deaf and hard-of-hearing audiences) captions first-run movies and schedules them with cooperating theaters anywhere in the country. To help get first-run captioned films at your local theatre, call 310-242-5700 or visit its Web site at www.insightcinema.org.

Theme parks and other entertainment venues

Many theme parks, concert halls, sports arenas, and fairgrounds have "guest relations" or customer service offices. Contact these entertainment venues by telephone or check their Web sites before visiting. Finding out in advance about available accommodations can make the outing more enjoyable for you and your elder. For example, Disneyland's Web site (www.disneyland.com) states that the park has listening devices for many attractions and two types of captioning for those with hearing problems as well as wheelchair accessibility and rental.

Although organizers at many local events like flower shows and county fairs often do their best to have wheelchairs available, the demand often overwhelms the supply. Bringing along your own wheelchair is a good idea.

Traveling

Here is a typical caregiving quandary. The local senior center is sponsoring an escorted trip abroad for older adults — or your older person wants desperately to visit her baby brother out West. It may be safer for your older person to stay put, but is it right to deny such wishes?

Grandpa's wheelchair makes the day

The grandkids, from 3-year-old Bobby to 13-year-old Ryan, regularly asked, "Grandpa, can you go to Disney World with us this weekend?" When the parents decided to make the trip, three generations found themselves at a theme park when the gates opened. The grandkids took turns pushing his wheelchair and laughing at his corny jokes. Grandpa enjoyed being included, but he had to admit that part of his popularity had to be attributed to the wheelchair advantages he added to many family outings. For example, his wheelchair enhanced the family experience at Disney World where wheelchair users get special parking (closer to the entrance). Grandpa and his group were invited to proceed through auxiliary entrances for many of the attractions, bypassing long waiting lines. They also got the best seating at shows and attractions — not to mention the fun it was for the little ones to be pushed about on Grandpa's lap when they got tired.

My general rule for deciding about whether an elder should travel (alone or escorted) is first to listen to your gut. If you know in your heart that a trip is too much for Mom to handle, it probably is. But the conditions that led you to the first assessment can change, and planning ahead (on your part) can alter your opinion about your elder's ability to travel. The first step is to shop around for a travel agent who has experience arranging travel for seniors or anyone with special needs. After you've listened to the travel agent's plan and considered all the tips in this chapter, ask yourself once again, "Is this trip doable?" If the answer this time is "Yes, could be, may be, might be okay," then go for it.

Next, protect your older person's travel dollars with trip insurance just in case the trip doesn't work out. Most travel packages have penalties for cancellation, and some tour businesses give no refunds at all. Compare different trip insurance offerings. The policy should cover all reasonable scenarios, including a family emergency, the tour company canceling the trip or going out of business, or an accident or illness that makes your elder and his or her companion unable to continue the vacation. Airlines generally will allow you to use the tickets another time or on another route, but you usually pay a rescheduling fee.

Uncomfortable shoes have ruined more vacations than stolen credit cards, rainy days, and expanding waistlines. Keep new shoes at home. The selection criteria are *comfort* and *support* — not color coordination, style, or packability. Sneak a peek into your elder's luggage just to be certain sensible shoes are in there.

When Jake fulfilled his lifelong dream to visit China, he remembered to pack comfortable shoes, but forgot the medicine that helped control his diabetes. Jake was not alarmed. He correctly thought, "I'll get a replacement from a Chinese doctor. After all, this medicine is a standard drug treatment." The problem was that the American pills were made for American-size people, and the Chinese pills were made for smaller Chinese people. The Chinese doctor had to find out just how large the American dosage was and then had to do some fancy footwork to convert what was available to an American-size dosage. It's better to be prepared — don't leave any medicine at home and carry medical information with you.

Have your doctor prepare a medical history that your elder can carry in a pocket, purse, or carry-on. The document should include your elder's name and address, contact information for a person to notify in case of emergency, a list of current medications and dosages (include generic names), blood type, reasons for prior hospitalizations, immunizations, and a list of drug allergies.

Another way to go is to wear a MedicAlert bracelet or necklace. MedicAlert is a worldwide 24-hour emergency response center. In an emergency, a medical team spots the bracelet or necklace and radios the emergency department of the hospital. Hospital personnel call MedicAlert. MedicAlert then transmits the patient's medical file to the hospital ER and notifies the person's family. Information relayed includes primary medical conditions, medications, allergies, and implanted devices (crucial information ER needs before providing treatment). The cost of MedicAlert is $35 for the first year and $20 each year after that. For more information, write Medic Alert, Box 1009, Turlock, CA 95381. You can sign up for MedicAlert by calling 800-344-3226 or going online to www.medicalert.com.

Planes

When you make your reservations (and then again 48 hours before the flight, and then *again* at the ticket counter on the day of travel), inform the airline about your elder's limitations and special needs, especially the need for wheelchair services at departure and arrival. Avoid surprises by finding out ahead of time the current security, boarding, and baggage reclaiming procedures. Most of all, steer clear of air travel at peak times, like Christmas and Thanksgiving. Also, flying into a small, manageable airport (if possible) rather than an overwhelmingly large one can make the difference between a stressful trip and a relatively stress-free one. (It may be cheaper, too!)

My mother once spent four uncomfortable airborne hours because she didn't know how to adjust the air-conditioning and didn't want to bother anyone for a blanket. Well before takeoff, review the flight attendants' duties with your older person so that he or she won't be reluctant to ask for something that would make the trip more pleasant. Duties include answering questions and providing magazines, pillows, and meals and water as needed. (Check the tickets beforehand to determine whether food and snacks are provided on that flight; if they're not, pack a lunch for your elder or purchase a carry-on meal at an airport restaurant.)

Check whether your airline offers an Adult Assistance Program. For example, Delta employs a full-time disabilities manager who can help plan the trip and provide the assistance that is needed. For a fee, Northwest provides supervision, escort, and sign-off transfer service similar in scope to the services provided to children traveling alone.

Here are more ideas for eliminating or diminishing problems your elder may encounter, whether flying alone or accompanied by a caregiver:

- ✔ Get permission to wait with your elder at the gate before boarding instead of having to say goodbye at the security checkpoint. (Remember to take advantage of early boarding for people who need extra time and assistance getting to and locating their seat and with overhead baggage.)

- ✔ Ask for a private screening at the security point if your age-advantaged person needs more time to get through a screening, needs assistance with his or her assistive devices, or just wants privacy.

- ✔ Request a tram ride from the security area to the gate. Even relatively healthy seniors find long walks to the gate too taxing.

- ✔ Order a wheelchair to take your elder to meet the tram or to go all the way to the gate if necessary. Personnel can page for one at the departure curbside. At the arrival end, an attendant may be able to push the wheelchair all the way to the parking garage.

Pride may cause your senior to refuse a wheelchair or tram to the gate. Appeal to his or her sense of practicality. For example, "A wheelchair will get us to the gate faster, and then we'll have a better chance for priority seating."

- ✔ Request bulkhead seating (assigned at check-in time). This location is great for people with knee problems or who must do medically necessary leg stretches. (Bulkhead seats usually face a partition but have more than the usual leg-room.)

- ✔ Pack all drugs and syringes for the trip (not just the ones needed for the flight) in a carry-on bag so that if the elder's luggage is lost, the medication will still be available. Bring a small cooler for any medicine (for example, insulin) that needs to be kept cool. On lengthy flights, flight attendants may be willing to put the medicine pack in the plane's refrigerated area.

- ✔ Request a seatbelt extender for heavy oldsters. An aisle seat with a moveable armrest is another comfort-enhancing feature to ask for.

- ✔ Request a seat as close as possible to the front of the plane for easy access to the bathroom.

- ✔ Pack a snack, a light throw-blanket or shawl, and a neck pillow in your elder's carry-on bag to avoid having to depend on the airline to provide healthy snacks and an adequate supply of pillows and blankets.

Let your doctor know about anticipated air travel. Some seniors are at higher risk for blood clots from long stints in economy-class seating. Swelling of the feet and lower legs is common. The doctor may recommend compression stockings, stretching exercises during flight, or another remedy.

When an elder travels alone (for example, to spend three months with her son in Chicago or a month at the New Jersey shore with her old sorority sister), consider having her bag picked up and shipped to the destination. It's pricey, but it eliminates waiting in long baggage check-in lines, hand searches at security checkpoints, and retrieving luggage from a conveyor belt. Figure on $50 to $100 to ship a bag, depending on weight, dimensions, and distance. FedEx and United Parcel Service are two ways to do it. Luggage shipping services have popped up in the last few years and may offer additional services — for example, monitoring the bag en route and calling you to let you know your bag has arrived at its destination. Luggage Express (866-744-7224, www.usxpluggageexpress.com) and Skycap International, which specializes in shipping luggage for airline passengers (877-775-9227, www.skycapinternational.com), are two private services. Always ask whether insurance is included in the price.

Ships

Cruises (really floating resorts) are especially good for older folks because, once onboard, everything is provided (including dozens of activities, a selection of restaurants and entertainment and — should it be needed — a ship's doctor and medical facility.)

It's best to work through a travel agent who willingly takes pains to find the perfect match between your older person's needs and a particular ship and cruise. For example, larger ships accommodate special diets best (including low-fat, diabetic, and low-salt).

Newer ships tend to have the largest number of wheelchair-accessible cabins. Older ships and small ships may be less adaptable to passengers with limitations.

Here are some questions to help you determine whether a particular ship or cruise meets your elder's needs:

✔ Does the ship have a dedicated gangway for wheelchairs?

✔ Is "casual dining" offered for those who dislike going formal?

✔ What level of exertion do the shore excursions require? (A popular destination for seniors is Alaska, where visitors can best view the natural wonders from the deck.)

Inform the cruise line of any chronic health problems in advance so that their medical services can be properly prepared to offer assistance.

✔ Are there likely to be waiting lines for dining or events because of the large number of passengers?

✔ Is the number of passengers small enough so that socializing is easy?

✔ Will tendering be required at any ports of call? (A *tender* is a small craft that makes frequent round trips from the ship to the dock when ships are too big for the local docks. Even if crew members help, getting on and off a tender may too difficult for your elder.)

✔ Are public rooms wheelchair-accessible? Can they be reached by elevator?

✔ Does the cruise line have special policies regarding travelers with disabilities — for example, requiring people with disabilities to be accompanied by an able-bodied companion?

✔ Are shipboard activities available when the ship is in port, in case your elder chooses not to go ashore?

Accessible Journeys is a travel agency that specializes in booking cruises and tours for slow walkers, wheelchair users, and their families and friends. They can also provide licensed health-care professionals to accompany your elder. Call 800-846-4537 or visit online (www.disabilitytravel.com). A great information source for mature travelers and people with disabilities is Frommer's (www.Frommers.com).

Trains

I was recently introduced to the joy of riding the rail when I took the train from Los Angeles to San Diego rather than flying (less than an hour flight and nearly four hours by train). The ride was leisurely and oh-so-civilized — plenty of aisle and leg room and ever-changing scenery out of the window. Planes get you to your holiday; trains are *part* of the holiday experience.

Travelers over 62 receive a 15 percent discount on most Amtrak trains. Call in advance to request assistance (including help boarding and detraining, oxygen transport, and station accessibility). Call 800-USA-Rail to talk to a customer service agent or visit online at www.amtrak.com.

Buses

Many community groups sponsor senior day trips to botanical gardens, malls, historical sites, and museums, using buses and vans for transportation. Excursions to discount outlets are popular with the ladies, especially before the holidays. Unlike tours designed for tourists, senior day trips are intended to accommodate those with mobility problems, including slow walkers. Look for postings of day trips for seniors in community newspapers (usually under Community Events). My eyes are always peeled for copies of free community papers (sometimes called throw-aways) in drug stores, supermarkets, and libraries. If you accompany your elder (and interact with others on the jaunt) the first time out, your elder may feel comfortable about going on the next day trip alone.

Call your local Department of Public Transportation (listed in the telephone directory) to discover what transportation services are available for people with disabilities in your community.

When making reservations on a bus line, always tell the agent about your elder's needs for assistance. When booking bus tours, ask about two-for-one fares and deals on regional fares good for one, two, or three sections of the country.

For a $5 annual membership fee, anyone 62 and over can become a member of Greyhound Seniors Club and get 10 percent off regular Greyhound passenger fares, 10 percent off food items at Greyhound restaurants, and 10 to 30 percent off room rates at certain hotels. Nonmembers can still get a 5 percent discount on regular fares. All you have to do is show your ID and ask for the discount. Call 800-229-9424 for more information about the Greyhound Seniors Club or information about traveling with a disability or visit online (www.greyhound.com). Click Travel Planning and then choose Seniors from the drop-down menu that appears.

Paratransit services

Every community has a different deal on transportation for the elderly and individuals with disabilities. Unfortunately, some have no deal at all. Your Area Agency on Aging can provide referrals to transportation services in your area. (See Chapter 8 for more ideas about locating transportation services.)

According to the law (The Americans with Disabilities Act of 1990), a person has a disability if he or she has a physical or mental impairment that substantially limits one or more of such person's major life activities (in other words, the person is unable to perform a major life activity that an average person in the general population can perform), has a record of such an impairment, and is regarded as having such an impairment. There is no such thing as an ID card that verifies that the carrier is disabled, nor do national standards define a disability.

Laminate a doctor's note that indicates the nature of your elder's disability and carry it for proof of his or her handicap.

Cars

Getting in and out of cars presents challenges to many elders and their caregivers. The act requires bending, sliding, and coordination — not to mention nerves of steel from the caregiver.

The following strategies may help:

- ✓ Place a piece of plastic on the seat before your elder gets in, to make sliding in and out easier. A heavy trash bag works well, too. Of course, if you have access to a car with leather seats, take that one!

   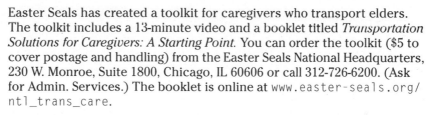

   Easter Seals has created a toolkit for caregivers who transport elders. The toolkit includes a 13-minute video and a booklet titled *Transportation Solutions for Caregivers: A Starting Point.* You can order the toolkit ($5 to cover postage and handling) from the Easter Seals National Headquarters, 230 W. Monroe, Suite 1800, Chicago, IL 60606 or call 312-726-6200. (Ask for Admin. Services.) The booklet is online at `www.easter-seals.org/ntl_trans_care`.

- ✓ Remind your elder to put his bottom in first when entering the car and his feet out first when exiting the car, in order to eliminate some awkward and potentially hazardous body positioning.

- ✓ Provide a small seat cushion to raise your elder up and give him or her a better view out of the car window. (It's so easy to forget that your elder has probably shrunk in height over the years.)

- ✓ Carry a little stepstool in the car to help your elder climb in and out of minivans and SUVs. (Be careful — the cheap plastic ones are unstable. You can often purchase sturdy footstools at yard sales and thrift shops for a song.)

- ✓ Put a gait belt around your unsteady elder's waist so that you'll have a secure place to grab hold while you're helping him in and out of the car. Gait belts are sold in medical-supply stores, but luggage belts (for securing suitcases) work just as well and are cheaper.

- ✓ Make sure that your elder or whoever drives your elder to outings has a cell phone and membership in a roadside assistance program, to ensure that your elder will not be stranded on the road.

If your older adult's health problems or impairments limit the distance he or she can walk, obtain a note from your elder's doctor and visit the local Department of Motor Vehicles to obtain a handicapped placard for the car. You can use the hangtag to transport your elder.

The largest not-for-profit motor club in the United States is the American Automobile Association (AAA), which has network of 79 clubs in the United States and Canada. Costs and benefits of membership vary, depending on the club, but basic memberships range from $38 to $76 per year. Benefits may include travel services (vacation planning, maps with routes marked, free traveler's checks, travel books), DMV services, safe-driving classes for seniors over 55, and discounts on rental cars, hotels, theme parks, restaurants, and retail stores). Find your local AAA club in your local telephone directory or go online (www.aaa.com).

Confused elderly may forget what a seatbelt is for or how to fasten one. Once you're in the driver's seat, you'll have difficulty leaning over your elder to grasp her seatbelt and pull it across her body to fasten it. In that case, get your elder seated, hand her the long end of the belt, and ask her to hold onto it. Then, when you get into the driver's seat, you can easily take the long end from her hand and fasten it. (See Chapter 18 for more tips on transporting confused elderly.)

Discovering Senior Discounts and Freebies

Arm your elder with her ID, and before purchasing services or buying tickets get in the habit of saying, "Do you have a senior citizen discount?" Then ask, "Are there any other promotional discounts available?" Sometimes limited-time specials are superior to senior discounts. Discounts and promotions aren't always posted or advertised and — unless asked — clerks don't often volunteer the information. I took my own advice recently at a Borders bookstore. To my surprise, the clerk said, "Oh yes, we give 20 percent off to people over 55 on Wednesdays. After I received my $16 discount, I asked her whether she would have offered the discount if I hadn't asked about it. The young women said, "Oh no, I wouldn't want to offend anyone by assuming that they're a senior."

When there's no discount, extra services may be offered. For example, many banks give free benefits to seniors. (Benefits may include free safe deposit boxes, checking accounts, checks, and notary service.)

Look for free health screenings for cholesterol, blood pressure, glaucoma, asthma, breast cancer, and prostate cancer. Screenings can occur at hospitals, private physicians' offices, churches, synagogues, and community centers. Take advantage of free or very reduced flu shots at community centers or even at pharmacies.

Together Rx is a prescription-savings program that can save your elder approximately 20 to 40 percent off the usual amount paid right at the pharmacy counter. Your elder must be a Medicare enrollee, have an annual income of less than $28,000 (or $38,000 for couples), and have no public or private prescription drug coverage. There's no membership fee. Obtain an application by calling 800-865-7211 or download an application form online (www.Together-Rx.com).

Senior discounts are more plentiful than most people realize. Many government institutions offer discount cards. For example, seniors 62 and older can purchase The National Park Service Golden Age Passport. This lifetime pass costs $10 and entitles the holder (and anyone else in the car who happens to be along) to free admission to all national parks, monuments, forests, and recreational areas. Purchase the Passport at any national park or through the mail from National Park Service, Office of Information, P.O. Box 37127, Washington, DC 20013-7127 or by phone (202-208-4747).

Seven major cities offer a CityPass. The one for New York gets you into seven famous New York City attractions (American Museum of Natural History, Guggenheim Museum, Intrepid Sea, Air, and Space Museum, Museum of Modern Art, Empire State Building Observatory, Circle Line Harbor Cruise, and Whitney Museum of American Art) and costs $38. You have nine days to visit each attraction (once), beginning the first day you use the CityPass. Best of all, you can avoid those pesky lines by flashing the pass. You can buy a CityPass for each participating city online at the Web site (www.citypass.com).

Elders who are eligible for certain government programs (including Food Stamps, Home Relief, Home Energy Assistance Program, Supplemental Security Income, Medicaid, Veteran's Disability Pension, or Veteran's Surviving Spouse Pension) qualify for Bell Atlantic's Life Line, which provides reduced or discounted rates on basic telephone service. For more information, write to Bell Atlantic Community Affairs, Room 3410, 1095 Avenue of the Americas, New York, NY 10036.

AARP is a nonprofit organization whose mission is to help older Americans achieve lives of independence, dignity, and purpose. Membership, a bargain at $12.50 a year, includes a bimonthly magazine and access to a cornucopia of services and discounts. Check out the discounts online (www.aarp.org/benefits).

My Dad stuck to the old-fashioned way of taking advantage of coupons. After breakfast, on Sunday mornings, Mom gave Dad the newspaper and a pair of scissors, and he clipped coupons. Dad didn't have to have a good memory for this job, and he loved contributing to their financial welfare by saving money at the market. Later in the day, he organized the coupons. The third task — the most difficult — was Mom's. She had to remember to bring the coupons with her when she went food shopping.

Although coupon use isn't limited to seniors, older people often enjoy clipping. Shopping at markets that pay double on coupons, using manufacturer's coupons, and taking advantage of rebates can produce substantial savings.

Inquire about special senior shopping days (10 percent off on Tuesdays or Wednesdays is common) at supermarkets and other large chain retail stores.

My favorite Web site for senior discounts (www.seniordiscount.com) prompts you to type your city and state or your zip code. Then it prompts you to pick the categories you're interested in (including airlines, car rental, restaurants, entertainment, public transportation, and retail stores). Another click, and you're given a number of discounts for each of those categories right in your own neighborhood. Amazing!

Part IV

The Blues, the "Good Old Days," and Other Senior Moments

The 5th Wave   By Rich Tennant

"Well, Dad, if you're feeling down, why don't you watch some TV. Let's see, there's 'Silent Killers at the Salad Bar,' 'When Puppies Attack,' and 'War of the Worlds.'"

In this part . . .

Remember the 1980s hit "Don't Worry, Be Happy"? If achieving happiness were as simple as musician Bobby McFerrin made it sound, everybody would be floating blissfully above the clouds like lovers in a Chagall painting. In real life, sadness, fearfulness, and confusion persist, despite your best intentions. What's needed are explanations in plain English with advice about how to cope with or fix the painful feelings — that's exactly what you find in this part.

Chapter 15

When the Clouds Roll In: Dealing with Depression

From time to time, most everyone experiences gloomy feelings. A disappointment or loss may cause a dark cloud to roll in. Usually, the clouds drift away in a few hours or days, and the sun shines once more. For some elders, clouds roll in, refuse to budge, and the older person (and his family) are at a loss to explain why he feels so bad for so long.

It's estimated that 15 to 20 percent of elders suffer from some kind of depression — everything from the passing mood to the kind that requires medical attention. This chapter explains the differences between the various types of depression and explores some remedies.

The Blues

Winston Churchill called it the black dog. Most people know it as the "blahs," being "down in the dumps," or the doldrums. You wish you had stayed in bed. You're downhearted, and everything's going wrong. Sometimes you can point to a cause. Often, you haven't a clue about what's behind your misery. Fortunately, it doesn't last long — that's "the blues."

One way to deal with a down-in-the-dumps feeling (either in yourself or in your elder) is to ignore it and carry on as usual. Or you can adopt the hibernation approach — reduce activities and wait for the arrival of a sunnier day. A third path is to build a storehouse full of "blues busters" and try each one until you find one that works!

The following "blues busters" are worth trying:

- Keep a list of your elder's favorite activities (for example, taking long car rides, going to the movies, playing cards, or baking) and ask her to choose what she'd like to do. If she can't or won't choose, you pick.

- Organize a visit from someone who always lifts her spirits (for example, a grandchild, a clergy person, a best friend).

- Arrange an outing. My mom calls it "giving her an airing." (See Chapter 14 for tips on making getting out and about with an elder easier.)

- Get your age-advantaged person up and moving. A regular walk (outdoors, if possible) provides a physiological lift that often shoos the blues away for a little while, especially if someone else goes along. (See Chapter 7 for more about exercise and the elderly.)

- Appeal to the child inside every grown-up. Prepare a bubble bath, read a story, put an old slapstick comedy on the VCR, and make some popcorn.

- Ask for help with a task your elder is good at but that you've never mastered. One caregiver asked her artistic client to show her how to paint. The caregiver's awkward attempts brought the oldster to laughter and ended with a painting lesson.

- Perk your elder up with a beauty-shop appointment to get her hair and nails done.

- Ask for help with gardening, drying dishes, or sorting socks. Not only does the task distract an elder from low feelings, it allows her to contribute to the upkeep of the household.

- Encourage activities that stimulate self-expression, including dancing, singing, drawing, and painting.

Grief

Grief is the overwhelming sorrow that accompanies various losses (including the loss of a beloved person, a pet, health, and self-confidence). Given sufficient time — grief usually gets better on its own accord. Recovery from a loss requires time. The elder must absorb the reality of the loss, endure the emotional pain that goes with it, and eventually figure out how to survive (and even live well) in spite of the loss.

Using time as healer

A mourner passes through various emotions and stages. There's no one right way to do it! Your elder may exhibit an array of emotional reactions to her loss or only a few. She may jump from one emotion to another or proceed through her grief in a more predictable fashion.

Most people take a year or more before the worst is behind them. The length of the grieving period depends on many things. For example, if her loved one was ill for a long time, your elder may have started mourning long before the actual death occurred, so the grieving after the death appears relatively brief.

On the other hand, if your elder experienced a series of losses, never fully mourning one before another hit in the face, her grief may be especially long and difficult. Many people don't allow themselves to cry, to take days off to recuperate, or even to take time to reflect. In their later years, a single loss can throw them into deep melancholy. Now they must mourn the fresh loss as well as the decades of unresolved losses. This kind of persistent sadness can turn into a serious depressive illness deserving of medical intervention. (See the section "Clinical Depression" later in this chapter for more ways to help your clinically depressed elder.)

For most people, the intensity of the grief gradually lessens, with shorter periods of intense feelings alternating with longer periods of better mood. Although the passage of time takes the edge off the sadness, it doesn't stop survivors from missing their loved ones.

Knowing how to comfort

How do you console a grieving person? You can use the following list as a guideline when you're not sure what to say or do.

Things you *should* do:

- ✔ Acknowledge the loss in as many ways as possible. Go to the funeral, call frequently, send notes, visit, and honor the departed with donations or memorials.

- ✔ Mention the deceased, remembering special moments, pleasing personality traits, and shared events.

- ✔ Understand that anger (directed at clergy, doctor, God, rescue teams, relatives, and you) is likely to be but a temporary stage in the grieving process. Don't take it personally or argue about it.

- ✔ Acknowledge that anyone in the same position as the mourner would be in similar emotional pain.

- ✔ Encourage your oldster to find solace in spiritual, cultural, and religious practices. (See Chapter 22 for more information on the elderly and faith.)

- ✔ Bring prepared food that is easy to warm up or freeze for later use. Include comfort food like chicken soup, mashed potatoes, and the elder's personal favorites.

✔ Give your elder extra attention during the anniversaries, birthdays, and holidays that fall during the first year after the loss.

✔ Be available when your elder wants to talk about her feelings or reminisce. Talking lessens the pain. (See Chapter 9 for tips on good listening.)

✔ Encourage participation in a bereavement group. (Check your elder's house of worship, local hospital, hospice, mental health or counseling center, and funeral home for an appropriate group.)

✔ Have your elder call the AARP Grief and Loss Support line (866-797-2277) as often as she likes. Volunteers offer support, information, and referrals to support groups across the country and can suggest helpful books on grieving.

Things you should *not* do:

✔ Discourage crying.

✔ Suggest that he ought to be over it by now!

✔ Say "At least he's not suffering any more" or "At least he lived a long life."

✔ Say "I know how you feel" (even if you think you do).

✔ Avoid mentioning the deceased.

✔ Say "Call me if I can do anything." Instead, offer to do specific things like going to the store or cooking dinner.

✔ Be overprotective. You risk making her angry — or worse, fostering dependency.

✔ Push for major changes such as selling the house and moving in with a child.

Widownet is an online site (www.widownet.org) featuring a message board and a host of resources for widows and widowers.

Clinical Depression

Clinical depression is a deep sadness that persists over weeks and months, playing havoc with sleep and appetite, and the quality of your oldster's life and relationships. Clinical depression can cause your age-advantaged person's health to decline often leading to premature institutionalization as his ability for self-care becomes compromised.

The blues and grief can develop into a full-blown clinical depression.

Finally, because depression can run in families, some people may have a biological predisposition that puts them at high risk for depressive illness.

Signs of clinical depression

If your elder exhibits any of the following symptoms for more than two weeks, he or she needs to be seen by the doctor:

- ✔ Complains of feeling "empty," hopeless, sad, or scared

- ✔ Shows lack of interest in everyday activities

- ✔ No longer enjoys formerly pleasurable pastimes

- ✔ Cries often (sometimes for no apparent reason)

- ✔ Complains of lack of concentration, faulty memory, and trouble with decisions

- ✔ Expresses feelings of worthlessness or guilt

- ✔ Has thoughts of suicide or has made an attempt

- ✔ Complains of headaches, backaches, or stomachaches that don't respond to treatment (when physical problems hide

depression, the condition is called a *masked depression*)

- ✔ Uses more alcohol, drugs, and tobacco

- ✔ Pays less attention to grooming and hygiene

- ✔ Sleeps too little or too much, has trouble falling asleep, and may wake up early, unable to fall asleep again

- ✔ Appears tired and sluggish

- ✔ Eats more or less than usual, resulting in significant weight gain or loss

- ✔ Frequently becomes agitated, hostile, or disoriented

- ✔ Adopts depressive positions and gestures (including sad facial expressions, being stooped over, and staring across room) that indicate sadness

The NIMH Public Inquiry Line can help you determine what type of information you need and send you appropriate free publications about depression and other disorders. Call 301-443-4513 to talk to a trained information specialist.

Searching for causes

A depressive illness can be triggered by an upsetting event or a series of upsetting events, such as moving to a new place, experiencing financial problems, or coping with a newly diagnosed disease. Unrelenting stress also breeds depression. (See Chapters 3 and 8 for ways to prevent or reduce caregiver stress.) Worry, loneliness, and living in a situation in which no amount of effort improves your circumstances are additional depression-makers. And the list goes on. All sorts of medical conditions and the drugs to treat them may cause depressive symptoms. (See Chapters 10 and 11 about how illness and medications contribute to depression.) And if an illness doesn't cause depression, worrying about it may!

If your elder has had a heart attack and is depressed, see the doctor to determine whether counseling and antidepressant medication are needed. Twenty percent of heart attack patients end up severely depressed. What's worse, coronary patients who become severely depressed are three times as likely to develop additional cardiac problems or die than those who don't become depressed.

Seniors who display memory problems, confusion, disorientation, and difficulty concentrating are often mistakenly assumed to have dementia when the real problem is untreated depression. This situation is so common that it has its own name — *pseudodementia*. Left untreated, it can result in premature institutionalization for the senior and heartache for him and his family. Be aware that depression can also co-exist with other psychiatric illnesses, including anxiety disorders.

Elders in the early stages of Alzheimer's disease often suffer from depression. (See Chapter 18 for more information about depression that accompanies dementia.)

Healing through reminiscence

Reminiscence is the work and play of old age. It's not only an enjoyable pastime, it also serves the elder well by helping him forgive, forget, and re-cast past transgressions and disappointments by highlighting the positive events and reshaping the negative events of the past. For example, an elderly mother laments that she often didn't have enough food for her children and many times they went to bed hungry. Her caregiver, hearing this sad reflection, comments that on the contrary, the old woman's cleverness and risk-taking surely kept the children from perishing. "Furthermore," she reminds the oldster, "The 'proof is in the pudding.' You must have done an awful lot that was right, because your children grew up to be such fine adults." Interactions like this one can help raise an elder's self-esteem, restore pride, and reduce depression.

The older people get, the more time they tend to spend reflecting on the past. Done well, reflection decreases depression. Scientists studying reminiscence in the elderly have learned that recounting the past is therapeutic, especially when a listener points out how the elder was loved and admired and notes his accomplishments and other positive qualities. Reminiscence brings the past into the present and reminds the older person that he isn't just an old man but also a father, a businessman, a teacher, and a sportsman.

Psychologists call this uplifting reconstructing of the past "a life review." Encourage your elder to recall the past. Acknowledge his sacrifices and help him to give more positive meanings to the more troubling parts. And when the remembering is filled with sorrow, remind the elder he did the best he could with what he had available at the time.

Capturing your loved one's memories to pass down to family members underscores the importance of your elder's reminisces and creates a family legacy. Suggest that your older person record her memories in a journal. Work together on a scrapbook with photos, newspaper clippings, letters, postcards, greeting cards, sketches, and poetry. You can even get song sheets from the music popular in her youth. Create a video or audio recording of her stories. These activities affirm for your loved one all the positive things she has done in her life. (See Chapter 20 about helping your elder create a family history.)

Although reminiscence is useful for most elders, be aware that for some the process only intensifies their despair and low self-esteem. In this case, don't encourage reminiscence. You may have more luck after your elder has received medical treatment for depression.

You can use a "memory box" or chest that contains old photos, tools, kitchen utensils, magazines, newspaper clippings, and even vintage clothing and toys to stimulate a confused person's memory.

Healing through re-igniting interest in others

Most depressed people (at all ages) turn their attention inward, obsessing about their own shortcomings and problems, the ills of society, and their dismal future. Any time you can redirect your elder's attention outward, away from his own misery (even for a short time), you have made an inroad to elevating his depression. Gently convince, cajole, and persuade your elder to participate in a support group, become a volunteer, and stay involved in the lives of family and friends. One senior who was depressed for several years turned the corner when he got all fired up about the city's plan to bring down a half-dozen magnificent old trees in the local park. He organized a sit-in and a schedule of protests. Somehow, he became too busy and too involved in changing the world to remain depressed.

For a list of local support groups and additional information on depressive illness, write to the National Foundation for Depressive Illness, P.O. Box 2257, New York, NY 10116-2257. This nonprofit agency requests a $5 donation for materials, but it drops the charge for those who include a note stating that they cannot afford the fee. Enclose a business-size, self-addressed stamped envelope with $1.06 postage affixed.

Talking sadness away

Although depression almost always responds to treatment, yet 75 percent of elderly sufferers never get treatment. A medical evaluation is the first step to

Depressed elders and suicide

It may surprise you to know that when an old person decides to end his life, he is more likely to be successful than a younger person who attempts suicide. For example, 25 percent of seniors who attempt suicide succeed, whereas only .5 to 1 percent of adolescents who attempt succeed. People over age 65 commit approximately 5,500 suicides a year, which is 50 percent higher than the rate of the general population. The group with the highest suicide rate in America is widowed white men in their 80s. Unlike younger people, suicidal elders tend to threaten less and do it more — all the more reason to seek medical treatment for depression, especially when the treatment has such a high success rate.

determine whether illness (including cancer, diabetes, Parkinson's disease) or side effects of drugs (including drugs used to treat high blood pressure and arthritis) are contributing to the problem. Once the doctor rules out those possibilities, he may suggest *psychotherapy* (talk therapy), which involves counseling with a social worker, psychologist, or psychiatrist individually or in a group. Talking with a trained therapist can give the elder a less pessimistic view of life, enhance his coping skills, and assist in finally setting to rest things that have troubled for him for decades. Often milder depressions improve with only a few sessions of such psychotherapy.

Taking medicine

Left untreated, a severe depression can debilitate your elder, worsening his medical conditions and affecting his ability to care for himself. Fortunately, 80 percent of people treated for severe depression respond to medications. Most people do best on a combination of antidepressants and talk therapy.

Medication generally takes about two weeks to kick in, and it may be as many as four to six weeks before the elder feels better. In the meantime, talk therapy helps your elder to discover more effective ways to deal with life's problems, including depression.

Some age-advantaged people resist going to a doctor for depression because they believe depression comes from moral weakness or that it's punishment for the sins of their youth. Explain that it's an illness, not a reflection of a character flaw. Remember that depression left untreated can lead to ever more serious problems, including deteriorating health, abuse of alcohol and drugs, and suicide.

The American Association of Suicidology sponsors Hopeline. Your depressed elder can call 800-SUICIDE to talk to a trained and certified suicide counselor 24 hours a day, seven days a week. Visit the Web site www.suicidology.org for a comprehensive listing of support group resources in each state.

The following are the most common classes of medications prescribed for depression. They must be taken regularly for several weeks before they work.

✔ **Tricyclic antidepressants.** (The two most common ones are Tofranil and Elavil.) These pharmaceuticals can cause weight gain and sedation. Doctors have to be careful in prescribing and monitoring them because elders are more prone to some of the adverse side effects, including increased heart rate, confusion, constipation, decreased blood pressure when a person stands up, and difficulty initiating urination. (See Chapter 11 about taking drugs safely.)

✔ **Selective serotonin reuptake inhibitors (SSRIs).** (The two most common ones are Prozac and Zoloft.) SSRIs produce fewer adverse side effects than the tricyclics, and the side effects that are present are mild and disappear with continued use. Most important is that they're safer for people who have both a physical disorder and depression.

✔ **Monoamine oxidase inhibitors (MAOIs).** These drugs are rarely prescribed anymore (except for depressed people who don't respond to the other medications for depression). The dietary restrictions and special precautions that must be followed when taking these medications are stringent. Patients can't drink beer on tap or red wine. They must avoid certain foods (including over-ripe foods, salami, aged cheese, and soy sauce) as well as over-the-counter cough and cold remedies. If these precautions aren't followed, the consequence may be a sudden severe rise in blood pressure. Patients on MAOIs must carry an antidote, take it if they get a throbbing headache, and then go to the nearest emergency room. The Food and Drug Administration recently approved a transdermal patch to reduce side effects. The new patch may result in more people using MAOIs.

Chapter 16

Managing Anxiety

. . . .

In This Chapter

▶ Knowing the difference between normal anxiety and an anxiety disorder

▶ Reducing anxiety with nonmedical remedies

▶ Benefiting from psychotherapy and medication

. . . .

F anny sat on the edge of her bed waiting for someone to come for her. She was near hysteria. Her heart was pounding. She was so shaken that she could hardly speak. Fanny had been abruptly awakened at 6:30 a.m. by a nursing aide who quickly dressed her and gave her a breakfast tray. The aide urged Fanny to eat her breakfast quickly. Medical transportation was already parked outside, waiting to take her from the nursing home to the clinic to get a mammogram. Fanny was beside herself. Why had the test been ordered? Why didn't anyone tell her before today? Why were they rushing her so early in the morning? Did she have cancer?

It turns out that the mammogram was a routine test ordered by her doctor. If someone had informed Fanny about the test in advance and answered her questions, she would have been spared from anxiety-producing uncertainty. Incompetent handling caused the frail elderly woman unnecessary (perhaps harmful) anxiety.

This chapter explains anxiety reactions and presents a variety of remedies.

Recognizing an Anxiety Disorder

When worrying or nervousness is so intense, extreme, and long-lasting that it interferes with the ability to carry on, your elder may have an anxiety disorder. On the other hand, if your elder's state of mind doesn't get in the way of performing daily tasks and the anxiety is intermittent and related to real-life problems such as money, health, or safety, your elder's anxiety may be no more than harmless fretting!

Anxiety (like depression) can range from a temporary passing state (triggered by an upsetting event) to a disabling, persistent condition that requires

The anxiety disorders

Symptoms of anxiety that persists over many months (or years), interfering with your elder's normal activities, may be described by:

Generalized anxiety disorder. This condition affects up to 5 to 7 percent of seniors and is more common in women than men. It's characterized by at least six months of constant, exaggerated worrisome thoughts and thinking that the worst is going to happen (despite the fact that little evidence supports such an expectation).

Phobia. This disorder is marked by intense irrational fear of something that poses little or no real danger (for example, fear of confinement or of public places). The fear leads to avoidance of objects or situations and may seriously restrict an elder's social interactions.

Panic disorder. Sufferers experience repeated episodes of intense fear that strike suddenly. Chest pain, heart palpitations, shortness of breath, dizziness, abdominal distress, feelings of unreality, or fear of dying that accompanies the attack may convince the victim that he's having a heart attack. Fortunately, panic attacks in the elderly are rare, and when they occur, they tend to be less severe than they are in younger adults.

Obsessive-compulsive disorder. This disorder is identified by repeated, unwanted thoughts or repetitive behaviors (including checking things over and over again) that seem impossible to stop or control. If your elder has obsessive thoughts and compulsive behaviors, they probably started when he was a whippersnapper.

Post-traumatic stress disorder. Persistent nightmares, flashbacks, numbing of emotions, depression, and irritability are among the symptoms that may occur after experiencing or witnessing traumatic events (such as a rape, war, child abuse, or natural or human-caused disasters). In elders, symptoms may appear decades after the original event, often because the senior has more time to think about past events or has recently been exposed to a situation that awakened buried memories.

medication, talk therapy, or a combination of both. And also (just like with depression) certain people are more vulnerable to anxiety because of their genetic make-up. In other words, worrywarts run in families!

Anxiety disorders can co-exist with or be induced by other illnesses (including cardiovascular disorders, respiratory problems, high blood pressure, irritable bowel syndrome, an overactive thyroid, migraine headaches, and depression). A medical evaluation can sort out the ailments. In some cases, the anxiety may subside after the medical condition is treated.

Estimates are that 10 to 20 percent of elders living in the community (and perhaps a greater percentage of those living in institutions) suffer from anxiety symptoms that require treatment.

If any of the following symptoms persist, a doctor's visit is in order:

- Agitation, shakiness, trembling
- Irritability (being on edge)

- ✔ Apprehensiveness

- ✔ Rapid heartbeat

- ✔ Uncomfortable awareness of heart rate *(palpitations)*

- ✔ Shortness of breath

- ✔ Faintness and dizziness

- ✔ Upset stomach (butterflies or cramps)

- ✔ Nausea

- ✔ Diarrhea

- ✔ Hot and cold flashes

- ✔ Frequent urination

- ✔ Exaggerated response when startled

- ✔ Extreme watchfulness

- ✔ Insomnia

- ✔ Concentration difficulties

The NIMH Public Inquiry Line has a selection of free publications on anxiety, depression, and other disorders. Call 301-443-4513 to talk to a trained information specialist who can send you useful information.

The NIMH Web site has downloadable publications about anxiety disorders. It also links to sites that provide fact sheets, information about medications, and a step-by-step self-assessment form called "Does This Sound Like You?" Go online to www.nimh.nih.gov/anxiety/anxietymenu.cfm or order from the Publication Ordering Line (888-826-9438).

Calming Down

Over time, chronic anxiety can wreak havoc on your age-advantaged person, including damaging arteries, weakening the immune system, and causing memory problems. Fortunately, you can help an anxious older person calm down in a number of ways.

Milder forms of anxiety may respond to pleasurable pastimes. Most people have a hard time painting a picture, shaping clay, or stitching a quilt and worrying at the same time. Music can also help, particularly if the music is non-heavily percussive and dates back to the elder's teen and young-adult years. In one recent study, background music successfully reduced anxiety in heart patients after surgery.

In people with Alzheimer's disease, the part of the brain that's involved with musical memory and coordination is one of the last parts to deteriorate, which may be the reason that music also soothes confused elders.

Outdoorsy, fairly fit oldsters may find some relief from their worries by getting involved in nature walks. The Sierra Club sponsors various outdoor activities, many of them for people over 65. To locate a chapter in your area, visit online (www.sierraclub.org), click the My Chapter link on the right side of the page, and search your state's Web site for senior groups.

The following activities have been shown to have calming effects:

- **Relaxation training.** The elder is taught how to "let go" of muscle tension. The theory is that you cannot remain anxious if your muscles are relaxed.

- **Meditation.** Studies show that meditation can reduce blood pressure and slow the heart rate in elders who suffer from anxiety. (See Chapter 22 for more information on the benefits of meditation.)

- **Prayer.** Besides inviting calmness, studies have shown that people who pray regularly tend to live longer. (See Chapter 22 for more information about the benefits of prayer.)

Seeking Professional Help

Older people tend to focus more on the physical symptoms than the psychological ones — a good reason to start the search for relief with your elder's primary care physician. (See Chapter 25 to find out how your elder may be hiding her feelings.)

The Center for Mental Health Services (through the Department of Health and Human Services) provides referrals to facilities and programs that treat mental disorders. They cannot refer callers to specific physicians but can provide names and contact information for hospitals, outpatient clinics, inpatient programs, support groups, patient advocacy groups, and low-cost services. The phone number is 800-789-2647, or you can log on to its Web site (www.mentalhealth.org).

Cognitive-behavioral therapy

Cognitive-behavioral therapy (CBT) is a particularly well-suited form of psychotherapy for older people who don't want or can't afford long-term counseling to rid themselves of crippling anxiety. It's a practical, brief method of treatment that's highly successful with anxiety disorders.

CBT helps people replace their anxiety-producing thoughts with more realistic, less catastrophic ones so that they can react differently in the situations that cause them anxiety. The elder may also learn to relax while being exposed to feared objects or situations. The principle is ingenious. CBT patients rid themselves of phobias because they can't be relaxed and fearful at the same time!

The National Association of Cognitive-Behavioral Therapists can refer you to a therapist in your area who is trained and certified in cognitive-behavioral therapy. Visit online at www.nacbt.org or call 800-853-1135.

Anti-anxiety drugs

Your elder's physician may determine that drug treatment makes sense. She may prescribe one of the benzodiazepines to relieve symptoms quickly. These drugs have relatively few side effects. Drowsiness and loss of coordination are most common, but fatigue, mental slowing, and confusion can also occur.

Certain benzodiazepines — including Diazepam (Valium), flurazepam (Dalmane), and chlordiazepoxide (Libruim) — have extremely long-lasting effects and can cause prolonged drowsiness. Some experts believe that these drugs shouldn't be prescribed for older people because they increase the danger of falls. Discuss such safety concerns with your doctor.

There's also a good chance that the doctor will prescribe one of the selective serotonin reuptake inhibitors (SSRIs), especially if the problem is generalized anxiety disorder, a panic disorder, or obsessive-compulsive disorder. (See Chapter 15 for more information on SSRIs.)

Another medication specifically for anxiety disorders is buspirone (BuSpar). Unlike the benzodiazepines, buspirone must be taken consistently for at least two weeks to achieve an anti-anxiety effect, which disqualifies it as a "use-as-needed" medication.

Chapter 17

All About Alzheimer's Disease

*I*magine walking into your mom's kitchen and finding her frying fish — oil sputtering around the cellophane-wrapped frozen flounder. An incident like this one is easy to ignore. It could happen to anyone. You grow a little more worried when she neglects her hygiene and grooming — clothing spotted, hair greasy and uncombed. For a while, you can blame her disheveled appearance on her poor vision and arthritis. Then unpaid bills pile up, and she gets lost on the way home from the supermarket. Finally, someone close to her — maybe you — can no longer deny that something's very wrong.

In this chapter, I help you determine whether you have cause for concern. I explain how the physician diagnoses Alzheimer's disease, the course of the illness, and the medical treatment that may slow down the mental decline.

Understanding Alzheimer's Disease

Alzheimer's disease, an incurable degenerative illness that destroys brain cells, affects 4 million Americans (mostly people over age 65). The destruction begins deep in the brain, impairing memory. As the illness spreads to other parts of the brain, it destroys language skills, affects judgment, and makes simple, everyday tasks difficult, if not impossible, to perform. Eventually sufferers lose additional mental functions, including the ability to control their basic physical urges.

More than 70 different kinds of illnesses cause dementia (which is not a specific diagnosis but a collection of symptoms). The most common illness is Alzheimer's disease, which accounts for about 50 percent of the cases. Stroke (vascular dementia) is responsible for 20 percent, and elders who have both

Alzheimer's disease and vascular dementia make up another 20 percent. Parkinson's disease, Creutzfeld-Jakob disease, and Pick's disease account for another 5 percent.

The brains of people with Alzheimer's disease are distinctive. As brain cells degenerate, the brain shrinks in size. *Plaques* (sticky material mostly made up of an abnormal type of protein) are scattered in between the remaining living nerve cells. *Tangles* (stringy twisted bits of fibers) are found within the nerve cells. Scientists don't yet know whether the plaques and tangles cause Alzheimer's disease or whether the great numbers of plaques and tangles are a result of the disease.

New symptoms surface gradually or rapidly, but the overall picture is the same — increasing dependency for the elder and escalating challenges for the caregiver. (See Chapter 18 for ways to manage the troubling behaviors and emotions that are so common in Alzheimer's disease and many other forms of dementia.)

Death occurs between 2 to 20 years after a diagnosis of Alzheimer's disease is made. (The average is about eight years.) However, Alzheimer's disease is rarely the cause of death. Pneumonia (resulting from a severely weakened physical condition) is the most common cause of death. (For more information on the stages of Alzheimer's, see the next three sections.)

Not all Alzheimer's patients exhibit the same symptoms. For example, despite a fairly advanced case of Alzheimer's disease, Diana is docile, sweet, and attentive to her husband. Although she likes restaurants, she has no idea what to do with a menu and needs help cutting her chicken. However, she shows genuine wifely concern when her spouse doesn't finish his meal. On the other hand, Esther, another Alzheimer's patient in the same stage of the illness, accuses her husband of cheating and poisoning her. In a recent bout of anger, she attacked him with an umbrella.

The following sections divide the most common symptoms of Alzheimer's disease into three stages. (Some symptoms may not appear at all, while others can occur in more than one stage.)

Recognizing the Warning Signs of Alzheimer's Disease

The following warning symptoms (adapted from the Alzheimer's Association checklist of warning signs) signal that a complete medical evaluation should be conducted. Some of these symptoms are also present in other dementing illnesses. The doctor can sort it all out — the sooner the better!

✔ **Persistent (and worsening) memory.** Memory loss that is not an inter-mittent problem (as when it accompanies stress, sleep deprivation, or illness, such as depression) is usually the first *noticeable* sign that some-thing is amiss. The forgetfulness (especially memory loss for recent events) gets to a point where it can no longer be brushed off as a "senior moment" (such as having a word or name on the tip of your tongue). One or two of the other symptoms in this list often accompany this one.

✔ **Trouble with familiar tasks.** People with dementia often find it hard to complete everyday tasks that used to be second nature to them — for example, doing the laundry or hanging a picture.

✔ **Problems with language.** People with this disease, at some point, suffer from shrinking vocabularies. They forget simple words and use substi-tutes. For example, your elder may ask for a glass of wet instead a glass of water.

✔ **Disorientation about time and place.** Forgetting the time or the day of the week can be minimized, but becoming lost on your own street or losing your way on a route you have taken regularly for 30 years demands attention. A person with Alzheimer's disease may even forget where he is, how he got there, and how to get back home.

✔ **Poor or decreased judgment.** Individuals with Alzheimer's may dress inappropriately for the weather (wearing several sweaters on a warm day or a summer frock in the snow). Individuals with Alzheimer's dis-ease and other types of dementia often show poor judgment about money, giving away large amounts to strangers or paying for home repairs or products they don't need.

✔ **Problems with abstract thinking.** This symptom becomes obvious when the elder can no longer take care of his checkbook and has trouble fol-lowing the news or movie plots.

✔ **Confusion with placing things.** A person with Alzheimer's disease may put things in unusual places — for example, an iron in the freezer or a wristwatch in the sugar bowl.

✔ **Changes in mood or behavior.** The elder may, at times, seem like a dif-ferent person. For example, a person who has always been known as even-tempered or docile becomes emotionally unpredictable, flying off the handle for no apparent reason one minute and then humming con-tentedly the next moment.

✔ **Changes in personality.** A person with Alzheimer's disease may show extreme personality change — for example, becoming surprisingly dependent on a family member or uninterested in the grandchildren who once occupied the center of her life.

✔ **Loss of initiative.** The person with Alzheimer's disease may become pas-sive, sitting in front of the television for hours, sleeping more than usual, and refusing to partake in his usual activities.

Becoming Familiar with the Alzheimer's Disease Stages

The following sections divide the most common symptoms of Alzheimer's disease into three stages. (Some symptoms may not appear at all, while others can occur in more than one stage.)

The first stage

This phase is also known as mild or early Alzheimer's and lasts about two to four years. It includes the period leading up to the diagnosis. Symptoms include

- Showing any of the warning signs of Alzheimer's disease listed earlier in this chapter, in the section "Recognizing the Warning Signs of Alzheimer's Disease"
- Asking the same questions over and over again
- Being unable to follow a conversation, especially if more than one other person is involved
- Demonstrating an inability to concentrate (which may result in abandoning former hobbies and pastimes)
- Becoming confused about directions or money management
- Being unable to come to decisions when indecisiveness was formerly not a problem
- Losing interest in surroundings
- Allowing personal appearance and common courtesies to slide
- Getting lost while driving on familiar streets
- Appearing depressed (from being aware that something is wrong but not knowing what it is)

The second stage

This period is also known as moderate or middle-stage Alzheimer's disease and lasts about two to four years. Symptoms include

- Showing more and more forgetfulness, such as not turning off the oven or taking medication
- Appearing to have trouble recognizing friends and family

✔ Wandering away from home (sometimes in the middle of the night)

✔ Becoming restless or easily upset in the late afternoon (known as *sundowning*)

✔ Exhibiting increasing inability to organize and express thoughts in a logical way

✔ Having difficulty with tasks that require planning (going shopping, putting together a meal)

✔ Having *hallucinations* (seeing or hearing things that aren't there) or *delusions* (holding irrational or false beliefs)

✔ Losing basic skills (tying shoelaces, setting the table)

✔ Exhibiting inappropriate behavior (taking clothes off in the presence of other people)

✔ Sleeping excessively long or hardly at all

The third stage

This period is also known as severe Alzheimer's disease or the final stage and lasts about three years. Symptoms include

✔ Having difficulty recognize family members or even recognizing oneself in the mirror

✔ Appearing to have little or no memory (not recalling what occurred minutes before)

✔ Having difficulty understanding or speaking (may become mute)

✔ Making grunting, screaming, or groaning noises

✔ Grasping objects and people (compulsively touching or putting things in the mouth)

✔ Experiencing incontinence (bladder and bowel)

✔ Becoming totally dependent for all personal care (including toileting, bathing, eating)

✔ Having difficulty chewing and swallowing (contributes to weight loss)

✔ Becoming severely weak and bedridden (increasing susceptibility to infections, seizures, and additional health problems)

Getting a Diagnosis

When you or your age-advantaged person forget a name or a word, you needn't worry that Alzheimer's disease is lurking behind the corner. Such "senior moments" are normal. I find it comforting that researchers say it's a good thing when you sense that the missing word is sitting on the tip of your tongue. That phenomenon is not likely to be experienced by people with Alzheimer's disease (or the *sometime* precursor called Mild Cognitive Impairment). (See Chapter 2 for more information on Mild Cognitive Impairment.)

On the other hand, any uneasiness about increasing memory lapses (and seeming attempts to make excuses for the lack of memory) warrants a complete medical evaluation.

The doctor, with the help of appropriate testing, can make a positive diagnosis of Alzheimer's disease that is 95 percent accurate. He also rules out every treatable disorder that mimics dementia or causes the worrisome symptoms, including multi-infarct dementia (ministrokes), depression, brain tumor, Parkinson's disease, chronic alcohol abuse, thyroid disease, viral infection, anemia, dehydration, medication toxicity, vitamin deficiency, poor nutrition, and head injury.

When the doctor has exhausted every possibility, the diagnosis is probable Alzheimer's disease. At the moment, the only way to be 100 percent certain is to allow someone to take out a slice of brain tissue, put it under a microscope, and discover the telltale plaques and tangles. Trust me, no one is volunteering for that test! The only time this procedure is done is at autopsy.

An early diagnosis can make a difference

Family denial, the elder's lack of cooperation, and a physician's attitude are three obstacles that may stand in the way of getting to the bottom of your elder's symptoms. Everyone needs to understand that a medical evaluation is the first step to peace of mind or possible improvement with drug treatment.

In one study, caregivers of people with Alzheimer's complained that it took many months (even years) to have the disease diagnosed. Nearly 30 percent of the caregivers reported that their doctor didn't take their concerns seriously, suggesting that the symptoms were due to normal aging. If your elder's primary care physician doesn't seem to take your concerns seriously, press for a referral to a *neurologist* who specializes in dementia or a *geriatrician* (a physician who specializes in the diagnosis and treatment of diseases and problems affecting older people).

Seeking an early diagnosis makes good sense for the following reasons:

- ✓ Reversing impaired thinking and loss of memory may be possible when the diagnosis is found to be something other than Alzheimer's disease (for example, thyroid disease).

- ✓ Slowing down the progression of Alzheimer's disease with drugs is most effective when they're administered in the early stages of the illness.

- ✓ Finding out what's wrong (although often traumatic) may be a relief to your elder, motivating him to learn about the disease and become involved in treatment decisions and long-term care planning.

- ✓ Uncovering and treating disorders (such as depression, sleeping disorders, and anxiety) that may coexist with Alzheimer's disease can improve the quality of your elder's life.

- ✓ Adjusting emotionally to the illness requires time. Knowing that he has Alzheimer's disease as early as possible allows your older person to get valuable emotional support, prepare for the changes ahead, and do some of the things he always wanted to do — while he is relatively well.

- ✓ Having no explanation for his memory loss, your elder is likely to continue desperately to try to remember (getting ever more frustrated and depressed in the process).

A medical evaluation doesn't have to be mysterious

Typically, the doctor conducts an evaluation, including some or all of the following tests, to consider all possible causes for the symptoms:

- ✓ **Medical history.** The doctor interviews the older person and a family member (separately and together) about the elder's present and past health problems, current over-the-counter and prescription medications, and the family history of illnesses. The doctor attempts to construct a chronology of the symptoms and events that cause concern.

- ✓ **Physical examination.** This exam helps identify medical conditions that may be contributing or causing the symptoms such as heart failure.

- ✓ **Neurological examination.** The doctor evaluates coordination, muscle tone and strength, eye movement, speech, and sensory abilities, testing the nervous system to rule out disorders such as stroke, brain tumor, and Parkinson's. The doctor assesses the older adult's sense of time and place, level of understanding, memory, and ability to do simple calculations through a series of questions.

- ✔ **Brain scans.** The doctor may order several different tests that take a picture of the brain (MRI or CT scan) or brain activity tests (EEG or PET) to detect tumors, ministrokes, or other structural abnormalities.

- ✔ **Blood and urine tests.** Laboratory tests can help detect whether the symptoms are due to thyroid problems, anemia, infection, diabetes, kidney or liver disorders, AIDS, or nutritional deficiencies.

- ✔ **Psychiatric or neuropsycohologic evaluations.** A psychiatrist, psychologist, or clinical social worker can determine the presence of depression, which often mimics the early stages of Alzheimer's disease (*pseudodementia*), or other mental illness.

Considering Treatment

Unfortunately, the treatment options are limited. Even so, starting early may buy your elder a longer period of independence.

Drugs may help

Currently, four medications (all of them *cholinesterase inhibitors*) can, in some cases, temporarily slow down memory loss, cause modest memory improvement, and have a positive effect on the behavior of elders in the early stages of Alzheimer's disease. The brand names are Reminyl, Exelon, Aricept, and Cognex (the first one developed, but no longer marketed).

Researchers haven't completely figured out how cholinesterase inhibitors work, but here's a layman's explanation. Acetylcholine, a chemical found in the brain, is essential to memory and thinking. The brains of patients with Alzheimer's disease and other types of dementia are deficient in acetylcholine. Scientists have observed that the longer acetylcholine hangs around in the brain (in the gaps between the nerve cells), the better the memory. An enzyme called acetylcholinesterase breaks down acetylcholine, but the inhibitors slow down the process, allowing acetylcholine to remain in the little gaps between the nerve cells much longer. The result? Improved memory and thinking. Generally, the higher the dose, the better the response, but the doctor has to start with a low dose and go slowly because high doses increase the likelihood of side effects (including nausea, vomiting, weight loss, and stomach ulcers). Eventually the person with Alzheimer's disease produces less and less acetylcholine, and the cholinesterase inhibitor loses its effect. The bottom line is that when the drug does help, it's only for about a year or so, and it also doesn't help everyone.

Other symptoms (including hallucinations, depression, anxiety, agitation, and sleeping disorders) may be managed with other drugs, but — as my own primary care physician says about many drugs — "They come with a price." For example, drugs prescribed to eliminate visual hallucinations may cause fairly serious side effects, including sedation and development of a shuffling gait, rigid movements, or tremors. (See Chapter 18 for ways to manage the symptoms of Alzheimer's disease with nonmedical techniques.)

Scientists are investigating other remedies

Many scientists believe that the damaged brains of Alzheimer's sufferers produce an excess of *free radicals.* In order to buffer the brain from more damaging effects of free radicals, your elder's physician may suggest taking vitamin E (an antioxidant). *Ginkgo biloba,* an herb that's also believed to sweep up pesky free radicals with its antioxidant properties, has been approved for treatment of dementia in Germany, but scientists in the United States are still investigating the usefulness of both vitamin E and ginkgo biloba for treating Alzheimer's disease. In other words, here in the United States the jury is still out!

Vitamin E and ginkgo biloba should only be taken with a doctor's supervision. Vitamin E can cause bleeding and gastrointestinal problems. Ginkgo has an anticlotting effect that can be dangerous if it's taken with blood thinners. (See Chapter 10 for more about using vitamins and herbs to treat illnesses.)

Scientists are also investigating whether estrogen or nonsteriodal anti-inflammatory drugs may help prevent Alzheimer's disease.

To find out about the clinical trials in your area, go online to www.clinical trials.gov. Type the word "Alzheimer's" and the name of your state in the search box and then click the Search button. A list of studies that are recruiting volunteer participants appears. Check off the studies that seem appropriate and then click Display Selected Studies to view the details, eligibility requirements, and contact information for each one. Research studies usually have multiple sites in several cities across the country. Discuss the pros and cons of participation with your elder's doctor.

Participating in research studies

Alzheimer's disease is a red-hot research topic. Scientists are closing in on finding out how it does its dirty work, ways to prevent it, and how to treat it. *Clinical trials* (research studies in which potential treatments are evaluated) are crucial. Every new medication (or new combinations of medicines) goes through clinical trials before the government decides to give it a thumbs-up, making it available to the public. These studies establish the correct dosage, investigate whether the drug does what it's supposed to do, and uncover any possible harmful side effects.

Clinical trials (which often take years) need volunteer participants. Your physician may tell you about a clinical study your elder may be eligible for, or you may hear or read about a study that needs volunteers. In the case of Alzheimer's disease, the decision to enroll the elder in a study is often a family decision because the older adult is too impaired to make such a choice.

Before jumping in, consider all the pros and cons. The strongest motivator for most families is that the medication under study may help their elder or that what is learned from the study may eventually help thousands of other sufferers. On the other hand, there is always a risk that the drug will be harmful or that your elder will be selected for a comparison group (also called a *control group*) that receives a *placebo* (an inactive pill, liquid, or powder that has no treatment value). Being a volunteer usually requires a large time commitment (including visits to the testing site and questionnaires to fill out) and interviews. Many research studies offer some free follow-up medical care and monitoring for the elder.

Planning for the Future

If ever there was a time to provide emotion support to your elder, this is it! Reassure your elder of your continued love and respect and the fact that you are all in this together. Expect yourself and other close people to respond to the Alzheimer's diagnosis with deep sadness, anger, horror, feelings of helplessness, and even guilt (because before the diagnosis, they may have reacted to your elder's forgetfulness with impatience and criticism).

When the dust settles, the family (including the older person) needs to address the following questions. (See Chapter 3 for tips on conducting a family meeting.)

- ✔ **What legal and financial matters need attention?** Because the illness eventually robs sufferers of their ability to handle their own affairs, get everything in order while your elder can still express her wishes. (See Chapter 20 for information on estate planning, wills, advance directives, and naming a durable power of attorney.)

- ✔ **Who will be the primary caregiver?** Someone has to be ready to step up to the plate. (See Chapters 3 and 8 about long distance caregiving, rotating caregiving, and hiring home-care help.)

✔ **What living arrangements have to be made?** Your elder may be able to live on her own at first (see Chapter 12 for ideas about making the home safe), but as the disease progresses, more supervision will be necessary. (See Chapter 3 about living with an adult child and Chapter 4 about nursing home care and other options.)

✔ **How will healthcare be paid for?** Medical care will be an increasing expense. (See Chapter 21 for help in determining your elder's medical benefits.)

✔ **What should be done right away?** Find out what your oldster was hoping to do "someday" and make it happen now.

My mother was just diagnosed with Alzheimer's disease. What do I do now?

The following resources can arm you with information and support:

The Alzheimer's Association. This organization offers information about Alzheimer's disease and other types of dementia, including the latest in treatment and research findings. Staff members can help you locate board-and-care facilities, skilled nursing homes, in-home care, adult daycare, respite care, and support groups. Chapters present free or low-cost workshops and trainings and provide referrals to physicians and attorneys. Calling 800-272-3900 automatically connects you to your local office. Or visit online (www.alz.org); you can find local events, workshops and support groups by clicking Your Chapter at the top of the home page. This site has a worthwhile feature called I Have Alzheimer's, which contains tips for the newly diagnosed Alzheimer's patient about self-care, helping loved ones adjust to the diagnosis, coping with changes, making job decisions, and planning for the future.

The Alzheimer's Disease Education and Referral Center (ADEAR). This center provides information about Alzheimer's disease, its impact on families and health professionals, and prevention and treatment research. To speak to an information specialist about the disease and the latest research findings on current clinical trials or to request publications or help in locating support groups, call 800-438-4380. The Web site www.alzheimers.org links you to fact sheets, research and technical reports, other federal resources, a clinical trials database, and a newsletter. Contact ADEAR by e-mail (adear@alzheimers.org) or write to ADEAR, P.O. Box 8250, Silver Spring, MD 20907-8250.

The Mayo Clinic. For practical answers to the most common questions and concerns about Alzheimer's disease, the Mayo Clinic Web site (www.mayoclinic.com) can't be beat. Click Ask a Specialist ☞ Alzheimer's disease" to view the questions and answers. In addition, *The Mayo Clinic on Alzheimer's Disease* is available at your bookstore or can be ordered online from the Mayo Clinic Web site by clicking Books and Newsletters.

The Eldercare Locator. This national directory-assistance public service can connect you to an Alzheimer's hotline and resources for transportation, home-delivered meals, legal assistance, adult daycare, respite services, in-home health care, support groups, and housing options. Call 800-677-1116.

Chapter 18

Managing the Distressing Behavior and Emotions of Confused Elderly

Chen's lower lip trembled, and his voice quivered as he spoke about his 70-year-old mother's attempts to take off her clothes in public. He knew that she had Alzheimer's disease, but he didn't understand how his modest and proper mother could shame her family in such a way. Behaviors like this one are hard to understand.

This chapter sheds light on your confused elder's disturbing behaviors and emotions, giving you an arsenal of management strategies that you can put into practice immediately.

Coping with Difficult Behavior

If you're like me, your chief coping strategy for illness is offering chicken soup. As powerful as chicken soup is, the behavioral symptoms of dementia demand much more! How do you comfort an 85-year-old who is crying for her mama? How do you hold your temper when your father has swept his breakfast off the table in a fit of anger for the third time in a week? How do you stop your older person from wandering away from home in the middle of the night?

The following general suggestions set the stage for coping with the specific problems discussed in this chapter:

- ✔ **Try to understand what's behind every distressing behavior.** Did your elder have little sleep the night before? Could she be having a drug reaction? Is she in pain? Is she cold or hungry but unable to communicate it? Figuring out the reason behind the behavior can sometimes help you curb the behavior and improve the quality of your life and your elder's life — at least for a little while longer. Some caregivers find it helpful to keep a behavior log to uncover patterns. For example, when angry outbursts occur only at mealtimes, poorly fitting dentures or too much food on the plate may be among the causes.

- ✔ **Accept that your confused elder is not doing what he's doing (whatever it is) to intentionally hurt or annoy you, even though it may seem that way at times.** Separate the behavior from your older adult. The illness — not your oldster — is responsible for the disturbing actions. Consider making "He can't help it, he can't help it" your mantra.

- ✔ **Consider telling white lies.** (I think of them as small kindnesses.) Should your confused elder repeatedly ask about her dead parents, don't try to convince her that her folks are dead. If you succeed in convincing her, she is likely to mourn for her parents over again and again. You have a couple of options. Some experts say that you should merely acknowledge that she misses them and change the subject (avoiding the issue, but committing no lie). Other professionals support a reply such as, "They're fine, and they'll come 'round when they're not so busy." Do what makes *you* most comfortable.

- ✔ **Become a yes man (or woman).** Avoid the "no" word at all costs. Saying yes and then using distraction is a superb strategy. For example, a home-care worker went to change her client's diaper (as was her custom) at 2 a.m. only to find his bed empty. After a frantic search, she found him sitting in her car. When he spied her, he insisted on being taken to the movies. She said, "Yes, of course we'll go to the movies, but let's go make pancakes [his favorite] first." By the time they got back into the house, he forgot the movies and the pancakes. She led him back to bed.

- ✔ **Appreciate the humor in everything.** After the events of September 11, 2001, a confused older woman (who had spoken nothing but disconnected words for more than a year) heard on the radio that gas prices were likely to rise sharply. She dressed herself and told her daughter that they had to "go for gas" immediately. Off they went. Afterward, the mother retreated to her confused state, and the daughter smiled as she recalled the image of her mom — in a hat, high-heeled pumps, and her housecoat — in command of the journey to the gasoline station.

- ✔ **Speak slowly, clearly, and in simple sentences, expressing one idea at a time.** Break down instructions into small manageable steps. For example, instead of "Brush your teeth," try "Pick up the toothbrush." When that action has been accomplished, "Squeeze the toothpaste on the bristles." When your elder has done so, "Raise the brush to your mouth." And so on.

✔ **Try not to let your anger show and control your body language.** Despite severe limitations, confused elders sense negative feelings in others. You can bet that your elder will react to your reddened face, clasped fists, and taut lips with fear, anxiety, or combativeness. She may cry or even strike out, but she surely will not cooperate if she senses your anger or frustration.

✔ **Create routines.** Oldsters who suffer from dementia tend to get upset by anything new (including places, people, and demands on them). Navigating the familiar is difficult enough. Predictable meals, activities, and bedtime rituals are comforting in a confusing world. Try to avoid changing home healthcare workers or the scheduled days at the adult daycare center.

✔ **Streamline the environment.** Get rid of clutter. Give away clothes that aren't worn regularly. A closet with lots of choices is overwhelming for a confused elder. Make the rooms bright and safe and the atmosphere calming. Remove anything that is troubling. For example, if your elder no longer recognizes his own image in the mirror and is frightened because he thinks a stranger is looking at him, cover or get rid of the mirror. On the other hand, if he enjoys talking to the reflection, keep the mirror and consider hanging a few more!

✔ **Cultivate a laissez-faire attitude about things that don't put your elder in harm's way.** Wearing mismatched clothes or clothing on top of pajamas, hoarding bottle caps, or eating mashed potatoes with her fingers won't hurt her. The cliché about choosing your battles wisely applies — in spades!

✔ **Report any sudden changes in behavior to the doctor.** The changes may be due to a treatable condition and not the dementia. For example, increased visits to the bathroom without producing anything may indicate a urinary tract infection, rather than being a sign that the older person forgot that she already urinated.

I've organized many of the behaviors seen in elders with dementia under separate sections in this chapter. Real life isn't arranged so neatly. One of your elder's behavioral symptoms may fit several categories, and the solutions for one problem may apply to quite a few different symptoms.

Aggression

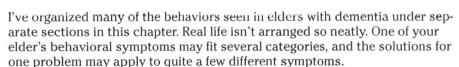

Verbal attacks (insults, curses, threats) and physical assaults (grabbing, pushing, striking, kicking, and biting) are often generated by frustration. For example, the bewildered older person is asked to do something he can't do at all — or can't do fast enough — and lashes out at his caregiver with a barrage of curses. Fear also sparks aggressive responses. A confused elder afraid of running water may turn bath time into World War II. In this case, drawing the water *before* inviting the oldster into the bathroom can greatly reduce the risk for violence.

If your elder has a tendency to strike out verbally or physically, keep the following ideas in mind:

- ✔ **Don't scold for failures.** Instead move in subtly to assist where you can. Your elder may not be able to do today what he could manage yesterday.

- ✔ **Mind your approach.** Avoid coming up to a confused older person from behind. Always approach slowly, giving one instruction at a time without rushing him.

- ✔ **Use distraction (changing the subject, offering a favorite snack or a favorite activity) to deescalate the situation.** For example, a caregiver reported that when her husband held a hammer over her head and said, "I am going to kill you," she responded with "Let's do it after lunch." He dropped the hammer and said "Okay." (This example is extreme, but you get the idea!) Call 911 and leave the house immediately if you're being attacked. Or leave first and call 911 from a neighbor's house or cell phone to protect your well-being.

- ✔ **Acknowledge your elder's anger over losing control of his life or whatever emotion seems to underlie the aggression.** Validating an upset person's feelings is often enough to take the wind out of his sails and calm him down.

- ✔ **Remove heavy and sharp objects from reach if aggression is a concern.** Securing dangerous items protects your elder from hurting himself as well.

- ✔ **Have your elder evaluated medically if the aggression persists despite your efforts to avoid it.** Angry attacks may be a consequence of pain that your elder is unable to express verbally. A simple procedure to correct, say, a painful hernia, may transform a tiger into a kitten.

Delusions

Delusions are false beliefs (sometimes paranoid in nature). For example, an older adult becomes convinced that her family has abandoned her, the person she lives with is an imposter disguised to look like her daughter, or her spouse is unfaithful. I interviewed a woman who was under the delusion that the house she lived in was not her home. Because she no longer recognized her house or anything in it, she *had* to believe it belonged to someone else.

Once formed, delusions are difficult to budge. It's best to use the following strategies when dealing with false beliefs:

- ✔ **Don't argue or try to convince your elder out of her delusion.** Such an endeavor only exhausts and frustrates you and upsets your older person.

> ✔ **Demonstrate that you take her concern seriously by responding to the emotion that's underneath.** For example, fear of abandonment may come from an awareness that she is a burden to the family. The words, "I can see that you're worried. You needn't be afraid. We love you and want to take care of you," address her fear without arguing with her.

Hallucinations

A *hallucinating* elder sees, hears, smells, tastes, or feels something that's not there. You can usually tell when an elder is hallucinating. For example, Mom may be happily picking blooms from the front yard — but no flowers are there. If the hallucinations are pleasant (seeing and hearing children at play), your older person may enjoy the experience. On the other hand, the visions may be horrifying. I can recall my dad hallucinating that the walls of his "brick" house were crashing down around him as bombs dropped from above. My wise brother beamed floodlights on the solid plaster walls of Dad's apartment, and the hallucination disappeared. Dad went to sleep peacefully, and the floodlight went back into the garage — for the moment.

The following ideas for coping with hallucinations are worth trying:

> ✔ **Reassure a frightened elder.** Hold his hand and tell him, "You're safe, I'll take care of you." If he asks whether you hear something, say, "I don't hear it, but I know you're frightened, so I will check the house to make sure that everything is okay." Frightening hallucinations often subside in the presence of another person and when the lights are turned up.

> ✔ **Ignore the hallucination if it's not upsetting to the elder.** If the fact that your elder is enjoying a drink with his old school chum (when the beer and the friend are imaginary) disturbs you, try to see the humor in the situation and realize that the event is very real to your elder.

> ✔ **Have your elder checked for kidney and bladder infections, dehydration, and intense pain, all of which can cause hallucinations.** When those problems are treated, the hallucinations will likely disappear.

Drugs to treat hallucinations sometimes help, but side effects and medication interactions can be worse than the hallucinations and increase the danger of falling. When hallucinations aren't disturbing, leave well enough alone.

Hiding things

Confused elders often hide items to protect them from being stolen. Hiding objects may make older adults feel more secure (unless, of course, they remember that they hid them but forget where).

If hiding items makes your elder less anxious, try the following strategies:

- ✔ **Provide objects for hiding (things of little value that will not be needed later).** You can replace valuable jewelry with inexpensive costume necklaces, bracelets, and earrings bought at thrift shops and garage sales.

- ✔ **Limit the number of potential hiding places by locking closets, cupboards, and unused rooms.** Outfit drawers with childproof locks, which you can purchase in hardware stores or baby stores.

- ✔ **Check wastebaskets before emptying them and clothes pockets before laundering.** Make it a habit to periodically look in the oven, trash compactor, and refrigerator, under the mattress, and between the sheets and towels in the linen closet.

- ✔ **Try to recall your loved one's favorite places for hiding gifts.** Check them regularly — especially if he likes to hide food.

- ✔ **Keep spares of important items.** Keep duplicate keys, glasses, hearing aid batteries, and medications on hand.

Hoarding

Squirreling away items and bits of food can be a harmless activity that provides the same sort of security that comes from hiding items. Some older people fear that they'll be abandoned and will need the items later. *Hoarding* (and other behaviors) may be rooted in the elder's history. For example, a woman in a nursing home was constantly hoarding pieces of bread in her room. Whenever the aides tried to take away the stale, moldy scraps, she protested bitterly. Eventually, the staff learned that the woman was a Holocaust survivor. Bread had been a valuable commodity in the death camps.

Some caregivers find that providing a place for hoarding items and thinning out the stock now and then helps keep the behavior from getting out of hand. (See the section "Hiding things," earlier in this chapter, for more ideas.)

Misidentification

Mistaking a chair or a wastebasket for a toilet is a *misidentification*. The elder sees and hears okay but interprets what he sees or hears incorrectly. (In this case, he interprets the circular form as a toilet seat.) Often, the confused oldster constructs a belief to go along with the misperception. For example, a woman hears strange sounds coming from her basement at night. The noise emanates from a tired old heater, but she interprets what she hears as coming from someone living in her basement who is throwing a wild party (the phantom boarder phenomenon).

Vision changes in the brain, which occur in about 10 percent of elders with Alzheimer's disease, contribute to misidentification. Your elder may over-reach for an object or have trouble with depth perception or seeing objects that are in motion or in low light. The boundaries between light and dark may blur, leading to misinterpretations. Even with nondemented elders, the ability to discriminate differences in shades of color often declines in late life.

The following ideas may reduce the likelihood of misidentifications:

✔ **Don't contradict the interpretation.** Explain it without humiliating the elder. For example, say, "There is a lot of noise in the basement, but it's coming from the heater, not from a party."

✔ **Make misinterpreted objects easier to see.** Remember the man who urinated into wastebaskets and chairs? Replacing his pale toilet seat with a brightly colored one may help him identify the correct place to relieve himself.

✔ **Place signs and pictures on or near items that are frequently misidentified.** In my example, hanging a picture of a toilet or a sign that says "toilet" on the bathroom door may help. For that matter, the caregiver can try hanging a sign on the wastebasket that says, "This is not a toilet."

Negativity

Confused elders often complain, stubbornly resist, and downright refuse when you try to get them to cooperate with your caregiving.

Because every situation and every confused person is different, you'll have to experiment with the following suggestions to discover what works for you:

✔ Develop consistent routines, scheduling the activities (including bathing, dressing, and exercising) to match your elder's best times of day.

✔ Avoid arguing. Confrontation with a confused elder usually fails and may result in defensiveness, agitation, and even violent behavior.

✔ Back off. Try again later with another approach (perhaps a gentler or firmer manner, with different words). If all else fails, postpone what you're trying to get done or allow someone else to try.

✔ Simplify your instructions. Too many demands at once can overwhelm your elder, causing more resistance and defensiveness.

✔ Try announcing the next activity in advance. Knowing what's going to happen next may lead to greater cooperation (or increased anxiety). You won't know until you try.

✔ Offer fewer opportunities for negativity. Avoid questions that can be answered yes or no, such as, "Do you want your lunch now?" You may have less negativity with "It's time for lunch" or, better yet, "Let's have our salami sandwiches," or "After lunch we'll [fill in with a favorite activity]."

✔ Be sympathetic. Say things like "I know it makes you angry when you have to put a heavy coat on." Or, for the constant complainer, "Yes, life can be difficult."

Pacing, restlessness, and agitation

It's painful to observe your loved one pacing from room to room for hours on end, knowing that he's exhausting himself. Boredom, hunger, thirst, medication, the discomfort of a noisy, chaotic, or confusing environment, or the need to use the bathroom can trigger pacing, restlessness, and agitation of any sort. It can also simply be related to the changes in the brain. Introducing the following ideas may keep your elder from wearing himself out:

✔ Eliminate beverages that contain caffeine from your elder's diet.

✔ Give your older person tasks to do that instill a sense of purpose and accomplishment (sorting buttons or screws and bolts, or folding clothes).

✔ Establish a regular exercise program to minimize restlessness.

✔ Keep the environment quiet and calm. Lots of people in a room, clutter, and noise (even clinking glasses) can trigger agitation.

✔ Install a night light. Extra light often reduces the confusion that may trigger nighttime agitation. (On the other hand, a dark bedroom sometimes decreases nighttime restlessness for some confused older people.)

✔ Accept that you may not be able to stop the pacing. If that's the case, supply your oldster with supportive nonslip shoes, provide a secure area to walk in, and check his feet regularly for swelling, blisters, or bruises.

✔ Offer frequent snacks and fluids to avoid weight loss and dehydration.

Paranoia, suspiciousness and jealousy

Paranoia is especially common in the early stages of Alzheimer's disease. Like delusions, paranoia, suspiciousness, and jealousy stem from the elder's efforts to make sense of an increasingly confusing world. For example, an older adult who can't follow a conversation may assume that others are plotting against

Driving Miss Daisy: Keeping your elder calm and collected

You need a little planning and a lot of patience to get confused elders where they need to go. Chauffeuring a restless or bewildered senior can be extremely taxing. The following tips can help make the drive safer and more enjoyable for you and your older person:

✔ Have the elder use the bathroom before getting into the car. Giving step-by-step simple instructions for getting into the car saves time in the long run, because you avoid agitation and resistance. (See Chapter 14 for more tips about driving with seniors.)

✔ Make the inside of the car as comfortable as possible. Get rid of clutter, adjust the temperature, and reduce glare on bright days — or bring sunglasses.

✔ Seat your oldster in the rear passenger-side seat. This position is the safest, because it makes it less possible for an upset elder to grab the steering wheel or you. It also makes it easier for you to check on him or her without turning around.

✔ Calm your elder by playing relaxing music or a tape of grandchildren singing. A book or a snack can prevent unrest.

✔ Use the child-safety door locks if you have them. These locks keep the back doors from being opened from inside.

---

her. Paranoid seniors frequently believe that they're in mortal danger ("People are out to get me") or that they've been robbed ("My daughter has taken all my money").

He laughs about it now, but it wasn't so funny when Ted, a home healthcare worker, took his elderly client for their weekly Sunday dinner at a local Chinese restaurant. The elderly woman excused herself to use the bathroom. Instead, she went to the restaurant manager and told him that she had been kidnapped by the man at the table. The manager called the police, and it was some time before everything was sorted out.

The following tips may help you cope with paranoia:

✔ Remind family members and workers not to take the accusations personally.

✔ Respond to the feeling behind the paranoia. You might say, "It's frightening when you find your purse missing."

✔ Assist in looking for the missing object. Remember to check those favorite hiding places.

✔ Before hiring a personal aide or any worker, remove all valuables from your elder's home. This action protects the aide from being accused of stealing.

Repetitive questions

At some point during your elder's illness she may repeat the same questions over and over again. The repetitions can drive you batty. Your elder is trying hard to remember and may be frustrated or anxious about being unable to recall the important information.

If you possess a vast reservoir of patience, you'll manage this behavior very well, but if you're like most folks, you'll reach your limits fairly quickly. The following tips may help remedy the situation.

- ✔ **Don't remind your age-advantaged person that she asked that question ten times, and it was answered ten times.** It doesn't help — and only causes her emotional pain.

- ✔ **Try ignoring the question, changing the subject, or falling back on that old standby, distraction.** Give her tasks that she can complete, such as sorting socks or dusting furniture.

- ✔ **Put up signs — for example, "The dentist appointment is at 2:30" or "Sally will be here at 6 p.m."**

- ✔ **Write answers on a card and give it to your elder.** Direct her to look at the card before asking the question. If she's asking about an appointment date or time, mark that information on a calendar that she can carry around.

- ✔ **Wait until just prior to an upcoming event to discuss it.** This delay cuts down the time available for questioning.

Screaming, yelling

Screaming, yelling, and loud groans are among the most difficult behaviors to live with. They upset everyone else in the house and disturb the neighbors. In nursing homes, these outbursts lower staff morale and frustrate elderly residents and their family. Your elder may not even be aware that she's yelling or calling out words like "Help me, help me." When you talk to her, she stops and may even tell you that she's fine.

The loud vocalizations may stop on their own accord, but until then, you may want to try the following strategies:

- ✔ Have a regular schedule for meals, snacks, and toileting to eliminate screaming and yelling resulting from hunger, thirst, bathroom needs, or soiled diapers.

- ✔ Distract your screamer with music, videotapes of familiar faces, and favorite television programs.

✔ Obtain a complete medical and psychiatric evaluation to uncover treatable depression or physical distress. Medications may be considered in severe cases.

✔ Avoid sedatives that put your elder into a stupor-like condition. Everyone else does better — but at the cost of a greatly reduced quality of life for your loved one.

✔ Try arranging for extra help so that someone will always be around to talk to her, hold her hand, and be involved with her. In many cases, the yelling stops when constant companionship and interaction occur.

Sexually inappropriate behavior

Making provocative or tasteless sexual comments, touching people in sexual ways, disrobing, masturbating in public, and making inappropriate sexual advances are examples of a particularly distressing symptom that sometimes results from a dementing illness. Like many of the other behaviors in this chapter, you can manage sexually inappropriate behavior. Unfortunately, this behavior usually triggers more embarrassment and shock than most of the others.

Sexual disinhibition is the term that applies to the lack of impulse control and poor judgment and poor insight that fuel the inappropriate sexual behavior. Often the elder desires physical intimacy but can't carry out the usual social rules regarding proper sexual conduct. He may have also forgotten that he's married. Well spouses generally lose sexual interest in their partners as the disease progresses.

On the other hand, the behaviors may not be sexual at all. Your elder may disrobe because he's too warm, is tired, or wants to go to bed. Masturbation may be a response to boredom rather than a need for sexual stimulation.

Experts advise the following tactics to cope with inappropriate sexual behaviors:

✔ **Distract your elder and remove him from the scene without scolding, berating, or flustering.** (If you can treat the incident lightly, do so.) If he's masturbating at a family gathering, take him to his bedroom or give him something to occupy his hands (playing cards, shuffling photos).

✔ **Try touching your elder more often.** He may be suffering from "skin hunger." (See Chapter 7 for more about the need for skin contact.) If hugs or backrubs are sexually stimulating, switch to rubbing cream on his hands.

✔ **Outfit him in hard-to-open clothing.** Elders who expose themselves do better in one-piece outfits like overalls or jumpers that fasten in the back. You may even try turning your elder's pants backwards so that the fasteners are in the back, but remember to take him to the bathroom and assist with his clothing.

Shadowing

When someone follows you around the house, depends on you for every activity, and mirrors your moods and expressions, you can get frazzled. These activities make the elder feel more secure, especially if she's anxious or fearful of abandonment. Such clinging may also be the consequence of fatigue, not knowing what else to do, or insufficient sleep.

The following ideas may help:

- ✔ Present your elder with a stuffed animal or doll. Some, but not all, confused elders find cuddly objects comforting. If your elder rejects your gift, don't push it.
- ✔ Get a pet. When a dog or cat isn't feasible, try fish or birds. (They require less care but may have a calming effect.)
- ✔ Supply an engrossing activity that involves winding, shelling, sorting, lacing, stringing, or matching.

You need to have some privacy, if only in the bathroom. If you can trust your elder to be alone while you go to the bathroom, lock the door and set a timer. Just make sure that you tell her you'll be back out when the timer goes off.

Sleeplessness

Sleeplessness is a common feature of Alzheimer's disease. (See more about managing this problem in Chapter 5.) Neurological changes in the elder's internal time clock may alter sleep patterns — your elder may have difficulty falling asleep or may be up and ready to go in the wee hours of the morning.

The following suggestions may make a difference:

- ✔ Don't stimulate your elder by telling him about plans for tomorrow.
- ✔ Avoid power struggles. For example, if your elder resists getting into bedclothes, a cotton sweatsuit that she can wear during the day and sleep in at night may solve the problem.
- ✔ Don't be rigid about where he sleeps. Your older person may prefer sleeping in his recliner or on the couch and may get a better night's sleep that way.

Sundowning

The cause of *sundowning* (increased confusion in late afternoon and early evening) is still a mystery. Possibilities are fatigue, less light, and the presence of more shadows, which aggravates confusion. In institutions, noise and activity increases as the staff members change shifts. Sometimes a brief afternoon nap helps. Or try turning up the lights. (See Chapters 2 and 12 for ideas about keeping your elder safe during this period of heightened confusion.)

Wandering

Wandering seems like aimless walking about with no purpose, but in the case of confused elders, the person often has a goal — their caregivers just don't know what it is. Discovering the purpose helps change the behavior. For example, the older person may wander off to look for an imagined lost puppy.

A trigger in the environment may act like a switch, turning on the wandering behavior. For example, seeing a hat and coat hanging on a hook near a doorway may send your elder out the door, or he may follow someone who is leaving. Elders who no longer recognize the people they're with may take off to search for familiar faces. A sense of responsibility to go to work or care for a child may drive the wandering — even though the child is now an adult. Hunger, boredom, the need to use the bathroom, or discomfort from a hot or cold room may trigger the behavior.

Many of the ideas in this chapter for dealing with other problematic behaviors (for example, pacing) may be helpful in reducing wandering as well. The following solutions may also help curb this sometime dangerous behavior:

- ✔ Install locks that require keys to unlock them from the inside as well as the outside, or install deadbolts or chains out of reach of the elder. (Never leave an elder alone when using these measures.)

  Make sure that someone who can unlock these devices in order to provide quick exit in case of emergency remains in the home.

- ✔ Hang signs on the exit doors that say "Stop" or "Do Not Enter."

- ✔ Paint a two-foot black threshold in front of the door. Elders may interpret the area to be a hole that can't be crossed.

- ✔ Place childproof devices over doorknobs so that they won't turn.

- ✔ Inform neighbors of the wandering and give them your telephone number so that they can call you if they spot your loved one.

- ✔ Keep yards secure with fences and locked gates. (Make sure that your elder can't scale the wall.)

✔ Stop your loved one as he is about to leave and ask him where he's going. Instead of saying, "No, you can't go" distract him with discussion about the place or people he is seeking.

Wanderers usually follow the direction of their dominant hand. Left-handers go left, right-handers go right.

The Safe Return program helps to reunite lost elders with their families. Registered elders receive an identification bracelet or necklace, a wallet I.D. card, and I.D. clothing labels. When an elder is reported missing, Safe Return faxes the older adult's vital information and photograph to law-enforcement agencies and provides family support while police conduct the search. Anyone who finds the missing elder can call the Safe Return number found on the identification item on the senior. The responding operator alerts the family that their loved one has been located. The one-time fee for this program is $40. To register your older person, contact the Alzheimer's Association (888-572-8566) or register online (www.alz.org). Click Programs and Services and then click the line for the Safe Return registration form.

Consumer Medhelp, Inc., sells a variety of useful tools for dealing with wanderers. Products include alarms that are placed between the box spring and mattress and that go off when a person leaves the bed, pressure-sensitive mat alarms that can be placed anywhere in the home, door contact alarms that sound when a door is opened, chair-leaving alarms, and personal alarms that sound when the wearer is out of range. Call 800-556-7117 to ask about the products or visit online (www.consumermedhelp.com).

Understanding Your Elder's Emotions

The behaviors discussed in this chapter are the result of impaired brain function — the brain is just not working right! Emotions (including anxiety, fear, anger, and sadness) also play a role in how your elder acts, and they help shape the quality of your loved one's final years.

Anxiety

Confused seniors worry about things that may happen (real and imagined). They often fret needlessly about work and family responsibilities that they no longer have. Worries about money and being away from home top the list, even though they may never have expressed these concerns before their illness. Confused elders often become anxious when they're left alone, even when the caregiver is in the next room. Spouses routinely feel guilty when they run out to the market for an hour, because when they return the elder looks forlorn and may accuse them of being gone for hours.

The best approach is to find out what's worrying your elder and try to calm her fears. Reassurance ("It will be okay, I'll take care of you") can't be heard often enough. If possible, eliminate or reduce the use of caffeinated beverages or drugs that contain stimulants. Many of the suggestions given in this chapter are designed to calm down, or at least distract, elders from their worries. Some of them may help. You should discuss anti-anxiety drugs with your doctor if the problem is severe — but, once again, the side effects may cause other problems. (See Chapter 16 for more information about anxiety.)

Catastrophic reactions

A *catastrophic reaction* is a sudden fit of rage that usually comes in response to stress or an overstimulating environment.

Once the out-of-control older person starts cursing, shouting, threatening violence, hitting, biting, or kicking his caregiver, it's hard to stop him.

Avoid catastrophic reactions by following these suggestions:

- ✔ **Give one direction at a time.** Multiple directions such as "Finish your sandwich, wipe your face, put the dishes in the sink, and wait for me in the living room," delivered in a staccato voice, can initiate a rage reaction.

- ✔ **Never rush your elder.** Words like "Hurry up, we'll be late" create anxiety and can tip the confused elder into an emotional frenzy. Allow plenty of extra time to get ready for appointments.

- ✔ **Don't force your elder to participate in an activity that he's resisting.**

- ✔ **Protect your confused loved one from fatigue, which puts him at high risk for losing control.**

Restraining or criticizing his behavior only makes a catastrophic reaction worse. Try backing off, speaking in a soothing empathic voice, and using distraction. In the midst of a catastrophic reaction, be careful not to further upset the elder with any sudden movements he may consider threatening and that may escalate the episode.

Depression

Depression is common among elders with dementing illnesses, especially early in the illness when the elder is painfully aware of his losses. Later on, particularly with an Alzheimer's patient, it becomes increasing difficult for your doctor to diagnose depression because the elder's ability to describe how she is feeling declines. To complicate the diagnosis, some of the symptoms of depression (apathy, sleeplessness, loss of appetite, forgetfulness, and even the inability to concentrate) are also found in dementia. Depressed elders lose interest in previously pleasurable activities, are often tearful, and look sad. They may be irritable or overly sensitive and may experience insomnia or early-morning awakening.

Depression needs to be reported to your elder's primary care physician for evaluation and treatment. Words like "I wish I were dead" or "You'd be better off if I was dead" reveal suicidal thoughts. In my view, they should be treated as a medical emergency. (See Chapter 15 for more information about depressed elderly.)

Part V
Making the Final Years Golden

EINSTEIN–THE LAST YEARS

"Well, Dear, maybe you're just not the one to have an end–of–life conversation with your Uncle Albert."

In this part . . .

If a genie granted your frail elder one wish, what would he wish for? Seeing his first love one more time? Knowing that his personal treasures will be loved and cared for? Not being a financial burden to his family? Making peace with his Maker? Dying painfree, with loved ones near? I wrote the chapters in this part with these and similar wishes in mind.

Chapter 19

When "The Apple of Your Eye" Needs a Peer

· ·

In This Chapter

▶ Locating long-lost friends

▶ Helping your elder maintain an old friendship

▶ Nurturing new relationships

▶ Meeting other older adults online

· ·

As the years go by, it gets harder and harder for your elder to maintain his or her friendships. Friends move away to live with their children or enter assisted living arrangements or nursing homes. Poor health, disability, and lack of transportation make getting together nearly impossible. And, of course, old friends pass away.

This chapter is about maintaining old friendships, starting new ones, and reuniting with long-lost friends.

Long-Lost Friends

Best friends Sophie and Miriam quit school at 16. Sophia married so that her family would have one less mouth to feed. Miriam got a job in a factory to help support her family.

Then a terrible thing happened. Miriam's father died in an explosion at a construction site. The newspapers said it was arson and that he and another man "were caught in their own firetrap." Miriam's little brother was born three months later. Shortly afterward, Miriam's family disappeared without leaving a forwarding address with anyone. Rumor was that welfare workers were trying to take the new baby away. Someone else said that they couldn't pay their rent.

Locating childhood friends is easy when you know how

If you have access to the Internet, you can search for long-lost friends yourself. But, if you have more money than time (or little patience), you can hire a private investigator. Be aware, though, that private investigators these days start their searches on the Internet.

Good Web sites to try are `www.people.yahoo.com`, and `www.switchboard.com`. Should attempts come up blank, don't lose heart. Try again. The following strategies may make the difference between a successful hunt and a disappointing one:

✔ Include all possible spellings and variations of a name (Thomas S. Dodd can be listed as T. S. Dodd, T. Siegfried Dodd, or even Thomas Siegfried).

✔ Try nicknames (Thomas Dodd can be listed as Tom Dodd or Tommy Dodd).

✔ When correct spellings don't work, key in misspellings and typographical errors (Thomas Dodd can be Thom Dodd, Thomas Dod, or even ThomasDodd).

✔ Try to recall who a woman friend may have married when her maiden name doesn't work. (The majority of older women changed their names when they married.)

✔ Try different Web sites. Lots of online directories and databases are inaccurate or incomplete.

Sophie, now 86-years-old and ailing, spoke of her girlhood friend often, wondering what happened to her and whether she was still alive. On a whim, Sophie's daughter plugged Miriam's family name into a few online directories. Lo and behold, Miriam lived less than 50 miles away. A reunion was arranged. The two elderly women picked up right where they had left off 70 years earlier. Now they speak regularly by phone and get together every three or four months.

A reunion with a long-lost friend may do wonders for your older person. Searching for and finding people today is relatively easy — unless they don't want to be found.

Locating Lost Family Members and Friends (Betterway Books) by Kathleen W. Hinckley tells how to obtain the documents and out-of-date telephone directories that may be the keys to finding your elder's long-lost friend.

Old Friends

Jill is the primary caregiver for her mother, Estelle, who is a retired schoolteacher. After Estelle's stroke and the depression that followed, the older woman's social world shrunk. When Jill urged Estelle to call up one of her old schoolteacher friends, Estelle promised she would — but never did.

Jill watched her Mother's world get smaller and smaller. Finally, she decided to intervene by throwing a tea party — with English scones, Devonshire cream, jam, and little finger sandwiches. She kept the work manageable by buying the scones at the local bakery and purchasing the cream and jam at the supermarket. Putting the finger sandwiches together was a project she and her Mom easily tackled. The really clever part was that the invitations (sent to five of Mom's old friends) asked them each to bring a young woman (a daughter, a niece, or young friend) with them to the mother and "daughter" tea party.

The older women loved the invitation because it allowed them to extend an invitation to a young woman (who in most cases provided transportation). The event was unusual and elegant — Jill's husband volunteered to wear white gloves while he served the sandwiches and cakes. The party broke the ice, as Jill hoped it would! After the successful tea party, Estelle had no problem initiating more contact with her old friends.

To help your elder stay in contact with old friends, try some of these suggestions:

- ✔ **Help organize monthly get-togethers (for example, the first Tuesday afternoon of every month is for playing canasta).** You'll have an easier time arranging transportation when you know your needs well in advance.
- ✔ **Initiate get-togethers by including your elder's friend when you plan an outing.** (See Chapter 14 for ideas on getting out and about.)
- ✔ **Include an old friend in family celebrations.** When transportation is a problem, arrange to have someone pick the old friend up — you'd do the same for a beloved uncle. An old friend is just as important.

New Friends

A few elderly men and women have said to me, "Why should I make new friends when chances are they'll get sick and die?" Many elders who feel this way are still in the throes of grief for dear ones they have lost. If your elder expresses a similar thought, he isn't ready for new relationships until his past losses are fully mourned. (See Chapter 15 for more information about depression and how to help elders grieve.)

You don't need more work to do, but time spent helping your elder develop a new friendship has the potential to enhance the quality of your elder's life

Six reasons why your elder needs a friend

Decades of research show that friends are "good medicine." The following explains the reasons why:

✔ **A friend makes an excellent audience for an old person's reminisce.** Elders reminisce about their past experiences and relationships, which help them to come to terms with their lives. Sharing such a review with friends is often easier than sharing it with family members who often have a vested interest in denying the oldster's version of the past or in avoiding sensitive issues. (See Chapter 15 for more information on the importance of reminiscing.)

✔ **A friend supplies the fun that's so important to a sense of well-being.** Family members (often motivated by feelings of obligation) provide caregiving and financial assistance. Friends just want to have a good time.

✔ **An old friend helps an elderly person maintain a sense of continuity.** When friends who have known each other for decades look at each other's faces, they don't see old people. They see each other as they were when they met (for example, as young mothers who were introduced at a PTA meeting, coworkers who worked alongside each other, and soldiers who served together).

✔ **Having a friend forces an older person to be less self-absorbed and more altruistic.** Friendship compels an older person to shift his attention from his own worries and preoccupations to the concerns of his friend. Friends exchange favors, advice, information, and emotional support and assistance.

✔ **A new friend provides an opportunity to try new ways of being.** There's no need to maintain an old image with a new friend — unless you want to. Because there's no common past to draw on, a new relationship may be more exciting than an old one.

✔ **Having a friend to confide in helps an older person cope more effectively with problems.** Everyday hassles don't seem so bad when you have someone to commiserate with. In addition, friends offer encouragement, ideas for problem-solving, and often a fresh perspective on the problem.

sixfold. (Read the sidebar "Six reasons why your elder needs a friend" in this chapter.) The same suggestions I made to stay in contact with old friends can also apply to maintaining contact with new friends.

Also, your age-advantaged person needs to go where she can find other older adults — church and temple senior citizen groups, volunteer organizations, adult education classes, senior centers, and adult daycare centers. The hook to getting her there may be learning something new, helping other people, returning to a hobby, or just keeping busy. Once your elder has gotten involved, the likelihood of becoming friends with another oldster who has the same interests increases.

Elders who suffer from dementia eventually lose their language skills. So, when a confused elder returns from the adult daycare center and reports, "I ate lunch with Joe [her departed husband] today," it may simply be that she has substituted the name of someone dear for the words "my friend."

Phone Partners, Pen Pals, and E-Mail Buddies

Physical and mental illness, disability, and lack of transportation get in the way of sustaining friendships. But the very worst obstacle is relocation (moving in with an adult child or entering a facility far from home). When your elder and her friend are parted in this way, encourage your elder to stay in touch by phone. You can put the friend's telephone number on speed-dial to make it easier to call. Shop around for a long-distance carrier with a good deal so that your elder doesn't have to be concerned about cost.

Encourage letter-writing by addressing stamped envelopes and providing paper and pen. If your elder no longer can write, offer to write while he or she dictates. Getting your elder online will enlarge his shrinking world. E-mail makes communicating with friends across the country or across the ocean easy and cheap. If your elder's friends do not communicate by e-mail, don't worry — their children and grandchildren surely do!

Online Communities

Many people use the computer to reach out to others, creating their own little communities. They may be lonely, seeking information, or they may simply want to compare notes with people who are experiencing the same life difficulties as they are.

Chat rooms

Many elders (and some young folks) don't have a computer and don't want one. They're quite happy not to have to deal with the usual frustrations that come with these newfangled devices. But the older adults who do have computers, know how to get online, can type quickly, and can recognize scams and come-ons may want to experiment with *chat rooms.*

Chat room participants are on their computers at the same time, conversing "live," using the keyboard to type comments, questions, and answers. Chat room meetings on specific topics are usually scheduled and announced ahead of time. For example, in Military Chat, veterans and active military personnel reminisce about the old days, loyal buddies, and current military agendas. Examples of scheduled chats are wide-ranging (including everything from Grandchildren to Managing Chronic Pain). Chat rooms can be a little intimidating in the same way that walking into a room full of strangers engaged in a conversation can be. Chat room conversations move fast, and sometimes it seems that everyone is talking at once. The Web sites are designed to help beginners get comfortable and understand online etiquette before they enter a chat room.

You can find a good chat Web site for senior citizens by visiting `www.thirdage.com` and clicking Chat. Membership is free.

Discussions boards

Participants in *discussion boards* (also called message boards) are on their computers at different times. When an individual enters a discussion board site, various comments or questions contributed by other participants appear on the monitor. The individual can respond to those messages or post her own thoughts or questions (which others can respond to later). For example, an elder woman wrote about her frustration. She had been widowed for over a year, but she still spent much of her time crying and found it difficult to socialize. She expressed her fear of being a burden to her family. The next day, three widows posted their responses. One had suggestions. Another offered encouragement, and the third shared a similar story. Discussion boards are easier for newcomers to manage than live chat rooms because they can take their time composing what they want to say.

AARP hosts a discussion board Visit `www.AARP.org/community`. Clicking Message Boards takes you to a list of discussion categories. Clicking the category Health and Wellness takes you to discussions on caregiving. Clicking Grief and Loss takes you to a discussion on coping with your grief.

Eldercare Online (`www.ec-online.net`) has a caregiver support network that includes live chat rooms and the eldercare Forum (a discussion board where you can post your questions, give answers to others questions, request information, and share experiences).

Caregivers need friends, too!

One of the occupational hazards of caregiving is social isolation — or, in plain words, giving up your friends. You're so busy rushing to your loved one's home to clean up, cook meals, chauffeur him to appointments, and respond to emergencies that you have no time left to spend with friends. Or you've abandoned your social life because all your free time is spent at the nursing home. Your elder has grown to expect your visits, and your constant presence improves the quality of care. Or, after daily caregiving duties and family responsibilities are taken care of, you're too pooped to see friends.

Caregivers need friends for the same reasons that elders need friends. Friends enhance your coping abilities with their listening, understanding, and advice. Time spent with a friend produces a few laughs (or a good cry) and precious distraction from your caregiving burdens. Consider a night out with the guys or gals to be a much-needed mini-vacation.

Keep up your phone contacts. Schedule a regular lunch or coffee date with your best friend. Let your elder know in advance that you'll be going out with a friend on Wednesday so that you'll see her again on Thursday. Or, when necessary, get someone to stay with your elder. (Call on one of those folks who said, "Let me know if there's anything I can do to help.") A paid sitter may seem like an unnecessary extravagance, but it's vital to your continued well-being.

Chapter 20

Keeping Your Elder at the Helm

· ·

In This Chapter

▶ Helping your elder maintain a sense of control

▶ Understanding estate planning

▶ Passing on treasures while alive

· ·

*J*oshua likes to say, "I'm not old, I'm ancient!" He doesn't mind being 95. He doesn't even mind dying. He says that when the Lord calls him, he'll gladly go. What Joshua does mind (and fear) is losing control. He refuses to move into his son's home or a nursing home because he likes being his own boss — eating supper whenever he wants, taking a stroll outside without someone asking him how far he's going and warning him about cracked pavements, stray dogs, and the dangers of a strong wind. Most of all, he likes to leave his things lying around until he needs them and not worrying about having to lock them up in some dang nightstand in an old folks' home. Joshua protests, "If I can't be my own boss, I surely will kick the bucket." He may be right.

This chapter demonstrates how planning ahead can help your elder remain "captain of his own ship," allowing him to have a say in critical medical decisions and in the management of his financial affairs (even if he is incapacitated), as well as in determining what happens to his life's belongings after he dies.

Promoting Choice

Studies show that when elders are allowed (and encouraged) to control their environments (including rearranging the furniture in their nursing home rooms and determining when and if they want to see a movie), they're healthier, happier and more alert — and, yes, live longer than oldsters who have little or no choice or control over their own lives.

The end of life is a time when many elders must relinquish some control, but it's also a period when elders can assert their most important wishes — wishes that extend beyond their lifetimes.

You can increase your elder's personal sense of control with the following suggestions:

✔ **Don't take over your older person's responsibilities because it's more efficient that way (and he doesn't appear to mind).** For example, Sandy makes her father's appointments and then tells her dad about it. Because Dad no longer drives and depends on Sandy to take him places, he keeps his lips zipped. Secretly, he misses making his own schedule. If Sandy consulted with her father about his preferences and her availability before setting up appointments, Dad would feel a lot more in control of his life.

✔ **Be willing to trade a little safety for more autonomy.** In other words, don't push your elder into assisted living or nursing care prematurely. Sure, you'd get peace of mind knowing that people are there to watch over her, but her ability to govern her own life would diminish. (See Chapter 12 for ways to create a safe environment for a live-alone elder.)

✔ **Take advantage of assistive devices.** For example, Agnes's increasing difficulty with walking narrows her world. A cane, wheelchair, walker, or a strength-building exercise program can not only get her moving, it can give her a heightened sense of control. (See Chapter 12 for more about assistive devices.)

✔ **Understand that oldsters who can no longer make major decisions about things like finances can still make or contribute to other important decisions.** For example, Edna can't tell you the year she was born, but she can certainly voice her opinion about which of three nursing homes she likes best. Confused seniors can often participate in decision-making better at one time of a day than another. (See Chapter 18 about the phenomenon called sundowning.)

Making Last Wishes Come True with Estate Planning

Don't be put off by the term *estate planning*. I admit that it sounds like it belongs to the world of the well-heeled, but it doesn't. As long as you own something (including your home, what is in it, a car, clothes, objects of monetary and sentimental value, savings, and insurance policies), you have an estate. Creating an estate plan allows your elder to pass on the contents of his estate with a minimum of fuss and expense to the heirs — it's that simple.

An estate plan may include a living trust, a will, and durable powers of attorney for healthcare and finances. These legal documents allow your elder to state how and to whom he wants his belongings to be distributed, how he wants to be treated medically should he be unable to express those wishes himself, and who should manage his financial affairs if he can no longer do it himself.

It may never have occurred to your elder that he has an estate to protect or make decisions about. If he resists the notion of estate planning, explain that you don't want to pry into his private affairs, but planning ahead may ensure that his wishes are carried out, that he can save his heirs the expense and delay of probate, and that his assets may be protected from being shrunk by inheritance taxes. (See Chapter 23 for more information about probate.)

Consultation with an attorney who specializes in elder law or estate planning makes sense. Laws change all the time, and they vary from state to state. It takes experience and expertise to deliver a plan that meets an elderly client's needs. Most states have a Legal Services Department with a Division of Elder Law. These departments often provide legal services or a sliding scale. You can find your state's program by calling the court system in your state.

You can locate an elder law attorney in your area, get definitions of elder law terms, and obtain loads of other useful legal information (including information on estate planning) by visiting www.elderlawanswers.com.

AARP provides a list of attorneys screened by AARP who offer free and reduced-fee legal services. Call 800-424-3410 or go online to www.aarp.org/lsn.

Estate planning is yet another area for scam artists. Watch out for unscrupulous businesses that provide "free" estate planning services only to gain access to an elder's financial information. Beware of advertised do-it-yourself living trust kits. Cookie-cutter approaches are ineffectual and may do more harm than good.

You don't want to place every document in a safe deposit box because access to certain papers needed at the time of an elder's death may not be allowed to family members until much later. (See Chapter 23 for information about getting into safe deposit boxes.) Consider keeping a set of copies at the elder's home or in the possession of a person designated to serve as executor after the elder's death.

The Beneficiary Book: A Family Information Organizer is a nifty product to document your elder's preferences, wishes, and desires. The $29.95 version consists of a fill-in-the-pages three-ring binder that helps your elder express his wishes in every conceivable situation — from how he would like to be remembered to how he would like his pets cared for. A software version at $49.95 also includes a binder. In this model, information is filled in on the computer and printed. Call 800-222-9125 to order, write to Active Insights, P.O. Box 500028, San Diego, CA 92150, or visit online (www.active-insights.com).

Living trusts

One way a senior can protect assets from probate delay and expense (and perhaps from inheritance taxes) is to have a living trust drawn up. In short,

My elder's important papers

Gathering as much information as possible now (including account numbers and locations of stored documents) when things are relatively calm is far better than doing it later under pressure or in the midst of emotional distress. The following documents are required to create an estate plan, deal with medical emergencies, and settle final affairs:

Basic documents

Birth certificate

Divorce decrees

Military discharge papers

Social Security card

Spouse's death certificate

Bank safe deposit box and key

Spouse's will (original and copies)

Power of attorney for finances

Trusts

Certificate for cemetery plot

Recent income tax returns

Marriage certificate

Adoption papers

Citizenship/ naturalization papers

Passport or number

Safe location and combination

Will (original and copies)

Power of attorney for health-care decisions

Burial and cremation policy

Credit card information

Irreplaceable receipts for tax deductions

Assets

Checking account

Deferred compensation

Bond and stock certificates

401(k) plans

Keogh plans

Promissory notes owned

Debts owed to elder

Royalties

Judgments

Military retirement benefits

Savings accounts

Property owned in copartnerships

Mutual fund shares

IRAs

Mortgages owned

Contracts to sell real estate owned

Amounts due from claims

Annuities

Pension plans

Profit-sharing plans

Insurance

Life insurance policies

Homeowner's insurance policy

Liability insurance policy

Health/accident insurance policies

Disability insurance policy

Car insurance policy

Renter's insurance policy

Umbrella insurance policy

Long-term care insurance policy

Valuables insurance policies (art, jewelry)

Automobiles/Boats

Titles

Service records

Real estate

Real estate deeds

Vacation home or timeshare

Rents owed to elder

Real estate mortgages outstanding

Household inventory

List of stored and loaned items

Easements/Rights-of-way

Loans

Bank loans

Automobile loans and leases

Personal loans

Installment loans

Credit union loans

Finance company loans

Contacts (include names, addresses, phone numbers)

Doctors

Tax advisor

Stockbroker

Financial planner

Plumber

Electrician

Alarm company

Attorneys

Accountant

Clergy

Professional/social organizations

Maintenance people (cleaning, lawn-mowing, snow removal)

the elder transfers her property into an entity (called a *trust*) while she's alive. Once done, the property then belongs to the trust, not the elder — but don't worry, the elder can still control it and change the terms anytime she likes. When the older person dies, the property goes from the trust to the beneficiaries without any court involvement. The person creating the trust is the *settlor.* The person who manages the trust is called the *trustee.*

For example, Mrs. Smith can set up a trust, call it the Smith Family Trust, and act as her own trustee and manage the assets — or she can designate someone else to manage the trust for her. It's called a living trust because it's created when the settlor, Mrs. Smith, is alive. In the event that Mrs. Smith dies or is incapacitated, the trust provides for an alternate trustee who can be an individual, a bank, or a financial institution. In my example, Mrs. Smith's daughter is named as alternate trustee to manage the trust. The daughter (now the *successor trustee*) safeguards the trust assets and income and transfers the property to the beneficiaries named in the trust by Mrs. Smith according to the terms of the trust. No court supervision or probate is required, so the distribution of assets is generally faster and less costly than the distribution would be if there were no living trust and the assets were written into a standard will (which has to go through probate).

Although a living trust can substitute for a will (if every single asset is transferred into the living trust during the settlor's lifetime), most of the time, a *pour-over will* is also drawn up. A *pour-over* will ensures that at the time of death, any property that was not in the living trust is poured over into the trust.

Living trusts are good for some people but not for everybody. The best plan is to explore options with an experienced and licensed estate planning attorney or financial advisor. Generally, state law requires that an attorney draft any kind of trust.

Wills

In the absence of a *will* (a legal declaration of how and to whom a person wishes his or her possessions to be disposed of after death), state laws determine what happens to your elder's assets and belongings. If there are no relatives, the property may end up in the state coffers. Surely that piece of information will persuade your elder that a will or some other estate document, such as a living trust, is a necessity.

Many states, but not all, accept handwritten wills as long as they're signed and dated, but be aware that handwritten wills are more vulnerable to lawsuits. An attorney may charge only a few hundred dollars to prepare a simple will. You don't need a will notarized, but having notarized witnessed statements helps later if the will is challenged as it goes through probate — as all wills must. Place the original will in a safe deposit box, with copies in other safe places. Have a family member or trusted friend and an attorney hold a copy.

Partnership for Caring can provide you with state-specific forms for wills. If you order by telephone (800-989-9455), you pay a $10 fee (credit card okay). Get the materials for free by downloading them from the group's Web site at www.partnershipforcaring.org.

Often personal belongings (also called nontitled property) that have little monetary worth but hold great meaning for family members and friends cause the most problems. A phrase in a will such as "Divide my personal possessions equally among my children" seems fair at first glance, but it's worthless if Susie has adored the old English candlesticks since she was 9 and her brother says he wants them. Urge your elder to be as precise as possible in his will to avoid family eruptions. Many states allow nontitled tangible personal property (like the candlesticks) to be distributed according to a much less formal list referred to in the will. The list can be modified much more simply than the will and without any further attorney fees.

If you sense that your elder is resistant to discussing a will, planting seeds today makes talking about it later easier. For example, you can say, "I know it sounds silly, but I get the heebie-jeebies when I think that if anything ever happened to me, my kids would put my Persian carpet out with the trash — or worse, fight over it. Have you ever worried about such things?" Another technique is to move the discussion to a third person. For example, "Remember my friend Betty? Her mother passed away last spring, and Betty's sisters, who always got along so well, are fighting tooth and nail over who should have their mother's china. It's a terrible situation. Apparently, there was no will."

Once a will has been created, remind your elder to review it every couple of years. Stuff happens! Maybe he needs to consider new grandchildren, or he may have acquired a new valuable since the document was drawn up. Remind your elder that as long as he is mentally alert, he can change his will at any time.

If you need more help with raising the subject of wills, the University of Minnesota Extension Service offers a useful publication titled *Who Gets Grandma's Yellow Pie Plate: A Guide to Passing on Personal Possessions* (item #MI-6686-WG). It's a step-by-step workbook filled with worksheets, practical suggestions, proven strategies, and real-life stories. To order, call 800-876-8636 or place an order online (www.yellowpieplate.umn.edu). The cost is $12.50 plus shipping and handling.

Advance directives

Although it's a painful exercise, imagine your elder so ill or impaired that she is incapacitated, unable to understand the nature and consequences of health-care decisions and make an informed decision. Nevertheless, urgent critical medical decisions must be made. What would your elder want? Would she agree to major surgery? Tube feeding? A mechanical ventilator? Would she want to be resuscitated if she stopped breathing? Would she want antibiotics that may only delay imminent death? If no one knows, family members are left to guess and often to argue. When family members can't agree, health-care personnel tend to continue life support — extending suffering for everyone.

A scene like this one can't happen if, while your elder was well, she executed an *advance directive* (a legal document that says what to do in such a situation or names a person to act in her behalf). A *durable power of attorney* for healthcare (one type of advance directive) or a *living will* (another type of advance directive) would help.

Every adult should have an advance directive in place. Engaging your elder in conversations about the necessity for an advance directive is difficult because it forces everyone involved to face his or her own mortality. Carol Akright, author of *Funding Your Dreams: Generation to Generation* (Dearborn Trade), writes that the easiest way to start these conversations is to broach various "what if" scenarios. For example, "Mom, what if you had a stroke and couldn't talk? How would we know what kind of medical treatment you'd be willing to undergo?" Or, "Dad, if you were in a coma, we kids don't know if you would want a breathing machine to keep you alive or not."

If your elder just says, "Tell them to do everything" or "Tell them to let me go," that's not enough. You need to have specifics about feeding tubes, respirators, pain medications, antibiotics, and dialysis — just to name a few treatments.

Power of attorney

The broadest definition for a power of attorney is that it's a legal document in which your elder gives another person the legal authority to make decisions and act in her behalf. He can even give that person specific powers like selling a house or paying bills (a *limited power of attorney*).

A durable power of attorney is one type of power of attorney. The elder authorizes a specific person (sometimes called an *agent, proxy,* or *attorney-in-fact*) to make decisions for him. It can go into effect as soon as he signs it and remains in effect even after he loses capacity. But most often, the durable power of attorney is worded so that it only goes into effect when a doctor certifies that the elder is incapacitated. Should that unfortunate event happen, the durable power of attorney becomes a *springing* durable power of attorney. The springing event is the incapacitation. Two separate durable powers of attorney exist — one for managing finances and one for making health-care decisions.

Creating a durable power of attorney for healthcare is a daunting task because the elder is asked to state under what conditions she wants her life to be prolonged. If she doesn't spell it out in the document, she needs to tell her agent what she wants so that the agent can carry out her wishes.

The Five Wishes way

Five Wishes is an advance directive that's legal in 35 states. The document enables the elder to state what he wants done in very specific situations (including coma, near death, and brain damage without hope of recovery). Best of all, it contains no legal and medical jargon — only plain English. Wishes 1 and 2 allow your age-advantaged person to name an agent to make health-care decisions for him when he can't do it himself and puts into writing the kind of medical treatment he wants or doesn't want if he becomes seriously ill and can't communicate.

Wishes 3 and 4 provide the elder with the chance to say how he wants to be treated to maintain his dignity, and wish 5 tells others how the senior wants to be remembered. He also has an opportunity to express what may be in his heart — like forgiveness.

Contact Aging with Dignity at 888-594-7437 for more information. To preview the document and find out whether your elder's state honors Five Wishes, visit online at www.agingwith dignity.org. A copy of Five Wishes costs $5.

Executing a durable power of attorney for healthcare and another one for finances is the best way to avoid conservatorship. (When a responsible person is appointed by the court to handle another person's financial and personal affairs, the procedure is called a *conservatorship.* The responsible person named by the judge is called the *conservator,* and the elder who is in need of such care is called the *conservatee.*) With a durable power of attorney, the elder's handpicked agent makes decisions instead of someone chosen by the court in a conservatorship. (See Chapter 21 for more information about conservatorship.)

Every state has its own laws concerning revising or canceling advance directives. If your elder completes an advance directive in one state and moves to another state, find out whether the document he executed complies with the laws of the new state. A new document may have to be drawn up. Partnership for Caring can provide you with state-specific advance directive documents and instructions. If you order by telephone (800-989-9455), there's a $10 fee payable by credit card. Get the materials for free by downloading them from its Web site (www.partnershipforcaring.org).

Living will

A living will is another type of advance directive document in which your elder states, in detail, acceptable medical procedures and life-sustaining measures. In some states, it's called a *healthcare declaration* or *healthcare directive.* Unlike the power of attorney for healthcare, this document doesn't name an agent to act in the elder's behalf. Copies should go to you, the primary care physician, the hospital, and the nursing home or other institution where your elder resides.

A living will, unlike a durable power of attorney, is *not* necessarily legally binding. State laws vary widely. Some physicians and hospitals may refuse to honor a living will, opting for aggressive procedures to keep your elder alive despite the instructions in the living will.

Do Not Resuscitate Order (DNR)

A *DNR* is a physician's written order instructing healthcare professionals not to attempt cardiopulmonary resuscitation (CPR) on the elder in case of cardiac or respiratory arrest. This order is written at the request of the elder, or in some cases, the family, but it must be signed by a physician. Understand that this order is done when it's believed that resuscitation would only delay the inevitable and leave the person severely and permanently incapacitated.

Considering Funeral Preplanning

Preplanning, pre-need, and *prearrangement* describe arranging and paying for a funeral in advance of need. The funeral industry, through its marketing efforts, has succeeded in making this option more common, but be careful. Although many legal controls govern how the funeral industry handles and invests the funds collected from prepaid services, reports about mismanagement and stolen funds still occur.

In the pro column, preplanning allows your elder to comparison-shop, obtaining the best deal on the exact products and services she desires — and saving the family from having to make difficult choices during a stressful period.

On the other hand, your elder may lose her money in certain states if she moves to another state. Even when a refund occurs, a substantial penalty often goes with it. Also, the preplanned package may not provide for inflation. The funeral home may have to substitute with less expensive merchandise, or the survivors may have to pony up some funds — which is exactly what the elder wanted to avoid. When the time comes, the casket chosen by the elder may be no longer available or the mortuary may have shut its doors. Because of these pitfalls, you're wise to consult an attorney before signing a contract. (See Chapter 23 for more information about funerals.)

Some funeral directors will keep a person's wishes on file without advance payment.

Another way to pay for a funeral

A bank or savings institution can set up a *Trotten Trust* for your elder. It works like this: A sum of money that would cover funeral cost is deposited in a passbook, certificate of deposit, or money market account, payable to a beneficiary the elder chooses. At the time of death, the funds become immediately available without having to go through probate. The funds are earmarked for the funeral. The accumulated interest usually covers any increases in funeral cost caused by inflation. (Be aware, though, that the interest is taxable.) The elder controls the funds while she's alive.

The best part is that money in the Trotten account won't be counted for Medicaid eligibility. For example, to be eligible for Medicaid, you have to be down to your last $2,000. The funeral money in a Trotten Trust is not counted in that $2,000. If the funeral money was in a regular savings account, it *would* be counted, forcing your elder to use it up to qualify for Medicaid.

Creating a Living Legacy

Why wait until you're gone and buried to give your cherished possessions away? There's a lot to be said for encouraging your elder to transfer collections, heirlooms, sentimental items, and family history to his loved ones while he's alive!

Introducing your elder to the idea of giving away treasures while he's still kicking

Norman amassed a number of collections over his long life, including stamps, coins, pipes, cameras, artwork, and first-edition books. And, of course, he had his beloved wife's jewelry and her collection of ceramic angels. More than once, Norman observed the children and grandchildren of departed friends quarreling over the dead parents' belongings, despite a will.

Norman prevented such a disagreeable possibility in his own family by creating a *living legacy*. Norman kept a list of his prized belongings. Over the years, when someone admired something or commented on its special significance or meaning, he noted it on the list. Eventually, Norman had a name next to everything that had sentimental or monetary value. If there were several names next to an item, he had to do some hard thinking. When he turned 80, he gave each of his heirs the things they admired or that held meaning for them. He doubly enjoyed seeing his heirs with his possessions — they obviously valued them, and there would be no disputes because his intentions were indisputable!

Encouraging your elder to hand down precious family history

Your elder possesses another legacy — the family history. Encouraging your elder to share an oral history allows her to bestow one more treasure upon the family. Invite your elder to tell stories and be as long-winded as she likes. Record every word. Use questions to awaken memories. For example, ask "What was it like for you during the depression?" or "What were the funniest and saddest things that ever happened to you?" Ask her to describe all her relatives — especially the ones who are long gone. Video or audiotape it all (perhaps over several sessions). Transcribe the tapes, edit and organize the content, and voilà, you have a family history. Distribute it to the family members at a special moment.

One of the best times to capture memories is in the midst of packing items to be taken to a new home or given away. Start early so that you and your elder can sort and pack at a leisurely pace. Invite the elder to recall the history of each item. Record that history, put it in a loose-leaf binder, and attach a copy with the item. How else would young Susie know that her grandma's copper kettle belonged first to her great-great-grandmother who received it on her wedding day in Czarist Russia and carried it onto the ship that brought her young family to the shores of America? How else would Susie learn about the attacks against Russian Jews *(pogroms)* and about the teeming immigrant neighborhoods in the New World, or what it felt like to be a young mother (who spoke no English), stirring soup in a copper kettle in a new land? (See Chapter 15 for more about the value of reminiscence.)

Chapter 21

Keeping the Bill Collector from the Door

*F*ormaphobia is the anxiety you feel when a stack of forms is plopped down in front of you, and you wonder what you've gotten yourself into. If you've ever applied for a mortgage, you know what I'm talking about. The multitude of choices, rules, and exceptions to the rules can make you give up before you begin!

In this chapter, I describe several benefits programs. Having a basic understanding of these programs makes the application process (and any forms you encounter) a mere "piece of cake."

Paying for Health Care

The cost of a serious illness, surgery, or a lengthy stay in the hospital can easily wipe out your elder's nest egg. The more you know about health-care insurance plans (government and private), the better prepared you are to help keep your elder as physically, mentally, and financially healthy as possible.

Medicare

Medicare is a federal health insurance program that provides hospital and outpatient medical insurance for eligible people over age 65 (as well as younger people with disabilities or end-stage renal disease). The benefits, premiums, deductibles, and copay requirements are the same in every state.

Most older Americans who were employed or were married to someone who was employed are eligible. Everyone who qualifies for Social Security benefits receives an application automatically at age 65.

The Original Medicare Plan

The Original Medicare Plan is the heart of Medicare, the nation's largest health insurance plan. It's divided into Part A and Part B.

Part A helps cover hospital stays. It pays for nursing home care (for a *very* limited period following a three-day hospital stay). Part A also pays for hospice care and certain home health-care services. (See Chapter 8 for more about Medicare payment for home healthcare.) There are no monthly premiums for Part A.

When your elder is admitted to the hospital under Part A, she's responsible for an initial deductible ($840 in 2003) for every benefit period. (A benefit period begins on the day of hospital admission and ends 60 days after discharge.) Should your loved one be readmitted within those 60 days, she doesn't have to pay another deductible. However, if she's readmitted after those 60 days, then she's responsible for a second deductible. After a deductible has been paid, Medicare kicks in the full amount of eligible charges for up to 60 days. After that, your elder must share the burden of cost through hefty copays. In 2003, the copay was set at $210 a day for days 61 to 90 and $420 a day for days 91 to 150. After 150 days in the hospital, your elder is responsible for 100 percent of the cost for each additional day.

Part B covers medical bills, most doctor's fees, diagnostic tests, outpatient care, and some medical equipment. (See Chapter 12 for a better understanding of what equipment is covered.) Your elder pays a premium for Part B ($58.70 a month in 2003). The premium gets deducted from her monthly Social Security checks. A deductible of $100 must also be paid before Medicare covers any portion of physician fees. Once the deductible is satisfied, your elder pays 20 percent, and Medicare pays 80 percent of all eligible physician charges.

Before authorizing treatment, ask your physician and the local Medicare office if Medicare covers the proposed services or fees.

Medicare + Choice

Congress created the Medicare + Choice program to give older adults more choice. This program allows companies (under contract to Medicare) to manage Medicare services for its subscribers. It works like this: Medicare pays a set amount of money every month to a private health plan for your oldster's care. Medicare + Choice includes two different plans: Medicare managed care plans (HMOs) and Medicare private fee-for-service plans.

Accepting assignment

Medicare keeps its costs down by assigning a standard fee that it will pay for each medical procedure. When a doctor accepts the assigned fee as full payment for a particular service, it's called *accepting assignment*. The reason accepting assignment is so important is that if the doctor charges a fee higher than the fee set by Medicare (and he can charge up to 15 percent more than the approved amount), then your elder must come up with the difference.

For example, if Medicare sets $500 as the fee for a certain procedure, a physician who doesn't accept assignment can charge your elder up to $575. Medicare will pay $400 (80 percent of the approved fee), and your elder will pay $175 instead of the $100 she would pay if the doctor accepted assignment. You should always ask a doctor whether he accepts assignment to avoid surprises later.

If your elder chooses a Medicare HMO plan, she still has Part A and Part B in the Original Medicare Plan coverage and still pays the premium, but she may also have to pay an additional premium to belong to the HMO plan. In return, the HMO may charge lower deductibles and copays or eliminate them altogether. The HMO may also have benefits that don't exist in the Original Medicare Plan (such as prescription drugs, eyeglasses, and dental care). But in this plan, your elder usually must see the health-care professionals that are in the HMO's network of providers.

The other plan, the Medicare private fee-for-service plan, also covers everything in Part A and Part B of the Original Medicare Plan. Your elder pays a premium for the fee-for-service plan in addition to the usual Part B premium. This plan may also offer additional services and require deductibles and copays. One of the main advantages for some oldsters is that this plan allows them to see any provider that accepts Medicare.

Medicare + Choice Plans are not available in all states. Recently, many private insurance companies have stopped participating because they can't make a profit. Others have had to raise their premiums while cutting their benefits to stay in the game.

To find the Medicare + Choice plans in your area, go online (www.medicare.gov) and click Medicare Personal Plan Finder or call 800-633-4227.

The Centers for Medicare and Medicaid Services's free booklet "Medicare & You 2003" (publication CMS-10050) explains exactly what's covered and where to get help with specific questions. To request a copy, call 800-633-4227 or go online (www.medicare.gov/Publications/Pubs/pdf/nhguide.pdfl), click Publications, and then search for the publication by its CMS number.

The Medicare Helpline staff answers questions about the Original Medicare Plan and Medicare + Choice plans 24 hours a day. Call 800-633-4227. To get a directory of physicians in your area who accept Medicare, go online (www.medicare.gov) and click Participating Physician Directory.

Medigap (Medicare Supplemental Insurance)

Medigap is a cute nickname for the private health insurance policies your elder can buy to cover the costs that the Original Medicare Plan doesn't cover. Medigap policies in every state (except Massachusetts, Minnesota, and Wisconsin) are standardized (they're named A to J) so that you can compare them easily. Each of the policies offers a different combination of benefits. In addition, any one of the ten standardized policies may be sold as a Medicare Select policy. Medicare Select Policies require policyholders to use specific hospitals, and, in some cases, specific doctors, to get full insurance benefits.

If your elder is enrolled in the Medicare Managed Care Plan (HMO) or Medicare Private Fee-For-Service Plan, a Medigap policy isn't necessary. In fact, it may be illegal for anyone to sell your elder a Medigap policy if she's enrolled in one of these health plans.

Compare Medigap plans and get the names and contact information of the insurance companies in your area that offer them by visiting online (www.medicare.gov) and clicking Medigap Compare.

If your elder decides that a Medigap policy is the way to go, buy the policy during the open enrollment period (a six-month period that starts on the first day of the month that your elder is 65 or older and enrolled in Medicare Part B). During this period, coverage can't be denied due to existing medical conditions. If your elder doesn't enroll during the open period, she may not be able to buy the plan she wants later, or she may get charged more for the same policy.

For more guidance on Medicare and Medigap plans, you can access the Health Insurance Counseling and Advocacy Project (HICAP) offices by calling the Eldercare Locator number, 800-677-1116.

Medicaid

Medicaid (sometimes referred to as medical assistance) provides free medical care for people with low incomes and few resources. The federal and state governments share the costs for Medicaid, but the state manages the program. Eligibility requirements vary from state to state, and the complicated rules change frequently. To qualify, your elder must be a U.S. citizen (with some exceptions) and must meet income and asset requirements. The elder's home and car can be exempt in determining eligibility. Long waits and complicated application forms are the norm.

The good news is that every state must allow some choice of providers, and if your elder is on Medicare and Medicaid (Medi-Cal in California), most of her hospital stays and medical costs will be paid in full. Medicaid covers nursing home care and outpatient prescription drugs. If your elder is already in a nursing home, pays for care from her own pocket, and is almost out of money, the personnel at the nursing home can apply for Medicaid on her behalf. (See Chapter 4 for information about the elder's responsibility to share some of the nursing home cost from her fixed income.)

To find out more about Medicaid and locate your local Medicaid office, call Medicare at 800-633-4227 and choose option 2.

The National Council for Aging has a Web site that tells you what state and federal assistance programs your elder may be eligible for. Go online (`www.benefitscheckup.com`) and fill out an online confidential questionnaire A second Web site (`www.govbenefits.gov`), which is hosted by the government, has additional features. It, too, produces a list of potential benefit programs and then links you to specific information about each program with application instructions.

Long-term care insurance

Private insurance companies sell long-term care insurance to cover medical and nonmedical needs. The older your elder gets (and the more medical conditions she accumulates), the more expensive the policy will be. Investigate this option early, before a crisis occurs.

Obtain a copy of *A Shopper's Guide to Long-term Care Insurance* by calling the National Association of Insurance Commissioners at 816-842-3600. Ask for the publications department and request publication LTC-LP. Or write to the National Association of Insurance Commissioners, 2301 McGee St., Suite 800, Kansas City, MO 64108.

Taking Advantage of Retirement and Income Benefits

Income drawn from stocks, bonds, real estate, or the sale of cars, boats, or rare-coin collections can keep your elder on the financial high ground — but not everyone has such investments or owns luxury items. Millions of older Americans depend on government programs (such as Social Security) or employee retirement benefits to keep them afloat.

Other resources to finance health-care costs

Your elder may be eligible for other forms of government-funded health insurance. The following programs are worth checking out:

✔ **State Medicare Savings Programs.** These programs help low-income elders by paying part or all of their Medicare premiums, deductibles, and copays. Call your state's Medical Assistance Office to find out whether your elder qualifies.

✔ **Veterans Health Administration (VHA).** Veterans of the Armed Forces can enjoy complete health-care coverage as long as the care is received at a VHA facility (there are 1,300 locations nationwide). A copayment may be required if the condition isn't related to military service. For information on health benefits and to find out whether your age-advantaged person qualifies, call 877-222-8387 or go online (www.va.gov/health_benefits).

✔ **Military retiree benefits.** Medicare-eligible uniformed services retirees (including retired National Guard members and reservists and eligible family members) may be entitled to TRICARE for Life (TFL) medical benefits. TFL is a Medigap-type coverage that pays Medicare copayments and deductibles and covers most of the costs not covered by Medicare. To get more information, call 888-363-5433 or go online (www.TRICARE.osd.mil).

✔ **The Pace Program (Programs of All-Inclusive Care for the Elderly).** This program for frail elders features comprehensive medical and social services. The comprehensive service package enables many frail elders to continue living at home rather than be institutionalized. PACE is available only in states that have chosen to offer it under Medicaid. To find out whether your state has such a program and whether your elder is eligible, call your local Medical Assistance Office, which you can usually find in the community services pages of your directory under Medicaid (Medi-Cal in California), or visit online (www.medicare.gov/Nursing/Alternatives/PACE.asp).

Social Security retirement benefits

Social Security is the largest source of retirement income for people over 65. Every employee contributes to Social Security while he or she is working. The contribution (automatically deducted from the worker's paychecks) is matched by the employer, deposited into a fund, and managed by the government. The fund pays retirement benefits (and also survivor and disability benefits). How much you get depends on how much you put in.

To qualify for benefits, your elder must have accumulated 40 credits, which represents about ten years of work. If your elder's only income comes from Social Security, that money won't be taxed. But if your elder draws additional income, a portion of his Social Security retirement benefits may be taxable. For example, in 2002, half of Jim's Social Security benefits plus his other income totaled $30,000. That amount and the fact that Jim was single meant that he had to pay taxes on a portion of his Social Security benefits. The threshold is $25,000 for an individual and $32,000 for married couples who file jointly.

You can apply for Social Security benefits by telephone, in-person, or online (www.ssa.gov/applytoretire). Call 800-772-1213 to schedule an appointment for a telephone application or an in-person application.

Supplemental Security Income (SSI)

Social Security and Supplemental Security Income (SSI) are two different federal programs. Most people look forward to the time when they'll get something back for all the years that money was deducted from their paychecks and contributed to Social Security.

Most folks know about Social Security, but many Americans who are also eligible to receive monthly SSI cash benefits miss out because they don't know about the program.

SSI provides monthly cash benefits to help pay for food, clothing, and shelter for people who don't own much, have limited incomes, and are 65 or older, or are blind or disabled. Usually a home, a small burial fund, and one car are exempt when assets are calculated. Aside from those assets, eligible seniors can't have more than $2,000 ($3,000 for a couple) and must be United States citizens (with some exceptions). For example, certain noncitizens who are honorably discharged veterans of the U.S. armed forces, their spouses, and unmarried dependent children of a deceased veteran may qualify. SSI recipients frequently qualify for food stamps and Medicaid as well. People who live in city or county nursing homes usually cannot get SSI. But there are some exceptions. For example, if your elder lives in a public or private institution and Medicaid is paying more than half the cost of care, she may get a small SSI benefit.

The federal SSI benefit pays base rates ($552 per month for an individual in 2003 and $829 per month for a couple in 2003). Some states may add to that sum, but the amount differs from state to state. For example, Pennsylvania supplements the base rate (to the tune of $27.40 a month for an individual in 2003). California also supplements the base rate (up to $198 for an individual in 2003). Call Social Security at 800-772-1213 to find out whether your state supplements SSI.

Visit your local Social Security Administration office to find out whether your elder qualifies for SSI or call 800-772-1213. You can also apply over the phone. Be prepared to provide a birth certificate and proof of income, including two or three of the most recent bank account statements, deeds to property, stocks and bonds, and anything else that can be turned into cash. Applicants must also provide information about financial assistance received from family members or organizations. Telephone applicants can send in copies of documents or have someone drop them off at the local Social Security office (the preferred method).

Retirement pensions

Employer-sponsored pensions are the second largest source of retirement income for people over 65. Most adult children know whether their parent receives a monthly pension, but that may be all they know. When you first undertake the job of sorting out your elder's finances, you may wonder whether the amounts on the monthly pension checks are correct. Perhaps someone needs to double-check. Administrative and calculation errors can and do occur!

Complex rules determine a person's pension distribution. Request a copy of your elder's Summary Plan Description (the rulebook for your elder's pension). A written request to the Plan Administrator will get you this document, as well as the Individual Benefit Statement that describes your elder's total accrued and vested benefits, which will help you make sure that your elder gets what she's entitled to.

To find a local free pension counseling center, call The Pension Rights Center 202-296-3776 or go online (`www.pensionrights.org`) and click Pension Help.

The National Center for Retirement Benefits consists of actuaries and accountants who think of themselves as pension detectives. These sleuths will examine your elder's retirement plan distribution and pursue claims against the pension plan sponsors. They charge a portion of any recovered money for their services. In other words, if they don't recover anything, they don't receive a fee. For more information, call 800-666-1000 or visit online (`www.ncrb.com`). The organization's Web site lists 30 serious errors found in pension and profit-sharing plans.

Living benefits

Your elder may have a life-insurance plan naming someone as beneficiary when she dies. That's all well and good — but, boy, could your elder use that money while she's alive to pay bills! Many insurance companies will pay out the death benefit (now tax-free and called a living benefit) to a policyholder who is clearly at the end of her life rather than paying it to her beneficiary upon her death.

Tread cautiously before saying yes to this agreement. Some insurance companies pay out only part of the total benefit, while others pay almost the whole thing. Some may pay a lump sum, while others send monthly checks. Ask whether costs and administrative fees are involved.

Don't confuse a living benefit with a *viatical* settlement, in which a third party pays the elder cash for the privilege of owning and being the beneficiary of her insurance policy. The elder receives an immediate cash payment of up to 85 percent of the policy's face value. When your elder dies, the viatical company collects the death benefit. Be especially careful with this type of arrangement — it's fraught with potential problems. Scams have been reported. The income may be taxed or may affect Medicaid eligibility. Consult with a certified public accountant, a certified financial planner, or an attorney who specializes in elder law. (For additional sources of income, see Chapter 3.)

Every little bit helps! The Alzheimer's Family Relief Program provides emergency grants up to $500. To be eligible, the older adult must have less than $10,000 in liquid assets and a written diagnosis of Alzheimer's from a physician and must have exhausted other available services. For an application, call 800-437-2423, visit online (`www.ahaf.org`), or write to 22512 Gateway Center Drive, Clarksburg, MD 20871.

Getting Those Pesky Bills Paid

Your loved one may be relieved to have a family member keep track of her accounts and pay her bills. On the other hand, she may dig her heels in and refuse assistance — even when it's obvious that her financial affairs are in disarray. Unfortunately, bill collectors don't wait around until you and your elder work things out. Gently assure her that you don't want to interfere, you only want to make her life easier.

Many senior centers offer money-management programs for elders. Call the Eldercare Locator at 800-677-1116. The organization can give you the phone number for your local Area Agency on Aging, which in turn can refer you to a money-management or bill-paying program in your elder's community.

Whether your elder continues to handle her own finances, accepts limited assistance, or relinquishes the responsibility entirely, the following ideas may help organize and streamline money management:

- ✔ Figure out your elder's assets and debts and locate all her important financial papers. (See Chapter 20 for a list of documents that you need to evaluate your elder's financial situation and to access in an emergency.)

- ✔ Think about hiring a lawyer, financial planner, or accountant to do some financial planning or provide expert advice about complicated financial pictures (including multiple assets and joint ownerships).

- ✔ Consider a "durable power of attorney." In this legal document, your elder names the person she wants to manage her financial affairs should she become incapable of doing it herself. (See Chapter 20 for more information on durable power of attorney.)

✔ Share financial decisions with family members at regular intervals and keep everyone informed about income and expenses on the behalf of a confused elder. Meticulous record-keeping and open communication can forestall family squabbles, feuds, and emotionally painful lawsuits.

✔ Talk to your banker or attorney about the best way to authorize a trusted person to conduct transactions on your older person's behalf.

✔ Arrange to have recurring bills (such as utility bills, mortgage payments, and health insurance premiums) paid electronically. Electronic fund transfers protect against missed payments and the hassles they cause.

✔ Set up direct deposit of government benefit checks and pensions. For example, your elder's Social Security check can go directly into her account, avoiding delays and reducing trips to the bank.

✔ Arrange to have government benefits checks sent directly to a representative payee. This payee can be an individual authorized to manage an elder's finances or even an institution that's providing nursing home care.

Take advantage of tax assistance. Tax-Aide is an AARP program in which volunteers in senior centers, libraries, and malls assist with tax-return preparation and answer tax-related questions. To find Tax-Aid locations, go online (www.aarp.org/taxaide) or call 888-AARP-NOW.

The IRS provides two additional tax-assistance programs: The Volunteer Income Tax Assistance program (VITA) provides aid to disabled individuals and people with low to moderate incomes. Tax Counseling for the Elderly (TCE) is a program for people age 60 and over. TCE uses IRS-trained volunteers to provide tax counseling and basic income-tax-return preparation. (Some volunteers make house calls.) To receive services from the VITA or TCE, contact the IRS Taxpayer Education Coordinator at your local IRS office or call 800-829-1040.

If you believe that your elder is no longer able to make her own decisions, you may have to consider conservatorship to protect her financial welfare. (See the next section.)

Understanding the Ins and Outs of Conservatorship

A *conservatorship* may be the only means left to protect an incompetent elder's interests, if the elder can no longer manage her own life and has not executed a durable power of attorney. (See Chapter 20 for information about the steps your elder can take while she is still well to avoid conservatorship later.)

When a responsible person is appointed by the court to handle another person's financial and personal affairs, the procedure is called a conservatorship. The responsible person named by the judge is called the *conservator,* and the elder who is in need of such care is called the *conservatee.* When the process has been completed, the elder is referred to as *conserved.*

There are two types of conservatorship. A *conservator of the estate* collects assets, pays bills, collects debts, makes investments, and (under court supervision) conducts major financial transactions, such as borrowing money and buying and selling real estate — all in the elder's best interest. A *conservator of person* makes decisions about medical care, food, and clothing, and about where the conservatee shall live. (The conservator can relocate an elder to a nursing home even when the elder refuses institutional placement.)

What is competency?

Declaring in court that your loved one is incapable of making her own decisions and managing her own affairs is traumatic for you and her. It can feel like you're hurting your older adult when, in fact, you're trying to help.

Because mentally impaired elders are easy targets for financial abuse, you may have to petition for conservatorship to protect your elder from being preyed on by others (including members of her own family). In such cases, caring people like yourself may step forward to offer themselves as candidates for the position of conservator. Judges take great care to choose the most honest, qualified, and responsible person for this job.

Despite the legal definitions, competency is not a black-and-white condition. Your elder may be competent in some areas but not competent in others or may have periods of competency alternating with periods of severe confusion (due to illness or medications). Even if the court determines that conservatorship is warranted, your elder should be told what is happening or about to happen and be invited to contribute to decisions wherever possible. For example, a conserved elder may have ideas about where she wants to live or what doctor she wants to take care of her.

How does a conservatorship happen?

The details vary in each state. In some jurisdictions, the court calls the appointed person a *guardian* instead of a conservator, while in other states the terms are interchangeable. Sometimes the conservator is the one in charge of finances, and the guardian is the one who handles personal care.

The following steps are more or less the way it's done in most places:

1. **A relative, friend, or public official petitions the court for the appointment of a conservator.**

   The petition states why the elder can't manage his own affairs.

2. **The court assigns an investigator to interview the elder, assess the situation, and form an opinion about whether a conservatorship is justified.**

3. **A court hearing is held.**

   The potential conservatee appears in court if he's medically able and wishes to be present. An elder who contests the conservatorship may be represented by his own attorney or have one appointed to him. He may even request a jury trial.

4. **The judge determines (based on the information in the petition, a physician's declaration, the investigator's report, and evidence presented during the hearing) whether the elder should be conserved and, if so, what powers should be granted to the conservator.**

5. **The judge names a conservator based on her determination of the best candidate for the job.**

6. **The newly appointed conservator inventories the elder's assets, makes accountings, and files regular reports to the court.**

The conservatorship process can be complicated. You need to hire an attorney who knows your state laws and can navigate the process.

What are the pros and cons?

On the pro side, conservatorship provides a high degree of protection and oversight. The oldster's money is earmarked for her welfare and safe-keeping. Conservators aren't appointed lightly. I know of several cases in which a judge removed and replaced an inept conservator or one whose practices were questionable.

On the down side, filing fees, legal fees, investigator fees, and conservator fees (which come out of the elder's estate) are pricey. The conservator must return to court for approval for major transactions (such as giving significant gifts, sale and purchase of real estate, and borrowing money). Each return is time-consuming, requires additional attorney fees, and delays proposed financial transactions. In addition, the details of conservatorship become part of the public record (assets, income, expenses), making extremely private information available to anyone who cares to look. Another concern is that should the judge find all of the proposed conservator candidates unsuitable, he can appoint someone outside the family who may not even know the elder (for example, an attorney or a private conservatorship company). A major downer is the emotional and psychological impact that a conservatorship may have on some elders.

Guarding against scams and con artists

Seniors tend to be more trusting than younger folks — perhaps because they grew up in an era when they had less reason to distrust. Confused, depressed, or ill oldsters may have faulty judgment. And others (in need of money) may allow themselves to be taken in by a slick con man who promises them a financial windfall. Elderly people are easy marks, and the bad guys know it!

Warn your elder about investment scams. Investment swindlers mimic the sales approach of legitimate investment firms and salespeople. They may contact your elder by phone, mail, e-mail, or even claim to have been referred by one of your elder's friends. These referrals are often the result of a scam in which an initial investor (the friend) receives large, fast profits. The whole purpose is for the friend to tell his friends, so that soon people almost beg to enter the investment opportunity. Before long, all the friends have been victimized. (See Chapter 11 about scams that offer miraculous cures, Chapter 12 about home-repair scams, and Chapter 22 about religious scams.)

The following tips can help your elder avoid being a victim:

- ✔ **Investigate before investing.** Call the Public Disclosure Program at 800-289-9999 to find out whether a person is a registered broker, and whether the person or company may be involved in disciplinary action.

- ✔ **Avoid people (registered brokers or not) who promise large profits with low or no risk.** Most legitimate investments require risk in order to realize reward.

- ✔ **Understand that being told that you must invest right now or miss the opportunity is the best reason to be suspicious.**

- ✔ **Watch out for swindlers who tell you to keep this special opportunity secret because it wouldn't be such a deal if everybody knew about it.** They just don't want you to discuss the deal with people who recognize that it's a scam.

- ✔ **Remind your elder about the old saying, "If it sounds too good to be true, it probably is."**

Your elder may have already been stung and not told anyone. You have cause for concern if you have observed that your elder:

- ✔ Receives lots of mail for contests, sweepstakes, and prizes. (She's on a sucker list.)

✔ Gets frequent calls from people offering great deals or asking for donations to charities.

✔ Has a checkbook or credit-card statement that shows repeated or large payments to companies in other states or countries.

✔ Has difficulty paying bills and buying essentials.

✔ Subscribes to more magazines than anyone could possibly read.

✔ Has a houseful of cheap "prize" items like clocks, costume jewelry, or even water filters (items probably purchased to qualify to win more valuable prizes).

If your senior has been misled or deceived, call the National Fraud hotline (800-876-7060) or the Federal Trade Commission (877-382-4357); write to Consumer Response Center, Federal Trade Commission, Washington, DC 20580; or go online to www.ftc.gov and click File A Complaint. Your state attorney general also wants to know about con artists. Look for your state attorney general's office in the government pages of your telephone directory. You can also get the name, address, and telephone number of your state attorney general by visiting the National Association of State Attorneys General Web site (www.naag.org).

Unfortunately, being burned once increases the chance that your senior will be burned again. Con artists often share their lists of targets with other con artists. If con artists call your elder repeatedly, urge your elder to change her phone number. Change bank accounts or credit-card numbers if she's already been ripped off and these account numbers were given out.

Don't fill out contest entry forms at malls or fairs. They are a common source of leads for con artists. Beware of companies offering to recoup money lost in fraudulent schemes for a fee. (No legitimate organizations provide such services.) The caller can be from the same company that stole the money in the first place, or he may have bought your elder's name from the first scam artist.

If your elder has been taken in, don't humiliate her. Anyone can fall prey to these persuasive crooks. Arm your elder with information. Warn her not to invite door-to-door salespeople into the house. Practice what to say when telemarketers call, soliciting money or offering opportunities. For example, "I don't do business on the phone," or "I don't contribute to telephone solicitations," or just a quick "No, thank you" and a hang-up. Sometimes forgetting the "No, thank you" and just hanging up is the best strategy.

Chapter 22

Helping Spiritual and Religious Elderly "Keep the Faith"

In This Chapter

▶ Helping your elder observe his or her religion at home

▶ Reawakening religious traditions

▶ Fostering prayer and meditation

▶ Supporting your elder's spiritual journey

Some people find religion late, others find it early, and some not at all. For example, your elder may be a lifelong follower of his religion. On the other hand, he may have been well-schooled in his faith as a child but abandoned it as an adult. Whatever the case, as the end of life approaches, many frail older people are drawn to their religious roots for the comfort and courage that faith brings them. In the last part of life, many elders also want to become more spiritual — although they may not use that exact word.

This chapter is about helping your elder reconnect or stay connected with his or her religious roots — if that's what he or she desires. It's also about facilitating your elder's spiritual journey — if, in fact, that's what he or she wants.

Bringing the Church Home

When your elder can't get to church, temple, or mosque as frequently as he would like or can't get there at all, here are some ways that you can bring the essence of a house of worship home:

✔ **Request a home visit.** Clergy, seminary students, and lay ministers are usually happy to visit the elderly. For example, in the Catholic Church, certain congregation members are able to administer the Eucharist to the homebound. Many churches have volunteers who visit the sick and elderly. (Modest donations aren't usually required but are appreciated.)

✔ **Locate a volunteer to read your elder's favorite religious tracts aloud.**

The Braille Institute offers a national service in which callers have favorite sections from various newspapers read to them over the telephone. For a referral to a local program that will provide readings from other sources, call 800-BRAILLE. Also check local universities and public libraries. Many offer reader programs.

✔ **Ask your elder's pastor, rabbi, or spiritual leader to record a personal spiritual message that your elder can play over and over.** Discussing the contents of the message with family will make it even more meaningful.

✔ **Play religious music, especially on the usual days for religious observance.** (See the section "Revisiting Religious Roots," later in this chapter, for more ways to bring religion into the home.)

Reassure your homebound elder that "God knows that you aren't able to get to church." Help him or her understand that faith and belief don't need to have a holy place to be experienced. If your frail elder is religious, has been a churchgoer, and has been active in religious activities for most of his or her life, you may want to consider a faith-based nursing home or other facility (when placement is needed). Homes under the auspices of a particular faith will have their public rooms and common areas decorated with religious pictures, items, and books. They're more likely to have visiting clergy or have pastoral counseling and support, Bible study groups, hymn-singing sessions, and prayer.

Revisiting Religious Roots

Religion gives you membership in a group that worships a Higher Power (regarded as the creator of the universe) and a set of rules (often in a holy book) that tells you how to conduct yourself personally and socially. Practicing members attend formal services, read holy passages, and observe their religion's traditions and holy days.

Old age and illness seem to reawaken religious longings in many people — even among those who were not observant in their youth. Such elders report that they draw strength, meaning, and courage from their faith.

Here are some ways you can support and enhance your elder's religious life:

✔ **Purchase religious books for your elder.** Every major bookstore has a religion section (including texts from mainstream religions and lesser known religions). Ask your elder whether she would like to have any special religious item or picture.

✔ **Tune in to television and radio preachers.** Not everyone likes evangelical television ministries, but those who do seem to get great comfort from their favorite pastors. (Read the sidebar "A wolf in sheep's clothing: Avoiding religious scam artists" in this chapter before you or your elder make any donations.)

- ✔ **Reinstitute lifelong religious practices like lighting candles and saying grace.**

- ✔ **Give gifts of religious items (for example, religious jewelry, holy books, CDs) for birthdays and other special occasions.**

Many houses of worship (especially the larger ones) have gift shops on site. If these aren't convenient, look for freestanding religious gift stores or try online religious gift shops. Two good examples of online stores are www.familychristian.com and www.jewishsource.com.

- ✔ **Make contributions to a religious charity.** Most religious charities send thank-you cards or small religious items to show their appreciation. Your elder can make the donation directly, or you can honor him or her by contributing in his or her name.

Praying and Meditating

One of the most intimate or loving things that caregivers can do is to listen to elders' prayers, pray with them, or offer to pray for them. If praying is not your cup of tea, try holding hands and sitting in silence. It may have a similar effect!

A wolf in sheep's clothing: Avoiding religious scam artists

Older adults receive more telephone and mail solicitations for charitable donations than any other age group. Some of the pleas come from soft-spoken people who seem sincere but who are really unscrupulous con artists who consider older people easy touches. Warn your elder about these creeps! Your older adult should be suspicious when someone asks for a donation for a charity with a name that sounds similar to a well-known organization. Warn your elder against giving his credit-card number to any telephone solicitor. When the voice on the other end offers to send someone by to pick up the donation, say "No, thank you." (Read Chapters 11 and 21 for more information about scams and con artists and how to report these scoundrels.)

Investigate before you donate. You can check for legitimacy of charities online (www.give.org). This Web site offers evaluations of hundreds of charities that solicit donations, including religious charities. Each evaluation shows where your money goes, including how much goes to pay for fundraising activities and how much salary the CEO draws. This service comes from the Better Business Wise Giving Alliance, 4200 Wilson Blvd., Suite 200, Arlington, VA 22203, e-mail give@cbbb.bbb.org.

Millions of people all over the world pray daily because their religion requires it and because it's helpful to them. Pastor William R. Grimbol writes in *Life's Big Questions* (Alpha Books) that prayer isn't magic, but it does have a mysterious power to help the individual. Prayer can help you resolve feelings of anger, fear, and guilt. It can reduce tension, unleash love, and create hope as well as open your heart to forgiveness.

Caregivers report that prayer helps them cope with the difficulties of eldercare, grief for the loss of their former life, and the sorrow of watching a loved one deteriorate.

Meditation has been practiced since ancient times in various forms by all religions, but it was popularized in the United States during the 1960s and '70s when the Indian Maharishi Mahesh Yogi popularized a system called Transcendental Meditation (TM).

People who meditate generally focus their minds on a single point of reference — for example, a silent repetition of a prayer or a calming phrase. The goal is to engender tranquility by emptying the mind of thoughts.

More than 25 years ago, Dr. Herbert Benson and his colleagues at Harvard Medical School showed that 10 to 20 minutes of meditation each day can produce enormous physical benefits, including lowering blood pressure and reducing heart disease. The practice lessens the harmful effects of stress by decreasing levels of *cortisol* (a hormone released in response to stress). Meditation also enhances recuperation from illness and improves the body's resistance to disease.

Growing Spiritually

Spirituality is a broad concept, and difficult to pin down. People who seek to become more spiritual may or may not belong to a formal religion. Most people think of their spirituality as a journey in which their efforts will ultimately help them achieve some or all of these results:

- More self-understanding
- A feeling of peace
- A greater connection with nature
- A greater connection with a Higher Power
- An acceptance of the past and present
- A feeling of oneness with all humanity
- An understanding of the meaning and purpose of their life

✔ The contentment that comes from being a more loving, more moral, more forgiving person

You can assist your elder's spiritual journey by initiating certain activities. For example, encouraging your older person to share memories with friends and family (in person or on tape) helps him to achieve a sense of oneness with others. Most folks who survive to an advanced age, despite their current frailties, possess intriguing stories about overcoming war, discrimination, and the Great Depression — just to name a few hurdles. You can help him to see that his life has made a difference to the world, the community, or his family. (See Chapter 15 for additional techniques on guiding reminisce.)

You can choose from a huge selection of spiritually oriented books for your loved one to enjoy. An oldie but goodie, *The Prophet* (Random House), written by Kahlil Gibran, poetically expresses a philosophy of life that has helped many people on their spiritual path. When your elder can no longer read by herself, volunteer to read short stories to her. Inspirational tales can help her identify with the feelings expressed by the characters and stir a sense of wonder of nature and an acceptance of a Higher Power. Carefully selected stories can promote hope and validate your age-advantaged person's values. A good inspirational collection of very short stories is *Chicken Soup for the Golden Soul: Heartwarming Stories About People Over 60* (Health Communications, Inc.), edited by Jack Canfield, Mark Victor Hansen, Paul J. Meyer, and Amy Seeger.

The greatest spiritual and religious growth can emerge from the most difficult times. During a recent potentially debilitating illness, I was uplifted when I read *Still Here: Embracing Aging, Changing, and Dying* (Riverhead Books), by Ram Dass. When the author drove home the idea that humans are much more than the appearance and functioning of their bodies, it suddenly dawned on me that I can be wise, kind, tolerant, and generous (in other words, a blessing to others) despite the state of my health.

Facing death, disability, and chronic illness often stirs questions about death and the meaning and purpose of life. Some examples: What is the meaning and purpose of my life? Why is God making me suffer? Am I being punished for my sins with poor health? What will happen to me after I die? Questions like these mean that the elder is trying to make sense of illness, grief, pain, loss, and disability. Such questions may be beyond your ability to answer. Your willingness to create a climate in which an elder feels comfortable discussing these questions is far more useful to his spiritual growth than direct answers. If you feel unequipped for such discussions, find someone who can handle them.

Print daily e-mail inspirations for your elderly person to enjoy. Examples are daily Bible readings, daily Jewish wisdom, daily Muslim wisdom, and angel wisdom (inspirational thoughts from philosophers, novelists, and people who write about angels). Go to www.about.com and click Religion and Spirituality, click one of several religions, and then under Free Newsletters, click the daily inspiration you want to receive.

Chapter 23

Ensuring a Good Death

- -

In This Chapter

▶ Discussing death and dying with your older person

▶ Considering hospice care

▶ Facing the final hours

▶ Making sense of funeral choices

- -

*T*his chapter shows you how to help your elder have a good death. It tells you in plain words what to expect when your older person is dying. It also sheds some light on the complex business of funerals.

Dying is not easy for an elderly person who's alone, fearful, and in pain. On the other hand, dying can be a good experience — a period of personal growth — when the older person makes peace with his maker, finds meaning to his life, and deepens his close relationships.

Dying with Dignity

The words good and death aren't usually spoken in the same breath. While you may not be able to change the fact that your loved one is dying, you can help him have a good death by helping him accomplish the following goals:

- ✔ Retain some control of his life up to the very end
- ✔ Fulfill last wishes (visit a favorite spot, attend a family celebration)
- ✔ Be free from pain (and as lucid as possible)
- ✔ Be in an emotionally and spiritually supportive environment
- ✔ Feel physically comfortable
- ✔ Feel that he's not a burden to others
- ✔ Have opportunities to say goodbye to important people or resolve conflicts
- ✔ Die with loved ones at the bedside

Las Vegas or bust!

Twice a year, Jed and his wife vacationed in Las Vegas. The adult playground with its casinos and long-legged show girls helped Jed forget his ho-hum life and the job he hated. After Jed lost his wife, Las Vegas became his elixir. Frequent weekend escapes refreshed and restored him.

Then his metastatic cancer was discovered. From his hospital sickbed, Jed asked his daughter repeatedly, "When can I go to Vegas?" After an internal struggle, the daughter decided against it, concluding that the strain of the four-hour car trip and the excitement of Las Vegas would surely weaken her father, hastening his death. She asked the doctor to back up her decision — certain that he would agree.

Was she in for a surprise! The doctor asked her two questions. First, "Who is in control of your father's death — you or him?" She answered, "I want Dad to be in control." The second question was, "Do you care *where* he dies?" Her answer was "No."

Next weekend, she loaded Dad, his oxygen, wheelchair, and medications into her SUV, and off they went. Jed fulfilled his last wish, remained in control to the end, and — thanks to the medications and the distractions of the casinos and the dancing girls — suffered no pain. His daughter arranged to have his remains sent home for a proper funeral.

If your older person dies while you're visiting another city, ask the hotel or restaurant management to call emergency personnel or the police. The police will arrange to have the body taken to a hospital. From there, the body will be taken to a mortuary. The mortuary can obtain a permit from the local public health department that will enable you to get your loved one's body home. The local funeral home can arrange for your hometown funeral home to have the body transported. If you decide on cremation locally, you can carry the ashes on your trip home as long as you declare what's in your package and keep the permit with the ashes. You can also mail ashes through Federal Express or UPS.

If death occurs when you're traveling out of the country, contact the local American consulate.

Speaking About the Unspeakable

You may be faced with the dilemma of whether to inform your older person (or allow the doctor to tell her) that she has a terminal illness. Your decision may depend on the cultural and religious dictates of your elder and her family. For example, in some Hispanic groups, talking about death is forbidden because it's regarded as evidence of lost hope. In some Asian cultures, to talk about death is to invite it, which means that people will do anything to avoid the topic.

To help decide whether to tell your elder about her terminal condition, ask yourself whether you would want to know if you were in her situation — and why or why not. Your answer may build a case for or against informing your elder. Not telling requires some deception (acting as though she'll recover or pretending that you're not upset). Informing your older person that she has a terminal illness allows her to voice concerns and say her goodbyes.

On the other hand, many older folks (and younger ones) prefer to avoid painful or emotion conversations and scenes at any cost. If you're unsure about whether your elder would want to know, test the waters. Ask her what the doctor has told her and whether she'd like to talk about anything. Her response should give you a clue to how open she is to knowing about the truth of her condition.

If your elder becomes aware of her terminal condition (many people figure it out on their own, despite a conspiracy of silence), should you ask her about her preferences for the end of her life? For example, does she want to be kept alive even if she's not expected to regain consciousness? Does she want a feeding tube put in if she can't eat? Does she want a family member or close friend to make those kinds of medical decisions for her? If so, who and at what point? What kind of funeral or memorial does she prefer?

Studies show that the older you get, the more comfortable you are talking about death and dying. Your older adult may be more comfortable talking about death than you are. Caregivers who broach the subject with their elder are often surprised at how easy the conversation is and how it actually draws them closer. Talking about last wishes relieves anxiety and makes dying people feel less isolated and more connected. Knowing that someone cares is comforting. Oldsters who pride themselves on being independent and making their own decisions often welcome a thoughtful discussion about death and dying.

Keep these points in mind before initiating a discussion:

- Be willing to speak despite your own fears or discomfort about talking about death.

- Understand all the options — such as hospices, living wills, and advance directives — before you talk. (This chapter and Chapter 20 cover these topics.)

- After a diagnosis of a terminal illness, give the elder a chance to work through a host of reactions and feelings (including anger, denial, bargaining with a higher power for more time, depression, and resignation) before you initiate the discussion.

- Watch for clues that your elder is willing to talk. Comments such as "I'm going to join Daddy soon" or "Do I need to write a will?" are openings. Don't deny her feelings or give her false optimism like "Hush now, you're going to outlive all of us!"

- Take advantage of unexpected opportunities. For example, initiate a conversation when a death is covered in the media, when a friend or relative passes, or on the anniversary of a death.

- Leave the door open for a later discussion when your elder is reluctant to talk. For example, "This is something we can think about and talk about at another time."

Engaging Hospice Care

The doctor informs you that your elderly person has only a few more months to live. Do you want the doctor to continue medical treatment or conduct additional diagnostic tests? Do you want the doctor to try to extend your older person's life by days, weeks, or months with ventilators or chemotherapy?

Most experts believe that elders should be the one to make such decisions — not you! Unfortunately, she may be too ill to understand her condition or express her wishes. This situation can be avoided with a *living will* (a document prepared when the person is still alert and that spells out the life-sustaining measures and medical treatments that are acceptable should she become unable to make health-care decisions.) Another option is for the elder — while well — to complete a document that authorizes a trusted person to be his *durable power of attorney for health care.* This document gives the trusted person the legal authority to make medical decisions when the elder can't. A third document, called a *Do Not Resuscitate Order* (signed by the elder's physician), states that when the severely and irreversibly ill person stops breathing or her heart stops beating, no attempt should be made to revive her. Without one of these advance directives, the next of kin and physicians may be forced to make gut-wrenching and troubling choices for the dying person. (See Chapter 20 for more about the implementation of these options.)

Should your dying elder want to discontinue traditional treatments and refuse heroic attempts to prolong her life, consider *hospice care.* Being in hospice doesn't mean you've given up hope. Nor does it mean that your elderly person's death will be hastened. First of all, hospice is a concept, not a place. The goals are simple: Control the patient's pain, alleviate distressing symptoms like nausea and dizziness, and create a physically, emotionally, and spiritually comfortable environment for the elder and her family and friends. In short, provide a "good" death. Cure and rehabilitation aren't in the picture. The hospice team members (doctor, nurse, chaplain, social worker, therapists, and home-care aides, homemakers, and trained volunteers) make themselves available to the dying person and the family 24 hours a day. (That's not to be mistaken with *providing* 24-hour care.) Someone is always on call to answer questions and arrange emergency visits.

You can find out everything you want to know about the hospice concept (including managing pain and fulfilling spiritual needs of dying patients) online at www.hospicenet.org.

Medicare covers certified hospice programs. Most private insurance plans, HMOs, and other managed care organizations also have hospice benefits. To qualify for hospice care, a doctor must establish a prognosis of less than six months to live. If the elder outlives the six months, Medicare allows the hospice benefit to be renewed.

Sometimes, faced with an emergency, a family member of a hospice patient calls an ambulance instead of calling a hospice physician or nurse. (Hospice patients always retain the right to revoke hospice care and seek treatment at an emergency room.) In such a situation, the patient cannot be "kicked out" of hospice, but a member of the hospice program would probably meet with the patient and family to assess whether hospice care is the best choice at that point. Perhaps neither party is ready for hospice.

Hospice programs vary, but most include the following types of care:

- **Physician services.** In most cases, patients can keep their primary physicians.

- **Nursing care.** Registered and practical hospice nurses visit the hospice patient regularly.

- **Home-health aide and homemaker services.** These workers provide personal care and help with the activities of daily living.

- **Counseling.** Social workers guide the patient and family through the dying process and help resolve family conflicts. Bereavement counseling is available for the survivors for at least a year.

- **Chaplain services.** Pastoral counselors provide support to the patient and loved ones (but only if desired).

- **Therapy.** Physical therapy, speech therapy, occupational therapy, and dietary counseling are provided as needed.

- **Medical equipment.** Hospital beds and medical supplies (dressings, catheters, and oxygen) are supplied.

- **Drugs.** The goals are to relieve pain and control symptoms while minimizing grogginess and maximizing alertness.

Regrettably, many doctors wait too long to recommend hospice, typically putting off the referral until the last month or weeks of life. Bringing hospice professionals in so late limits their ability to help the dying person have a good death and assist the family and friends in coping with the impending death.

More than 3,000 hospice care programs are in the United States. To locate one in your area, look in the telephone directory under "hospice" or call the Hospice Foundation of America at 800-854-3402. You can also call the National Hospice and Palliative Care Organization at 800-658-8898 or visit online at www.nhpco.org.

In the home

Although patients can receive hospice care in hospitals, nursing homes, and free-standing hospice centers, 90 percent of hospice care is delivered in the home. Approximately 700,000 Americans moved through hospice programs in 2000.

Even with the help of a team of hospice workers, having your older person die at home can be emotionally and physically overwhelming. (See Chapter 8 for ways to prevent caregiver burnout.) To prevent burnout, hospice can arrange for your elder to have short respite stays in a hospital or nursing home.

Understand your elder's need for control. For example, insisting on having a blanket folded and placed on the end of the bed in a precise position may seem like irrational or demanding behavior but really may represent an effort to hold on to some level of control. On the other hand, some very frail elders (often in hospital settings) feel more comfortable relinquishing control, allowing others to make all decisions. In both cases, it's best to just do as asked and not to argue.

When you interview potential caregivers, ask them about how they think dying people should be cared for. For example, should care be focused on controlling pain and making the dying elder as comfortable as possible, or should care involve using whatever measures are possible to prolong the elder's life? You're best off hiring caregivers whose views are similar to your elder's. You don't want an elder to hire a home-health aide who believes that she will go to hell if she doesn't do everything possible to prolong your elder's life, even though your elder has chosen hospice care.

In the nursing home

Some nursing homes have hospice-care wings or designated rooms for hospice patients. Usually, these rooms are more homelike than regular rooms. Hospice workers perform the same services as they do in home hospice care, which means that your elder receives considerably more attention than she usually would have from the often overworked and short-staffed nursing assistants. Receiving hospice services in a nursing home is the ideal solution for older persons who have no family member or friends to care for them at home or for elders whose behavioral problems require the protective environment of an institutional setting. A primary caregiver, in need of a break from the emotional and physical stress of caring for a dying person, can place his loved one in a nursing home for respite care.

In the hospital

You may need to admit a hospice patient to a hospital for procedures necessary to control his or her pain or other symptoms or for respite care. The hospice can arrange for this care, stay involved with the elderly person and the family during the hospital stay, and then resume in-home care when the elder is discharged. Sometime a patient will spend the last days in a hospital-based hospice program because the care needed can no longer be managed at home.

Witnessing the Final Hours

Professionals who care for dying people are the best prepared to tell you when death is approaching. Each person's death experience is unique, but having a basic understanding of what happens in the hours prior to your elder's death helps you to remain calm and collected. I am forever grateful to the hospice nurse who told my mom it was time for her to call my brother and me to my father's bedside. When we arrived, she prepared us for my father's last hours.

Some of the following signs may not appear at all or may appear in a different order. (For example, my dad's skin stayed pink until the very end.) The following timeframe gives a general idea of what to expect.

During the last one to three months, the elder may exhibit some or all of the following changes:

- Lose interest in the outside world, including television and newspapers
- Be less interested in interacting with family and friends or want to be with only one or two people
- Nap more, but be awakened easily
- Refuse food, saying, "Nothing tastes good" or "I'm not hungry"

During the last one to two weeks, the elder may exhibit some or all of the following physical and behavioral changes:

- Sleep most of the time or prefer to stay in bed all day
- Talk about unknown events or talk to unseen people (often people who have died)
- Stop eating or drinking

- ✔ Become agitated

- ✔ Experience a drop in blood pressure, variations in pulse rate, and body temperature

- ✔ Have skin turn pale or bluish

- ✔ Perspire more and feel clammy

- ✔ Experience changes in respiration (increase or decrease in number of breaths per minute)

During the last one or two days, the elder may exhibit some or all of these dramatic changes:

- ✔ Experience a surge of energy and a brief renewed interest in food and people

- ✔ Become restless and make repetitive motions such as pulling at bed linen

- ✔ Suffer intermittent congestion that may produce a rattling or gurgling sound, sometimes called a "death rattle"

- ✔ Have tearing, glassy, half-open eyes

- ✔ Become unresponsive

- ✔ Lose control of bladder and bowel functions

- ✔ Change breathing patterns from normal to shallow, with periods of no breathing at all and then rapid shallow pant-like breathing

- ✔ Appear to take a last breath, pause, and take more breaths before the final breath

The last goodbye

Your elder may pass away while you're working, taking care of your family, having a meal, or frantically running through an airport. You shouldn't feel guilty about not being there — you did the best you could. Say your farewells in private or at the funeral or memorial service.

If you're present in the last moments, touch your elder. Hold his hand or stroke his face and speak lovingly to him. If you wish some private time, feel free to ask whoever is there for a few moments alone with your loved one. Because hearing is the last sense to go, be careful not to talk about him as though he weren't there. Speak in your normal tone, identify yourself by name, and say all the loving things he needs to hear before passing on. For example, remind him of accomplishments, of what he gave to you and how much his life has enriched yours. Reassure him that he's safe and loved, that he had a good life, and that he's free to go.

Parting rituals

Funeral services usually occur within a few days or weeks after the death, depending on the religious and cultural traditions and how quickly out-of-town mourners can get there. (See the section "Arranging the funeral," later in this chapter, for the ins and outs of funeral arrangements.)

A memorial service (held in addition to or instead of a traditional funeral) is often but not always less formal than a funeral service. The body or ashes aren't present at the memorial service, which is usually held well after the funeral. For example, a family may prefer to have an immediate solemn family-only graveside service followed by a more rollicking memorial service a month later for the former coworkers and poker buddies of the deceased. You can hold memorials anywhere that meets your fancy — the community room of the assisted-living center, the beach, or the game room at the senior center. I know one woman who jokes that she would like her memorial to be held at her favorite place in all the world — Bloomingdale's!

Whether formal or informal, religious or secular, funerals and memorial services are for the survivors. Traditional rituals (including prayers, eulogies, and music) provide mourners with opportunities to express their grief and honor the departed. But you can create your own rituals if you like. Here are a few ideas to inspire you:

✔ Invite guests to spontaneously share their memories of the deceased.

✔ Invite friends and family to write down their memories and send them to you well before the memorial and then compile the anecdotes into a booklet to distribute at the service.

✔ Create a videotape of the deceased, using still photos and old home movie footage to play at the service.

✔ Read something that your elder wrote that reflects his personality (a letter, an op-ed piece to the local newspaper, a funny or heartwarming e-mail message).

✔ Read one of the deceased's favorite readings aloud (a Bible verse, a poem, a short story, a limerick, or an oft-repeated joke or anecdote).

✔ Pull together a collage of photographs or mementos from the elder's life.

✔ Have each grandchild light a candle or place a flower in a basket.

In the book *Remembering Well*, Sarah York offers a touching ritual. The person who is leading the service tells the guests that she'll read several lines and asks them to say the words "We remember you" aloud after each line. (The lines are written to suit the unique personality of the deceased.) If I had done this for my father's memorial (and I wish I had), it would have gone something like this:

On each and every joyous occasion. . . . We remember you.

When we long for unconditional love. . . . We remember you.

When we have good news we yearn to share. . . . We remember you.

When we see ocean waves gently rolling in. . . . We remember you.

When we see someone with a smile that goes from ear to ear. . . . We remember you.

When we see an act of kindness taking place in an unkind world. . . . We remember you.

When we are in need of a strong and steady influence in our lives. . . . We remember you.

Taking Charge When a Loved One Dies

When an elderly person passes away, the responsibility for doing what needs to be done often falls to the primary caregiver.

As you read about the tasks that have to be accomplished when a loved one dies, keep in mind that you can make nearly everything easier if you do some advance work. For example, deciding on a funeral director prior to the death is extremely helpful so that you won't feel frazzled and can comparison shop. Consider it merely a fact-finding mission to inform yourself about this facet of life. You are not — I repeat, not — wishing for your elder's death, doing anything wrong, or being disrespectful. You are merely being prepared.

You may also consider creating a list of names and phone numbers of people who will need to be notified of your older person's death.

Call a funeral director to arrange for someone to come and take the body away. When an elder dies at home, you don't need to call immediately. You can sit with the loved one for a while. But if your older person has died in a nursing home or hospital, you'll be asked almost immediately for the name of the funeral home they should call.

The National Funeral Director's Association provides listings of local funeral homes. Call 800-228-6332 or visit online at www.nfda.org.

Notify other family members, friends, former coworkers, and neighbors. Look in the departed's personal telephone book for help. Don't forget people from the old neighborhood, childhood friends, and anyone who has had frequent contact (such as a hairdresser and anyone who helped provide care). When you make these calls, ask others whether they know of anyone else who should be called. Ask people to help you make some of the calls. Call sooner rather than later. Most folks want to get word as soon as possible. Who to call can be another item on the agenda when you discuss end-of-life decisions with your older person.

Writing obituaries, death notices, and eulogies

Some newspapers make no distinctions between obituaries and death notices, while others treat them quite differently. For example, in *The New York Times,* the editorial staff writes obituaries (usually about the death of someone famous), and death notices are written by family members who pay for their inclusion in the newspaper.

Obituaries and death notices do share a common purpose in that they notify family, friends, and others about the death and provide details about the funeral service.

Obituaries

Obituaries may include a photo of the deceased along with a good deal of detail, including educational background and degrees; religious affiliations; community and charity work; profession; employment (where and when); memberships in clubs, unions, and volunteer organizations; military record; hobbies; notable accomplishments; full names of spouse, siblings, children and other survivors; awards; compelling anecdotes; and date, time, and location of funeral or memorial services. They may also indicate where to send donations in lieu of flowers.

Death notices

Most of the larger newspapers charge for death notices, while some of the smaller ones do not. Charges range from newspaper to newspaper and depend on the number of lines in the notice. Families can write the death notices themselves or enlist the help of the funeral director. Death notices can include any information that the family would like, but minimally they should include the deceased's full name, nickname, and maiden name; date of birth, cause of death; survivors' names; donation requests; visitation information; and the date, time, and location of funeral or memorial services. They may also include a photo. Consider placing a death notice in a hometown newspaper. The death of an elder who grew up and raised her family in Ohio and then retired to Florida would be of interest to old neighbors and friends in her town in Ohio.

Typos and misspellings are especially upsetting in obituaries and death notices. The risk of errors increases when the task is left to a funeral director or newspaper reporter. Be sure to ask to proofread the obituary or death notice before it goes into print.

You can often reach people who knew the deceased by sending a copy of the obituary or death notice to clubs and organizations your loved one was a member of. Don't forget religious organizations, alumni associations, community newspapers, and the place of former employment. (Large companies often have newsletters.)

Eulogies

I like to think of a eulogy as a goodbye toast — but without the glass of champagne. If you've been asked to write a eulogy, accept. Delivering a public tribute is a great honor. Don't allow a fear of public speaking to get in the way — you'll never have a more empathetic and supportive audience. Don't worry about getting emotional, breaking down, or having less-than-perfect sentence structure. Your audience will admire you for standing up and speaking despite your own grief.

Brainstorming is the first step in writing a eulogy. Don't try to summarize the person's entire life. Instead, recall things your elder did, conversations you had, and times you shared. Write down what the departed meant to you and how the relationship made a difference in your life. Write from your heart. Jot down stories or recollections that characterize your loved one's personality. You may be surprised how many vignettes you can remember. When you're done, select the stories that best capture what you want to get across. Then edit. Don't worry about spelling or perfect grammar. Your eulogy should be no longer than five to ten minutes and should be written in conversational language. Make a final copy that you can read easily (in a large font or large hand-printing).

Sipping water before you start to speak and during the eulogy helps you relax. Have tissues with you. If you break down, stop, compose yourself, and start again. You may want a back-up person to finish reading your eulogy if you can't. Remember, no one will judge you; they will only admire and remember your heartfelt remarks.

Settling financial affairs

The daunting task of settling your elder's affairs may fall on you. It's a difficult job, especially when you're grieving. Try to get others to help.

In the weeks or months after your loss, the following tasks need to be attended to:

- ✔ **Look for a will.** If no will surfaces, contact the elder's lawyer. If he helped execute a will, he'll have it on file.

- ✔ **Gather all the departed's financial records, certificates, and documents.** (See Chapter 20 for guidance.)

✔ **Notify insurance companies.** You may need to handle other types of insurance benefits in addition to life insurance. For example, some loans, mortgages, and credit-card accounts are covered by insurance that pays off the account balance at death.

✔ **Notify insurance companies when there's a change in beneficiary.** For example, if the husband's life insurance named the wife as beneficiary and the wife died, a new beneficiary needs to be chosen.

✔ **Notify the Social Security Administration.** The spouse may receive survivor benefits or help with funeral costs. Call 800-772-1213 as soon as possible after the death.

✔ **Notify the Veterans Administration.** Survivors may receive benefits or help with funeral costs. To apply for benefits and get more information, call 800-827-1000.

✔ **Notify all past employers.** Family members may receive death benefits, continued health insurance for family members, or payments from a pension or annuity plan. Union members may have death benefits or forgotten credit-union balances.

✔ **Locate the most recent tax return.** A tax return for the year in which the elder died has to be filed. You may want to consult with a tax accountant to make sure that you're aware of all the legal tax deductions due.

✔ **Contact the elder's bank.** All accounts should be closed. Ask whether he had a safe-deposit box. You may be able to open the box to look for a will or a deed to a burial plot. The bank is allowed to deliver the will to the Probate Clerk or to the person named as executor. Usually, no other items may be removed until court authority is obtained.

✔ **Get at least ten copies of the death certificate.** You must have a death certificate in order to collect insurance proceeds and other death benefits. (Purchase copies from the funeral director, write to your local health department, or go in person to the county courthouse.)

✔ **List all debts, including mortgages, leases, and charge accounts.**

✔ **Cancel all credit cards and club memberships.**

✔ **Advise the surviving spouse that she has to have her will revised if her departed husband was the beneficiary.** In addition, when assets are in joint names and one person dies, titles (for example, to the house and car) must be adjusted.

If insurance policies elude you, look in the checkbook for premiums paid.

✔ **Contact the probate court in the state where the deceased lived for details on beginning the probate process.** (See the sidebar "What is probate?" in this chapter.) Unless your elder did some advance financial planning to avoid probate, this process must be initiated. (You may have to contact your elder's attorney to find out whether such planning took place.)

What is probate?

Probate is the legal process that finalizes a deceased person's affairs. Probate ensures that the will is genuine, all the assets are identified, appraised, and inventoried, and all debts and taxes are paid. Probate also sees to it that all the provisions of the will are fulfilled. (In other words, the beneficiaries receive their inheritance.) If the elder had a will, the executor named in the will files the necessary papers with the local probate court. If no will exists, the court appoints an administrator to take the estate through the process. Either way, a probate attorney can help by staying on the sidelines, answering the executor's questions, and reviewing documents before they're filed with the court. Or the executor can hire a lawyer to handle the whole shebang. The decision to hire an attorney really must depend on how complicated the estate is, how significant the tax

liabilities are, and — alas — whether potential heirs are at each other's throats. Probate attorneys may cost a pretty penny. (Fees can be 5 percent or more of the entire estate.) However, some lawyers will work for an hourly fee or a lump sum. Shop around.

During the time the probate process takes (typically a year), the executor or administrator manages the estate. The deceased's assets and the terms of the will are made public. The court notifies everyone who has an interest in the estate (family members and creditors) that the estate is about to be disbursed.

Once the elder has died, nothing can be done to prevent probate, but a good estate planner can advise your older person, while he or she is well, about various legal options to avoid the probate process.

Arranging the funeral

Following a death, survivors often feel a desire to do something. For many, taking care of the funeral arrangements satisfies that need. In fact, one of the main criticisms of the trend toward funeral preplanning is that prearranged funerals deprive the survivors of an activity that can help hold the initial overwhelming grief at bay. (You can find out more about the pros and cons of preplanned funerals in Chapter 20.)

Understanding the Funeral Rule

When your loved one passes away, you want to show your respect and demonstrate your love with a beautiful, perhaps elegant, sendoff. You depend on the funeral director to guide you in what you feel is a sacred responsibility — burying the dead.

Most of the time, funeral professionals are trustworthy and will try their best to meet your needs. But, sadly, some unscrupulous people are also out there who, given half a chance, will take advantage of you at your most vulnerable time. The *Funeral Rule* (enforced by the Federal Trade Commission) protects you from inflated prices, double charges, overcharges, and misinformation. The Funeral Rule requires funeral directors to quote individual prices for funeral products and services over the telephone. (This type of quote makes it easier for you to comparison shop.) Some places will even send you a price list, although the law doesn't require it.

Many funeral homes offer package deals with various combinations of services and types of goods. When you go to the funeral home in person, the funeral director must give you a written price list with each product and service individually priced, so that you can easily determine whether the packages are best for your budget and taste or whether it makes sense to individually select the goods and services you want.

If a funeral director says that the law requires you to purchase a service (for example, embalming), don't take his word for it. Ask him to reference the specific law. By the way, embalming is not mandated for most deaths. (Only a few states require it when the death occurs from a communicable disease.)

Often, the most expensive item for a funeral is the casket. The Funeral Rule states that the funeral provider may not refuse to handle or charge a handling fee for a casket that you bought elsewhere. In other words, you can buy a casket anywhere you please (online or at a retail store). You can even build one yourself. Thanks to the Funeral Rule, you can save hundreds of dollars on a casket.

Don't fall for claims that a particular casket has special features designed to help preserve the remains indefinitely. No such features exist. The Funeral Rule forbids such false claims.

Every funeral home is allowed (by federal law) to charge a basic services fee (it includes the services of the funeral director, consultations, paperwork, and overhead costs). The same fee is applied to the simplest funeral or the fanciest one. Fair enough. The good news is that when you comparison shop, you can also compare the basic service fees of different homes, potentially saving big bucks. Comparison shopping prevents what the unscrupulous are hoping for — emotional overspending. Another way to avoid paying more than you need to is to take a clearheaded friend with you when you make the arrangements. Better yet, do your comparison shopping in advance. Saving money doesn't mean that you're skimping on love. In fact, if your loved one was anything like my dad, he or she would be happy to know that you're using your noggin!

Call the Veterans' Administration at 800-827-1000 and ask to speak to the Enrollment Coordinator to find out whether your veteran is eligible for burial benefits or go online (www.va.gov). Click Burial ➪ Burial Benefits. Another good Web site is www.cem.va.gov.

Making choices

If you're really lucky, your elder told you exactly what he wished and may even have written it down to avoid mistakes or family squabbles. The so-called

Funerals with pizzazz!

Name a human interest (including outer space, rock-and-roll, and the circus), and someone has thrown a party with that theme. For example, brides and grooms have exchanged vows underwater, jumped out of airplanes together, and said "I do" perched on horses to further a theme. A mortuary in St. Louis is at the forefront of a new idea that is spreading across the country — themed send-offs for the dearly departed.

Caskets are placed in settings that are designed to celebrate the deceased's personality and passions. One of the most popular sets is "Big Momma's Room," in which a casket is placed in a cozy kitchen setting near an oven, stove, and a kitchen table set for dinner. Another example is a casket amidst a boxing ring — suitable for the funeral of a prizefighter. Still another design features a barbeque setting with grill and picnic tables. The mortician who put this one together microwaved a rib sandwich in the next room every hour so that the aroma of the barbeque would waft through the chapel. The St. Louis mortuary plans to open a national chain of funeral homes specializing in themed funerals. Coffin manufactures are also getting in on the act. For example, hunters can now be laid to rest in a casket lined with camouflage-patterned fabric.

When cremation is the choice, ashes can be mixed with other materials to form meaningful items, bird baths, wind chimes, or Frisbees. One woman mixed her mother's ashes with oil paint, used the paint to create a picture, and hung it on the wall in her living room. The idea may have some appeal until you consider how many paintings end up in garage sales.

traditional funeral usually includes a service, transport of the remains from the service to the cemetery, and either ground burial, entombment (burial in a mausoleum), or cremation. It may or may not include a visitation or viewing of the deceased. If a viewing occurs, then embalming is necessary, and you need to make decisions about dressing the body, such as shroud, favorite outfit, eyeglasses, makeup, hairdo, and what to place in the casket, if anything (pictures, favorite quilt, and military medals).

Another type of funeral is the immediate in-ground burial. Here the body is buried shortly after death in a simple container, and no embalming or casket is required. No viewing or service occurs with the body present. A memorial service may be held at graveside or elsewhere many weeks later.

If you want to have an expensive casket for the viewing, you can rent one (with a removable liner) for about one third of the retail price and then use a simple box for the burial. (Ask the funeral director about this option.)

Cremation has become popular in recent years. No casket is required. If the body is to be viewed at a funeral service, you can rent a casket for the visitation. Funeral directors must offer you an inexpensive unfinished wooden box or alternative container (made of fiberboard, composition materials, or heavy cardboard) that is cremated with the body instead of a casket. You may keep the ashes at home, buried in the ground, placed in a space in a *mausoleum* (a building in which remains are entombed), or scattered.

Another type of funeral is *direct cremation,* in which the body is cremated shortly after death. There's no viewing, although a funeral or memorial service may be held later. When a death occurs hundreds or thousands of miles away from home, for example, survivors may prefer a local cremation to the expense of transporting the remains across the country.

Burial vaults or grave liners are sort of boxes for boxes. Their purpose is to prevent the ground from caving in as the casket deteriorates over time. The grave liner covers the top and sides of the casket. The more expensive burial vault entirely surrounds the casket. State laws don't require vaults or grave liners, but some cemeteries do. Here, too, you can buy one of these liners from a third party and save money.

The Funeral Consumer's Alliance (FCA) is a nonprofit agency with 118 affiliate offices across the country. (It was formerly called the Funeral and Memorial Society of America.) The FCA can save you money! The agency negotiates with local funeral homes for lower fees for funeral services. The FCA provides educational materials about funeral homes, exposes funeral industry abuses, acts as a consumer advocate, and refers individuals to appropriate societies and agencies that supply local services. The membership fee varies from office to office and can range from $10 to $40 for a lifetime membership. The newsletter is free for the first year of membership; a donation of $10 a year is requested thereafter. Call 800-765-0107 for information or visit online (www.funerals.org).

Facing Life Without Your Elder

Hardworking caregivers, especially in the midst of a crisis, often long for the old days when they weren't so burdened with eldercare. When their elder dies, they may feel guilty because of those longings. Such feelings are common and normal. It's just the way human beings are made! Often caregivers will feel depressed and aimless once their caregiving responsibilities end. They may have trouble filling the day with meaningful activities. This reaction, too, is common and normal.

When your elder dies, you expect that you will grieve and feel sad (or, if the relationship was negative, feel relief). It's more than surprising when the feelings that emerge are guilt or a sense of emptiness. Bereavement groups can help. (See Chapter 15 for more information about groups for the bereaved.)

Part VI
The Part of Tens

The 5th Wave   By Rich Tennant

"Mom and Dad are definitely getting older. All the
signs are there. Mom relies more on a calculator
when she's doing her particle physics research,
and dad keeps forgetting where he put
his mountain bike."

In this part . . .

Move over, Sherlock Holmes and Sigmund Freud! The Part of Tens furnishes what every investigator needs — the facts, just the facts, ma'am. This part provides you with the clues you need to separate the good nursing homes from the bad ones. You also solve the mysteries of "life's little deceptions" (the things your elder may do and say to hide troubling feelings from himself and from others). Happy sleuthing!

Chapter 24

Ten Tests to Help You Assess a Nursing Home

. . . .

In This Chapter

▶ Safeguarding your elder's dignity

▶ Realizing that a home is more than four walls and three square meals

. . . .

Dad moved into a nursing facility when he was 88, and I flew across the country to visit him in his new home. The first thing I noticed when I entered the building was an old-fashioned ice-cream parlor, complete with white wrought-iron chairs with pink-and-white candy-striped seats and a blackboard advertising tutti-frutti and pistachio ice cream. The ice-cream parlor was empty. I visited Dad dozens of times at different hours and on different days of the week. I never saw a resident licking the drips off an ice-cream cone or enjoying a banana split. In fact, I never saw anyone in the ice-cream shoppe at all.

Ice-cream parlors and other flashy gimmicks are marketing devices to impress families. They're seldom used and don't even register on things to consider when evaluating whether a nursing home is a good one or not.

But does anyone really know what makes a home a good one? A group of very smart researchers asked nursing home residents, their relatives, and nursing home staff members (including nurses' aides) for their opinions on what factors contribute to a high quality of life in a nursing facility. Staff members extolled the virtues of the medical care, the importance of a shower twice a week, good meals, and activities to stimulate resident's minds. Relatives were certain that it was good food, a sense of security, and also access to medical care that distinguished the good from the bad. The elders said that the most important thing was their own attitude and morale! The physical surroundings were rarely mentioned by anyone — ice-cream parlors included.

In this chapter, I highlight the things you should look for when evaluating a nursing home. No home is perfect. There's always a trade-off, but as you go about considering various features, focus first on which features are most likely to buoy up your elder's morale. These plusses may include easy access to a telephone, transportation into the community, a compatible roommate, or a location that allows frequent visits from loved ones. — you (and your elder) are the best judges.

To get a realistic view of life in any nursing home, make several visits at various times — during mealtimes, in the evening, and on the weekends.

The Respect and Dignity Test

Nothing crushes one's morale more than being treated disrespectfully. A good nursing facility works at keeping your elder's dignity intact. After you visit a nursing facility, you should be able to answer the following questions:

- Do staff members (from nursing aides to office clerks) interact with the residents in a cheerful, pleasant manner? There's never any excuse for scolding, teasing, or humiliating the residents — these practices also constitute abuse.

- Do the rooms reflect the individuality of elders who live in them? Are there photos on the wall, personal memorabilia on the dressers, or items from home placed about the room?

- Are residents clean, shaved, and generally well-groomed?

- Have you spotted elders in partial dress (for example, in open nightgowns or only partially covered while being taken to and from toileting or bath)?

- Are residents helped to spend time out of bed if they're able? (For example, if your elder wears a prosthesis, make sure that several nursing aides know how to put it on so that your elder will be able to move about the facility.)

- Can the facility accommodate your elder's preferences (for example, make reasonable requests for wake-up time, time to eat, snacks, and time outdoors)?

- Are residents tied in their chairs or limited in mobility because obstacles (such as tables) are placed in front of their wheelchairs? Federal law states that restraints can be imposed only to protect the physical safety of the resident (or other residents) and then only with the physician's written order specifying the duration and the specific conditions for use. Restraints can never be applied for punishment or staff convenience.

The "Is It Just a Job or Do They Really Care?" Test

Most nursing facilities suffer from staff shortages. Nursing aides are overworked and harried. I recall one woman who pressed her buzzer repeatedly because she needed help to get to the toilet. The agitated aide who finally arrived said that she had no time and that the elder should just pee in her diaper. The comment was not just an affront to the elder's dignity — the aide was encouraging behavior that could lead to premature incontinence.

The following suggestions can help you decide whether staff members like their work and care about the residents or are merely putting in their hours for a paycheck:

- Observe whether the staff seem to know the residents and call them by their names.

- Listen for laughter and friendly chatter coming from residents' rooms and community rooms.

- Ask about turnover rates. High turnover indicates poor working conditions, including lack of respect toward staff on the part of administrators.

- Ask whether nurses are available around the clock.

- Check to see whether dishes are sitting around, hours after mealtime (which may indicate serious staff shortages).

- Note how quickly nurses' aides respond to call lights and buzzers. (A resident shouldn't have to wait 30 minutes to get another blanket or have the air-conditioner adjusted.)

The Rhythm of Life Test

Get a handle on the pulse of life in the home. This test can be difficult when you're merely passing through, but it's not impossible. Holidays, for example, should be marked with decorations and appropriate activities. Family members should be invited to participate in festivities and enjoy dinner with their elder at various times throughout the year. Find out whether active family councils exist and monthly residents' meetings occur. Are religious services held, and are special diets available for those with religious restrictions?

See what's posted on the activity board and then turn up in the appointed place to see whether the activity is happening. It's a very bad sign when residents are simply parked in front of a TV rather than doing what's described on the activity schedule. And just because your elder is bed-bound doesn't mean the facility is exempt from planning appropriate activities for her — she could still have her nails painted or enjoy a holiday visit from the first-graders at the local elementary school. Chat with residents. How do they like living in the home? Can they get outside to a lawn or garden with ease? Is someone available to help them walk or do range-of-motion exercises?

The Good Neighbor Test

Roommates are extremely important to most nursing home residents. Find out how rooms and roommates are selected. Do residents have a voice in the selection of roommates? Is a mechanism in place to make appropriate matches? Can residents have a say in where they sit in the dining room? Can they change places if they're not happy? Dining-room seating arrangements should be for the pleasure of the elders, not the convenience of the staff.

The Administrator Test

Good administrators emerge from their offices frequently, and they often leave their office doors open so that residents, staff, and family members can pop in. A good administrator knows most — if not all — of the residents' names and has pleasant relationships with staff members. Observe whether the administrator greets residents in a caring manner. Be wary of administrators who seem obsessed with the bottom line.

Ask the administrator how long he's been at the facility and how long the administrator before him was there. A revolving door of administrators deserves explanation. Gauge the administrator's attitude when you inquire about the deficiencies cited on the state survey or problems that you observed yourself. (See Chapter 4 for more information about survey investigation reports.)

In the best of all possible worlds, the administrator is someone with whom you feel comfortable when you talk about your concerns, someone who will take your complaints seriously.

You can get detailed information about the performance of every Medicare and Medicaid-certified nursing home in the country by visiting the Centers for Medicare & Medicaid Services at www.medicare.gov. Click Nursing Home Compare to discover the deficiencies found in any particular nursing home during its most recent state nursing home survey. You can find a wealth of information, including data on the percentage of residents with pressure (bed) sores and the average number of hours worked by registered nurses, licensed practical or vocational nurses, and certified nursing assistants per resident per day.

The Safety Test

Rooms, corridors, and community rooms should be uncluttered and well-lighted. Halls should be lined with handrails and be clear of mops, brooms, and unattended carts. Look for grab-bars in bathrooms and clearly marked exits. If you spot wet towels or the floor, paper towels and tissues spilling over the edge of wastebaskets onto the floor, unattended medical carts, and dirty over-the-bed tables, ask why. An occasional lapse may occur, but beware of a facility that is chronically cluttered and dirty and that presents dangerous obstacles for residents. If your elder is already in such a facility, complain to the administrator and call the ombudsman.

 To get the telephone number for your local ombudsman, call the Eldercare Locator (800-677-1116) and ask for the local ombudsman program nearest the nursing home or facility where your elder lives, or visit online (www.ltcombudsman.org).

The Sniff Test

As you walk through the facility, take several good sniffs. If it smells like urine or feces, residents aren't being changed frequently enough. Be concerned about strong orders of pesticides, ammonia, or thick air-freshener scents. Pleasant smells should waft from the dining room and from food trays.

The Taste Test

Nothing beats the ol' taste test for evaluating the dietary program. Food should taste good, look appealing on the plate, and be the right temperature. Ask whether aides have a way (such as a microwave oven) to reheat food that grows cold. Hungry residents or large residents should have their requests for extra food satisfied, unless the doctor orders otherwise. Alternative meals must be available for those who don't care for the scheduled meal.

At its best, mealtime is quiet and calm, allowing for socialization between residents. Observe and then ask the administrator and other residents questions about meals. For example, what kind of fresh fruit is distributed and how often? A tired banana a couple of times a week or canned fruit cocktail isn't "fresh fruit served regularly." Are residents who need help with eating getting adequate assistance — for example, getting help with cutting their food and cleaning up spills? Are residents who are being spoon-fed also receiving warm, supportive comments and being treated with patience?

Bedtime snacks are not a luxury, they're required by regulation. Someone's head in a doorway asking, "Do you want a snack tonight?" is not sufficient. The resident should be offered a choice of snacks. I'd like to see all facilities wheel around an attractive cart filled with nutritious and attractive treats in the evening.

The Cozy Test

Nothing's worse than a sterile institutional atmosphere devoid of personality and warmth. Lounges, lobbies, and other public rooms should be homey and welcoming. Look for well-tended, healthy plants and furniture in decent repair — it doesn't have to be expensive or fancy, but it shouldn't have rips, creaky frames, or bulging springs and stuffing. As you walk about, look for a sense of community and efforts to keep noise levels down. For example, walkers should have padded cushions on the bottom of the legs (or be fitted with tennis balls as padding) to cut the clatter.

Individual rooms should have window coverings, bedspreads, quilts from home, and individual cork bulletin boards or other means for displaying photos, greeting cards, and other mementos from home. Ask whether your elder can bring a piece of furniture from home (for example, a favorite rocking chair or dresser). Does the home maintain a comfortable temperature?

The Location Test

The best nursing home in the world isn't much good if it's too far away for family and friends to drop by or too difficult to get to because of traffic patterns or lack of public transportation. Elders who have more visitors tend to keep their spirits up and feel less lonely. They also receive more attention from nursing aides. When family members visit often and bond with nursing home staff, everyone benefits — relatives, workers, and, most of all, your elder!

Chapter 25

Ten Ways (More or Less) That Elders Hide Their Feelings

. . . .

In This Chapter

▶ Recognizing efforts to ward off distressing emotions

▶ Determining when self-deceptions help and hurt

. . . .

*P*eople frequently protect themselves from the pain of their own emotions (including anxiety, resentment, frustration, and depression) by hiding these feelings — from themselves and from others. They often do so without even being aware that they're doing it. Seniors are no exception.

Hiding feelings is not always a bad thing — it can be an excellent way to cope with a scary world and protect yourself from being emotionally overcome. Psychologists called these maneuvers "life's little deceptions." But life's little deceptions can be harmful as well as helpful. For example, an older man is told that he has severe emphysema. The prognosis is so frightening that he *deceives* himself into thinking his situation isn't as bad as the doctor claims (thus avoided emotional distress). He may fool himself about the seriousness of his condition, but he still follows the doctor's orders. Another man with the same diagnosis is so frightened that he too deceives himself. Choosing to believe that nothing is wrong with him, the second man continues to smoke, disregarding all medical advice and refusing medication. In this case, self-deception can take him to an early grave!

I offer this chapter, a primer on life's little deceptions, so that you can better understand why your elder may behave in puzzling ways.

 Don't rush to expose your elder's self-deceptions. If they help her cope and do no harm, leave well enough alone. On the other hand, if the self-deceptions harm her health or relationships, take it up with the primary care physician. A psychiatrist, psychologist, or social worker may help your elder develop healthier ways to cope with problems and their emotional fallout.

Denying the Truth

The act of denying the facts, even when the truth is obvious, usually serves a purpose. For example, denying bad news is common. ("Oh, no, it can't be true.") Otherwise, the news may so emotionally overwhelm you that you're unable to function. Acceptance takes time. Denying the truth for a little while allows a person to accept the reality gradually. On the other hand, continued denial can be risky. For example, the Department of Health condemns an elder's building and sends him an eviction notice, but the oldster insists that nothing's wrong with his building and that no one will force him out. His self-deception jeopardizes his health and safety.

Complaining of Aches and Pains

Bottled up emotions (especially depression and anxiety) are often expressed physically in headaches, stomachaches, backaches, and other physical problems. The conversion of feelings into physical complaints is especially common in older adults, who may find it unacceptable to complain of sadness or worry, which may be seen as signs of weakness. The physical symptoms persist despite medical attention but may disappear when the elder is treated for depression or anxiety. (See Chapter 15 for more about depression and Chapter 16 for more about anxiety.)

Displaying False Bravado

How can you explain it when a bright, usually levelheaded elder insists on climbing a ladder to hang his outdoor Christmas lights when he's subject to dizzy spells? Or when he shovels snowdrifts in below-freezing weather when the doctor warns him that his heart is too weak for such activity? Elders who boldly stare danger in the face do so in an effort to cloak their fears with sheer will. False bravado is one of the most potentially dangerous self-deceptions.

Exaggerating Helplessness

On occasion, elders act as if they're more needy than they are. The underlying feeling that's hidden here is fear of abandonment. Feigning helplessness induces caregivers to provide ever more care, which is comforting to the elder who's trying — usually outside her awareness — to shield herself from her fear of abandonment. At first, this self-deception is successful. The elder gets lots of attention; caregivers feel needed. Eventually, the elder grows increasingly passive, often complaining incessantly. The caregiver does more and more, but eventually gets weighed down with the mounting demands and becomes angry, causing the elder's fears to escalate and making her act even more helpless. The best approach to this downward spiral is to encourage your elder's independence while assuring her that she will not be forsaken.

Doing Busywork

Grover lives in a continuing-care retirement community. Unlike most of the examples given in this chapter, Grover is aware of the self-deception he employs to manage his fear. He fears losing his ability to think clearly, so he spends a good part of every day on his project — identifying every one of the 600 trees on the property, making signs of names of the trees in both English and Latin, and hanging the signs on the appropriate trees.

Grover's activity may be seen as productive and important work — and it is. But the giveaway that his work is caused by an underlying fear is that Grover doesn't really care about the goal — having every tree clearly marked for the nature lovers who live at the facility. Grover could care less about the goal. His goal is to keep himself so busy that his fear of losing his mental faculties won't overcome him.

Busywork is designed to take up time, not necessarily to yield productive results. Sometimes retirees immerse themselves in a flurry of activities, meetings, and hobbies to keep away guilty feelings about not producing in a society that has a strong work ethic.

Digging in Their Heels

Generally speaking, elders are as flexible as any other age group. If your elder seems obstinate, unreasonably unyielding, or rigid, she may just be trying to defend herself against feelings of powerlessness. Fear of losing control is often underneath refusal to accept help. (See Chapter 2 for tips on helping your oldster accept help.)

Remembering Selectively

Age-advantaged people and their teenage grandchildren may share a behavior that drives the middle generation batty — they seem to hear or remember only what they want to. Elders may tune out the painful features of the present, choosing instead to focus on past happier times or only pleasant current subjects. Come to think of it, almost everyone does this when real life gets hard to take!

Idealizing

Idealization occurs when an age-advantaged person glorifies her past, her status, or her importance in order to keep in check her feelings of regret about the life she led. This behavior can be healthy. (See Chapter 15 for more about the benefits of reshaping one's past at the end of life.) On the other hand, done to excess, this practice alienates the family that has to listen to it. For example, their mother's repeated stories about the kindness of their deceased father (who in reality was a cruel alcoholic who beat them unmercifully) causes the adult children to limit their visits.

Misdirecting Anger

This little deception consists of *redirecting* disagreeable feelings rather than hiding them. Sometimes an elder will find it too threatening to experience the anger she feels toward a particular person, so she shifts that anger to a safer person. For example, a mother may be angry at a son who rarely calls or stops by. If she directs her anger toward him, he may even visit less, so she vents her anger instead toward the steadfast child — often the hardworking child who provides most of the care and who can be relied on, no matter what!

Index

B

D

Notes

Notes

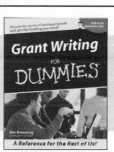

FOR DUMMIES®

A world of resources to help you grow

HOME, GARDEN & HOBBIES

Feng Shui FOR DUMMIES
0-7645-5295-3

Gardening FOR DUMMIES
0-7645-5130-2

Guitar FOR DUMMIES
0-7645-5106-X

Also available:

Auto Repair For Dummies
(0-7645-5089-6)

Chess For Dummies
(0-7645-5003-9)

Home Maintenance For
Dummies
(0-7645-5215-5)

Organizing For Dummies
(0-7645-5300-3)

Piano For Dummies
(0-7645-5105-1)

Poker For Dummies
(0-7645-5232-5)

Quilting For Dummies
(0-7645-5118-3)

Rock Guitar For Dummies
(0-7645-5356-9)

Roses For Dummies
(0-7645-5202-3)

Sewing For Dummies
(0-7645-5137-X)

FOOD & WINE

Cooking FOR DUMMIES
0-7645-5250-3

Cookies FOR DUMMIES
0-7645-5390-9

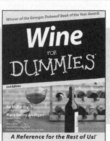

Wine FOR DUMMIES
0-7645-5114-0

Also available:

Bartending For Dummies
(0-7645-5051-9)

Chinese Cooking For
Dummies
(0-7645-5247-3)

Christmas Cooking For
Dummies
(0-7645-5407-7)

Diabetes Cookbook For
Dummies
(0-7645-5230-9)

Grilling For Dummies
(0-7645-5076-4)

Low-Fat Cooking For
Dummies
(0-7645-5035-7)

Slow Cookers For Dummie
(0-7645-5240-6)

TRAVEL

Italy FOR DUMMIES
0-7645-5453-0

Hawaii FOR DUMMIES
0-7645-5438-7

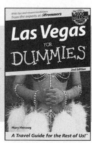

Las Vegas FOR DUMMIES
0-7645-5448-4

Also available:

America's National Parks For
Dummies
(0-7645-6204-5)

Caribbean For Dummies
(0-7645-5445-X)

Cruise Vacations For
Dummies 2003
(0-7645-5459-X)

Europe For Dummies
(0-7645-5456-5)

Ireland For Dummies
(0-7645-6199-5)

France For Dummies
(0-7645-6292-4)

London For Dummies
(0-7645-5416-6)

Mexico's Beach Resorts For
Dummies
(0-7645-6262-2)

Paris For Dummies
(0-7645-5494-8)

RV Vacations For Dummies
(0-7645-5443-3)

Walt Disney World & Orlan
For Dummies
(0-7645-5444-1)

Available wherever books are sold. Go to www.dummies.com or call 1-877-762-2974 to order direct.

FOR DUMMIES

Helping you expand your horizons and realize your potential

INTERNET

The Internet FOR DUMMIES

0-7645-0894-6

The Internet ALL-IN-ONE DESK REFERENCE FOR DUMMIES

0-7645-1659-0

eBay FOR DUMMIES

0-7645-1642-6

Also available:

America Online 7.0 For Dummies
(0-7645-1624-8)

Genealogy Online For Dummies
(0-7645-0807-5)

The Internet All-in-One Desk Reference For Dummies
(0-7645-1659-0)

Internet Explorer 6 For Dummies
(0-7645-1344-3)

The Internet For Dummies Quick Reference
(0-7645-1645-0)

Internet Privacy For Dummies
(0-7645-0846-6)

Researching Online For Dummies
(0-7645-0546-7)

Starting an Online Business For Dummies
(0-7645-1655-8)

DIGITAL MEDIA

Digital Photography FOR DUMMIES

0-7645-1664-7

Photoshop Elements 2 FOR DUMMIES

0-7645-1675-2

Digital Video FOR DUMMIES

0-7645-0806-7

Also available:

CD and DVD Recording For Dummies
(0-7645-1627-2)

Digital Photography All-in-One Desk Reference For Dummies
(0-7645-1800-3)

Digital Photography For Dummies Quick Reference
(0-7645-0750-8)

Home Recording for Musicians For Dummies
(0-7645-1634-5)

MP3 For Dummies
(0-7645-0858-X)

Paint Shop Pro "X" For Dummies
(0-7645-2440-2)

Photo Retouching & Restoration For Dummies
(0-7645-1662-0)

Scanners For Dummies
(0-7645-0783-4)

GRAPHICS

PowerPoint 2002 FOR DUMMIES

0-7645-0817-2

Photoshop 7 FOR DUMMIES

0-7645-1651-5

Macromedia Flash MX FOR DUMMIES

0-7645-0895-4

Also available:

Adobe Acrobat 5 PDF For Dummies
(0-7645-1652-3)

Fireworks 4 For Dummies
(0-7645-0804-0)

Illustrator 10 For Dummies
(0-7645-3636-2)

QuarkXPress 5 For Dummies
(0-7645-0643-9)

Visio 2000 For Dummies
(0-7645-0635-8)

Available wherever books are sold. Go to www.dummies.com or call 1-877-762-2974 to order direct.

FOR DUMMIES®

The advice and explanations you need to succeed

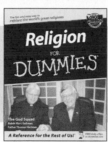